Earth Science

by
Robert H. Marshall
Allen B. Rosskopf

AGS Publishing
Circle Pines, Minnesota 55014-1796
800-328-2560

About the Authors

Robert H. Marshall, M.Ed., teaches high-school physics and algebra at the Baltimore School for the Arts. He is a coauthor of several AGS textbooks, including *Physical Science, General Science,* and *Matter, Motion, and Machines.*

Allen B. Rosskopf, M.L.A., has taught English, journalism production, and desktop publishing for 30 years in the Baltimore City Public Schools. He is a coauthor of the AGS textbook *General Science.*

Photo credits for this textbook begin on page 395.

The publisher wishes to thank the following consultants and educators for their helpful comments during the review process for *Earth Science.* Their assistance has been invaluable.

Susan B. Board, Exceptional Student Education Department Chair, Terry Parker High School, Jacksonville, FL; **Bonnie Buratti,** Research Astronomer, Jet Propulsion Laboratory, California Institute of Technology, Pasadena, CA; **Sean Madden,** Special Education Teacher, Summit School, St. Laurent, Quebec; **Suzanne McKinley,** Special Education Teacher, El Capitan High School, Lakeside, CA; **Esterina Mignacca,** Special Education Teacher, Summit School, St. Laurent, Quebec; **Harrison H. Schmitt,** Geologist and former *Apollo 17* Astronaut; **Lorraine S. Taylor,** Ph.D., Professor of Special Education, State University of New York at New Paltz, New Paltz, NY; **Wayne Wendland,** State Climatologist, Illinois State Water Survey, Professor of Geography, University of Illinois at Champaign-Urbana, Urbana, IL

Publisher's Project Staff

Vice President, Product Development: Kathleen T. Williams, Ph.D., NCSP; Associate Director, Product Development: Teri Mathews; Senior Editor: Julie Maas; Assistant Editor: Jan Jessup; Development Assistant: Bev Johnson; Senior Designer/Illustrator: Tony Perleberg; Creative Services Manager: Nancy Condon; Purchasing Agent: Mary Kaye Kuzma; Senior Marketing Manager/Secondary Curriculum: Brian Holl

Editorial and production services provided by Navta Associates, Inc.
Additional illustrations by Stephanie Pershing/John Edwards Inc.

© 2004 AGS Publishing
4201 Woodland Road
Circle Pines, MN 55014-1796
800-328-2560 • www.agsnet.com

AGS Publishing is a trademark and trade name of American Guidance Service, Inc.

Printed in the United States of America
ISBN 0-7854-3635-9
Product Number 93940
A 0 9 8 7 6 5 4

Contents

How to Use This Book: A Study Guide . . . . **xii**
The Nature of Science . . . . **xviii**

Chapter 1 | **Studying the Earth** **1**

Lesson 1 Earth Science 2
◆ Achievements in Science: Celebrating Earth Day 6
Lesson 2 Understanding Maps 7
◆ Science at Work: Cartographer 12
◆ Investigation 1-1: Making a Map 13
Lesson 3 Topographic Maps 15
◆ Science in Your Life: Mapping a Park 18
◆ Investigation 1-2: Reading a Topographic Map 19
◆ Chapter Summary 21
◆ Chapter Review 22
◆ Test-Taking Tip 23

Chapter 2	**Describing the Earth**........................ **24**
	Lesson 1 The Earth's Features 26
	◆ Achievements in Science: A Trip Around the World 30
	Lesson 2 The Earth's Rotation and Time 31
	◆ Science in Your Life: Time Zones................... 35
	◆ Investigation 2-1: Modeling the Earth's Rotation....... 36
	Lesson 3 A Grid System on a Map 38
	◆ Achievements in Science: Global Positioning Systems... 39
	◆ Investigation 2-2: Describing Location on
	a Round Surface 40
	Lesson 4 Latitude................................. 42
	◆ Science at Work: Air-Traffic Controller.............. 45
	Lesson 5 Longitude 46
	Lesson 6 A Grid System on a Globe 48
	◆ Chapter Summary................................ 51
	◆ Chapter Review 52
	◆ Test-Taking Tip 53

Chapter 3	**The Earth and Moon System**.................. **54**
	Lesson 1 The Effect of Gravity 56
	◆ Achievements in Science: Almanacs 57
	◆ Investigation 3-1: Making a Model of an Orbit 58
	Lesson 2 The Earth's Movement in Space 60
	◆ Science at Work: Space Shuttle and International
	Space Station Crews 62
	◆ Investigation 3-2: Exploring Light Angle 63
	Lesson 3 The Moon's Movement in Space.............. 65
	◆ Science in Your Life: Natural and Artificial Satellites.... 69
	Lesson 4 The Moon's Surface 70
	◆ Chapter Summary................................ 73
	◆ Chapter Review 74
	◆ Test-Taking Tip 75

Chapter 4 **The Solar System** **76**

Lesson 1 The Solar System 78

◆ Science in Your Life: A Solar House 83

◆ Investigation 4-1: Observing Sunspots 84

Lesson 2 The Inner Planets 86

◆ Achievements in Science: The Struggle to Accept
the Solar System 91

Lesson 3 The Outer Planets 92

◆ Science at Work: Astronomer 97

◆ Investigation 4-2: Modeling Distances in the
Solar System 98

Lesson 4 Other Objects in the Solar System 100

◆ Chapter Summary 103

◆ Chapter Review 104

◆ Test-Taking Tip 105

Chapter 5 **Stars and Galaxies** **106**

Lesson 1 Stars 108

◆ Science at Work: Telescope Technician 111

◆ Investigation 5-1: Observing Brightness 112

Lesson 2 Distances to Stars 114

Lesson 3 The Life of a Star 117

◆ Achievements in Science: Black Holes 120

Lesson 4 Groups of Stars 121

◆ Science in Your Life: Light Pollution 124

◆ Investigation 5-2: Making a Constellation Model 125

◆ Chapter Summary 127

◆ Chapter Review 128

◆ Test-Taking Tip 129

Chapter 6	**Earth Chemistry** **130**
	Lesson 1 Matter 132
	◆ Science in Your Life: Lasting Plastic. 134
	◆ Investigation 6-1: Measuring Physical Properties
	of Objects. 135
	Lesson 2 The Smallest Parts of Matter 137
	◆ Achievements in Science: Creating New Elements. 140
	Lesson 3 Compounds and Mixtures. 141
	◆ Science at Work: Chemical Engineer. 146
	◆ Investigation 6-2: Separating a Mixture 147
	Chapter Summary. 149
	Chapter Review 150
	Test-Taking Tip 151

Chapter 7	**Minerals** **152**
	Lesson 1 Minerals. 154
	◆ Achievements in Science: Working with Metals. 156
	Lesson 2 Properties Used to Identify Minerals 157
	◆ Investigation 7-1: Observing Color, Streak,
	and Hardness. 162
	Lesson 3 Other Physical Properties of Minerals 164
	◆ Science at Work: Jeweler. 167
	◆ Investigation 7-2: Finding Specific Gravity. 168
	Lesson 4 Common Uses of Minerals 170
	◆ Science in Your Life: Recycling Aluminum. 172
	Chapter Summary. 173
	Chapter Review 174
	Test-Taking Tip 175

Chapter 8

Rocks **176**

Lesson 1 Rocks and Rock Types 178

◆ Science at Work: Stonemason 180

Lesson 2 Igneous Rocks. 181

◆ Achievements in Science: Field Guides for Rocks
and Minerals 184

Lesson 3 Sedimentary Rocks. 185

◆ Science in Your Life: The Good and Bad of Coal 189

◆ Investigation 8-1: Making Calcite 190

Lesson 4 Metamorphic Rocks. 192

Lesson 5 The Rock Cycle 194

◆ Achievements in Science: The Rock Cycle Theory. 196

◆ Investigation 8-2: Identifying Rocks 197

Chapter Summary. 199

Chapter Review 200

Test-Taking Tip 201

Chapter 9

The Earth's Atmosphere. **202**

Lesson 1 Gases in the Atmosphere 204

◆ Science in Your Life: Ozone: Protector and Pollutant. . . 207

Lesson 2 Layers of the Atmosphere 208

◆ Achievements in Science: Balloon Pilots. 210

Lesson 3 Clouds 211

◆ Science at Work: Environmental Science Technician. . . 214

◆ Investigation 9-1: Observing Clouds. 215

Lesson 4 Precipitation 216

◆ Achievements in Science: Cloud Seeding 218

◆ Investigation 9-2: Making a Model of Rain 219

Lesson 5 Wind Patterns. 221

Chapter Summary. 225

Chapter Review 226

Test-Taking Tip 227

Chapter 10   **Weather and Climate**......................**228**

Lesson 1   Weather Conditions and Measurements 230

◆ Science at Work: Atmospheric Scientist 235

◆ Investigation 10-1: Measuring Air Pressure 236

Lesson 2   Weather Patterns and Predictions............ 238

◆ Achievements in Science: Doppler Radar 241

◆ Investigation 10-2: Using a Weather Map........... 242

Lesson 3   Storms 244

Lesson 4   World Climates............................ 247

◆ Science in Your Life: Your Climate Zone............ 250

Chapter Summary.................................. 251

Chapter Review 252

Test-Taking Tip 253

Chapter 11   **The Earth's Water** **254**

Lesson 1   The Water Cycle 256

◆ Science in Your Life: Your Water Budget............ 258

Lesson 2   Sources of Fresh Water.................... 259

◆ Science at Work: Hydroelectric Power
Plant Operator................................. 264

◆ Investigation 11-1: Exploring Evaporation........... 265

Lesson 3   Oceans 267

◆ Achievements in Science: Protecting the
Environment 272

◆ Investigation 11-2: Measuring the Effect of Salt
Water on Floating 273

Chapter Summary.................................. 275

Chapter Review 276

Test-Taking Tip 277

Chapter 12	**Weathering and Erosion**	**278**
	Lesson 1 Weathering	280
	◆ Investigation 12-1: Observing Chemical Weathering . . .	284
	Lesson 2 Erosion Caused by Water	286
	◆ Science in Your Life: Erosion Caused by People	291
	◆ Investigation 12-2: Comparing Erosion	292
	Lesson 3 Erosion Caused by Glaciers	294
	◆ Achievements in Science: Artificial Glaciers	299
	Lesson 4 Erosion Caused by Wind and Gravity	300
	◆ Science at Work: Floodplain Manager	302
	Chapter Summary	303
	Chapter Review	304
	Test-Taking Tip	305
Chapter 13	**Forces in the Earth**	**306**
	Lesson 1 Movement of the Earth's Crust	308
	◆ Achievements in Science: The Theory of	
	Sea-Floor Spreading	312
	Lesson 2 Volcanoes	313
	◆ Science in Your Life: Living on a Tectonic Plate	316
	Lesson 3 Mountains	317
	◆ Investigation 13-1: Making Models of Folding	
	and Faults	320
	Lesson 4 Earthquakes	322
	◆ Science at Work: Seismologist	326
	◆ Investigation 13-2: Locating an Earthquake	327
	Chapter Summary	329
	Chapter Review	330
	Test-Taking Tip	331

Chapter 14 | **A Record of the Earth's History** **332**

Lesson 1 The Rock Record 334

◆ Achievements in Science: Uncovering the
   History of Life 337

◆ Investigation 14-1: Making a Model of a Fossil 338

Lesson 2 The Ages of Rocks and Fossils 340

◆ Science at Work: Petroleum Engineer 344

◆ Investigation 14-2: Making a Half-Life Model 345

Lesson 3 Eras in the Geologic Time Scale 347

◆ Science in Your Life: Cutting Down on Fossil Fuels 352

Chapter Summary 353

Chapter Review 354

Test-Taking Tip 355

Appendix A: Metric and Customary Measurement **356**

Appendix B: Alternative Energy Sources **358**

Appendix C: The Solar System **364**

Appendix D: Space Exploration **366**

Appendix E: Constellations **368**

Appendix F: The Periodic Table of Elements **372**

Appendix G: World Map **374**

Appendix H: North America Map **376**

Glossary **377**

Index **385**

Photo Credits **395**

How to Use This Book: A Study Guide

Welcome to *Earth Science.* Science touches our lives every day, no matter where we are—at home, at school, or at work. This book covers the area of earth science. It also focuses on science skills that scientists use. These skills include asking questions, making predictions, designing experiments or procedures, collecting and organizing information, calculating data, making decisions, drawing conclusions, and exploring more options. You probably already use these skills every day. You ask questions to find answers. You gather information and organize it. You use that information to make all sorts of decisions. In this book, you will have opportunities to use and practice all of these skills.

As you read this book, notice how each lesson is organized. Information is presented in a straightforward manner. Tables, diagrams, and photos help clarify concepts. Read the information carefully. If you have trouble with a lesson, try reading it again.

It is important that you understand how to use this book before you start to read it. It is also important to know how to be successful in this course. Information in this first section of the book can help you achieve these things.

How to Study

These tips can help you study more effectively.

◆ Plan a regular time to study.
◆ Choose a quiet desk or table where you will not be distracted. Find a spot that has good lighting.
◆ Gather all the books, pencils, paper, and other equipment you will need to complete your assignments.
◆ Decide on a goal. For example: "I will finish reading and taking notes on Chapter 1, Lesson 1, by 8:00."
◆ Take a five- to ten-minute break every hour to stay alert.
◆ If you start to feel sleepy, take a break and get some fresh air.

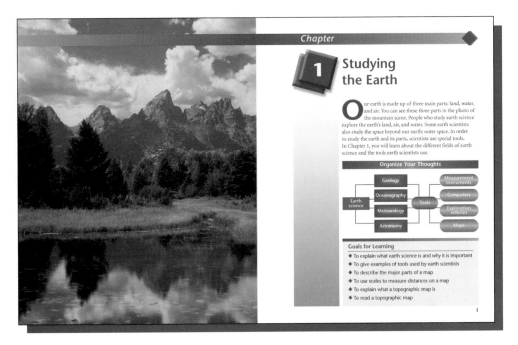

Before Beginning Each Chapter

◆ Read the chapter title and study the photo.
  What does the photo tell you about the chapter title?
◆ Read the opening paragraph.
◆ Study the Goals for Learning. The Chapter Review
  and tests will ask questions related to these goals.
◆ Look at the Chapter Review. The questions cover
  the most important information in the chapter.

Note These Features

Note

Points of interest or additional
information that relates to the lesson

Did You Know?

Facts that add details to lesson content
or present an interesting or unusual
application of lesson content

Science Myth

Common science misconceptions
followed by the correct information

Technology Note

Technology information that relates to the lesson or chapter

Science in Your Life

Examples of science in real life

Achievements in Science

Historical scientific discoveries, events, and achievements

Science at Work

Careers in science

Investigation

Experiments that give practice with chapter concepts

Before Beginning Each Lesson

Read the lesson title and restate it in the form of a question.

For example, write:
What are topographic maps?

Look over the entire lesson, noting the following:

◆ bold words
◆ text organization
◆ notes in the margins
◆ photos and diagrams
◆ lesson review questions

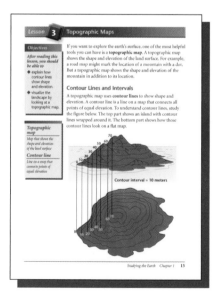

As You Read the Lesson

◆ Read the lesson title.

◆ Read the subheads and paragraphs that follow.

◆ Before moving on to the next lesson, see if you understand the concepts you read. If you do not understand the concepts, reread the lesson. If you are still unsure, ask for help.

◆ Practice what you have learned by completing the Lesson Review.

Using the Bold Words

Bold type

Words seen for the first time will appear in bold type

Glossary

Words listed in this column are also found in the Glossary

Knowing the meaning of all the boxed vocabulary words in the left column will help you understand what you read.

These words are in **bold type** the first time they appear in the text. They are often defined in the paragraph.

> **Earth science** is the study of the earth's land, water, and air. Earth science also includes the study of outer space and the objects in it.

All of the words in the left column are also defined in the **Glossary.**

> **Earth science** (ėrth sī´əns) Study of the earth's land, water, air, and outer space (p. 2)

Word-Study Tips

◆ Start a vocabulary file with index cards to use for review.

◆ Write one term on the front of each card. Write the chapter number, lesson number, and definition on the back.

◆ You can use these cards as flash cards by yourself or with a study partner to test your knowledge.

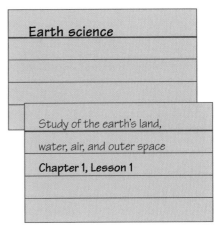

Earth science

Study of the earth's land,
water, air, and outer space
Chapter 1, Lesson 1

Using the Summaries

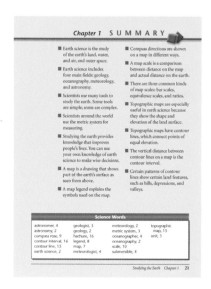

◆ Read each Chapter Summary to be sure you understand the chapter's main ideas.

◆ Make up a sample test of items you think may be on the test. You may want to do this with a classmate and share your questions.

◆ Read the vocabulary words in the Science Words box.

◆ Review your notes and test yourself on vocabulary words and key ideas.

◆ Practice writing about some of the main ideas from the chapter.

Using the Reviews

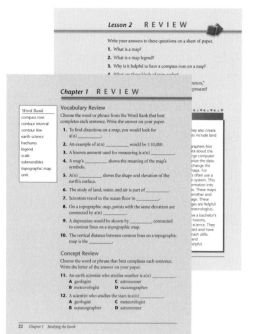

◆ Answer the questions in the Lesson Reviews.

◆ In the Chapter Reviews, answer the questions about vocabulary under the Vocabulary Review. Study the words and definitions. Say them aloud to help you remember them.

◆ Answer the questions under the Concept Review and Critical Thinking sections of the Chapter Reviews.

◆ Review the Test-Taking Tips.

Preparing for Tests

◆ Complete the Lesson Reviews and Chapter Reviews.

◆ Complete the Investigations.

◆ Review your answers to Lesson Reviews, Investigations, and Chapter Reviews.

◆ Test yourself on vocabulary words and key ideas.

◆ Use graphic organizers as study tools.

Using Graphic Organizers

A graphic organizer is a visual representation of information. It can help you see how ideas are related to one another. A graphic organizer can help you study for a test or organize information before you write. Here are some examples.

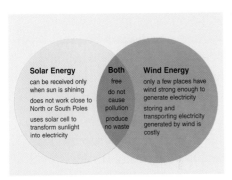

Venn Diagram

A Venn diagram can help you compare and contrast two things. For example, this diagram compares and contrasts solar energy and wind energy. The characteristics of solar energy are listed in the left circle. The characteristics of wind energy are listed in the right circle. The characteristics that both have are listed in the intersection of the circles.

Four Biomes

Tundra	Grassland	Tropical Rain Forest	Desert
cold, dry frozen below the surface	temperate humid	warm wet	very dry
lichens, low shrubs	grasses	palms, tree ferns, vines	cacti
polar bears, caribou, wolves	antelopes, bison, coyotes	bats, birds, monkeys	lizards, snakes, kangaroo rats

Column Chart

Column charts can help you organize information into groups, or categories. Grouping things in this format helps make the information easier to understand and remember. For example, this four-column chart groups information about each of the four biomes. A column chart can be divided into any number of columns or rows. The chart can be as simple as a two-column list of words or as complex as a multiple-column, multiple-row table of data.

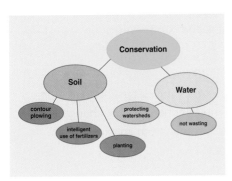

Network Tree

A network tree organizer shows how ideas are connected to one another. Network trees can help you identify main ideas or concepts linked to related ideas. For example, this network tree identifies concepts linked to the concept of conservation. You can also use network trees to rank ideas from most important to least important.

The Nature of Science

Science is an organized body of knowledge about the natural world. It encompasses everything from atoms to rocks to human health. Scientific knowledge is important because it solves problems, improves everyday life, and uncovers new opportunities. For example, scientists develop vaccines and antibiotics to prevent and cure diseases. Scientific knowledge helps farmers grow better and more crops. Science is behind the electricity we depend on every day. And science has launched space exploration, which continues to offer new opportunities.

Scientists use a logical process to explore the world and collect information. It is called the scientific method, and it includes specific steps. Scientists follow these steps or variations of these steps to test whether a possible answer to their question is correct.

1. Ask a question.
2. State a hypothesis, or make a prediction, about the answer.
3. Design an experiment, or procedure, to test the hypothesis.
4. Perform the experiment and gather information.
5. Analyze the data and organize the results.
6. State a conclusion based on the results, existing knowledge, and logic. Determine whether the results support the hypothesis.
7. Communicate the results and the conclusion.

As a scientist researches a question, he or she may do these steps in a different order or may even skip some steps. The scientific method requires many skills: predicting, observing, organizing, classifying, modeling, measuring, inferring, analyzing, and communicating.

Communication is an important part of the scientific method. Scientists all over the world share their findings with other scientists. They publish information about their experiments in journals and discuss them at meetings. A scientist may try another scientist's experiment or change it in some way. If many scientists get the same results from an experiment, then the results are repeatable and considered reliable.

Sometimes the results of an experiment do not support its hypothesis. Unexpected observations can lead to new, more interesting questions. For example, penicillin was discovered accidentally in 1928. Alexander Fleming observed that mold had contaminated one of his bacteria cultures. He noticed that the mold had stopped the growth of the bacterium. Since the mold was from the penicillium family, he named it penicillin. A decade later, researchers found a way to isolate the active ingredient. Since then, penicillin has been used to fight bacteria and save people's lives.

Once in a while, scientists discover something that dramatically changes our world, like penicillin. But, more often, scientific knowledge grows and changes a little at a time.

What scientists learn is applied to problems and challenges that affect people's lives. This leads to the development of practical tools and techniques. Tools help scientists accurately observe and measure things in the natural world. A new tool often provides data that an older tool could not. For example, computers help scientists analyze data more quickly and accurately than ever before. Our science knowledge grows as more advanced tools and technology make new discoveries possible.

Scientists use theories to explain their observations and data. A theory is a possible explanation for a set of data. A theory is not a fact. It is an idea. Theories are tested by more experiments. Theories may be confirmed, changed, or sometimes tossed out. For example, in 1808, John Dalton published a book describing his theory of atoms. His theory stated that atoms are solid spheres without internal structures. By the early 1900s, however, new tools allowed Ernest Rutherford to show that atoms are mostly empty space. He said that an atom consists of a tightly packed nucleus with electrons whizzing around it. This theory of the atom is still accepted today.

Theories that have stood many years of testing often become scientific laws. The law of gravity is one example. Scientists assume many basic laws of nature.

In this book, you will learn about earth science. You will use scientific skills to solve problems and answer questions. You will follow some of the steps in the scientific method. And you will discover how important earth science is to your life.

Studying the Earth

O ur earth is made up of three main parts: land, water, and air. You can see these three parts in the photo of the mountain scene. People who study earth science explore the earth's land, air, and water. Some earth scientists also study the space beyond our earth: outer space. In order to study the earth and its parts, scientists use special tools. In Chapter 1, you will learn about the different fields of earth science and the tools earth scientists use.

Organize Your Thoughts

```
                    Geology              Measurement
                                         instruments

                    Oceanography         Computers
Earth                              Tools
science
                    Meteorology          Exploration
                                         vehicles

                    Astronomy            Maps
```

Goals for Learning

◆ To explain what earth science is and why it is important

◆ To give examples of tools used by earth scientists

◆ To describe the major parts of a map

◆ To use scales to measure distances on a map

◆ To explain what a topographic map is

◆ To read a topographic map

Earth science
Study of the earth's land, water, air, and outer space

Geology
Study of the solid parts of the earth

Oceanography
Study of the earth's oceans

Meteorology
Study of the earth's air and weather

Astronomy
Study of outer space and objects in it

Earth science is the study of the earth's land, water, and air. Earth science also includes the study of outer space and the objects in it.

Fields of Earth Science

Earth science can be divided into many fields of science. The table describes the main fields, or subject areas, that make up earth science. Which field could answer the question, Why did it rain today? Which field would include scientists who learn about dinosaurs? Compare this table to the Table of Contents on page iii. Which chapters in this book deal with which fields of earth science?

Fields of Earth Science	
Field	**What Is Studied**
geology	the earth's land, including the surface of the earth and the inside of the earth; how the earth changes; history of the earth
oceanography	the earth's oceans, including what they contain and how they interact with the air
meteorology	the earth's air, including weather
astronomy	outer space, including planets, stars, and other objects in space

The land, water, and air of the earth are constantly changing and interacting with one another. For example, when rain washes mud off a hillside and into a river, the land and water interact with each other. When a puddle dries up, the water and air interact with each other. Because of these interactions, a change in one part of the earth affects other parts of the earth. In your local environment, how do land, water, and air affect each other? How do you affect your environment?

Tools Used by Earth Scientists

The earth's land, water, air, and living things make up a system. A system is a group of related parts that work together in an ordered way. Each part affects and depends on the other parts.

Scientists use many tools to help gather information about the earth. Some of these tools are simple. For example, a **geologist** can study the solid parts of the earth by using a rock hammer to break off chunks of fresh rock. A hand lens helps the geologist look more closely at the particles that make up the rock.

Some tools are complex and sensitive. They can measure small changes in the environment. For example, the geologists in the photo below are collecting data near an active volcano. They are using an instrument that measures distance with a laser beam. By collecting and comparing measurements, they learn more about the earth.

This surveying instrument sends a laser beam to a distant reflector. When the reflected beam returns, the instrument calculates the distance.

These and other scientific measurements are almost always based on the **metric system**. Scientists all over the world use tools that measure in metric **units**. For example, a scientist might measure something in meters, not feet. A meter is a metric unit of length. A foot is a customary, or ordinary, unit of length. Appendix A will help you become familiar with the metric system. As you will see, this is the measurement system used throughout this book.

Computers are important tools in science. They store information, make rapid calculations, and let scientists communicate with one another all over the world. What helps **meteorologists**, scientists who study the weather, provide those up-to-the-minute weather reports? Computers do. Weather information is continuously put into computers. Then the computers use the information to perform calculations for developing forecasts.

Earth scientists use other tools to explore places that are hard to study directly. The vehicle shown on the left is a **submersible**. This small underwater vessel carries **oceanographers** to the ocean floor. Oceanographers are scientists who study the oceans. Remote-controlled equipment attached to the submersible can explore small, deep, or dangerous places.

Submersibles can dive to 4,000 meters.

Exploration vehicles can be used to study planets.

Did You Know?

In 1999, scientists used the submersible *Alvin* to study the Gulf of Alaska. *Alvin* helped gather data about sea life along an undersea volcanic ridge.

The vehicle on the right is an exploration robot that collects data. It is being tested and prepared to roll across the surface of Mars. **Astronomers** are scientists who study planets and other space objects. In 1997, astronomers placed a vehicle like this on Mars to take photos and soil samples. Tools like these have helped earth scientists make important discoveries.

The tools described here are only a few of the many tools earth scientists use to gather information. What others can you think of? In Lesson 2, you will learn about one important kind of tool: maps of the earth.

The Importance of Earth Science

Earth science is important in your life. In fact, you probably use earth science in some way every day. Did you ride in a car or bus today? The fuel was made from oil that geologists located underground. Have you heard a forecast for tomorrow's weather? A meteorologist made this forecast.

The meteorologist in the photo studies climate patterns. By analyzing weather and ocean conditions, he can predict warming systems called El Niños. These systems happen every three to seven years and can cause drought or extra rain.

How is the work of meteorologists important to farmers?

You can use your own knowledge of earth science to make wise decisions. For example, knowledge about soils can help you when planting a garden. Knowing about the earth's underground water table can come in handy when buying a house. Communities often face questions about how to use the land and its resources. An earth science background will help you understand such issues.

Write your answers to these questions on a sheet of paper.

1. Write a definition of earth science.

2. What are the four main fields of earth science?

3. How do tools help scientists?

4. How are computers helpful to scientists?

5. Give two examples of how earth science is important to your life.

Achievements in Science

Celebrating Earth Day

Each year we celebrate our planet on a special day called Earth Day. The idea for having an Earth Day first occurred to Wisconsin Senator Gaylord Nelson in 1962. Because he was worried about the earth, Senator Nelson wrote a letter to President Kennedy. He urged the president to make the health of our planet an important issue. The president thought that was a good idea. He did his best to make people interested in taking care of our planet.

Even with President Kennedy's help, it took a while for the idea of Earth Day to catch on. Senator Nelson spoke at many college campuses. He tried to convince students that it was important to have a special day to celebrate the environment. Finally, the first Earth Day happened in 1970. Across the country, more than 20 million people, thousands of schools, and many local communities participated. Since then, Earth Day has been celebrated every year on April 22.

Objectives

After reading this lesson, you should be able to

◆ explain what a map is.

◆ describe the parts of a map.

◆ use a legend and scale to read a map.

When learning about the earth, you will use many models. A model shows how something looks or works. For example, a model car shows how a real car looks. Blow on a page of this book. You have just made a model that shows how wind works. A globe is a model of the earth. It shows the relative sizes and shapes of the earth's features.

Among the most useful models in earth science are **maps**. A map is a drawing that shows part of the earth's surface as seen from above. Maps are useful because they show and label information clearly. Compare the photo below with the map. They both show land, rivers, bridges, and roads. But suppose you wanted to know how to drive from Virginia to West Virginia. The map clearly shows which roads to take.

Map

Drawing that shows part of the earth's surface as seen from above

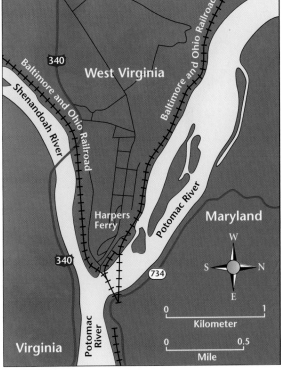

Both the photo and the map show where Maryland, Virginia, and West Virginia meet.

Map Legends

A map is useful only if you know how to read it. In order to read a map, you must understand the symbols used on it. Therefore, most maps include a **legend**, or key, that explains what the map symbols mean. Some symbols are shapes and some are colors.

What information does the map below provide? Look at the legend to find out. This map shows elevation, or how high the land is above sea level. Most of the southeastern United States is near sea level. You can tell this by matching the dark green color on the map with the legend.

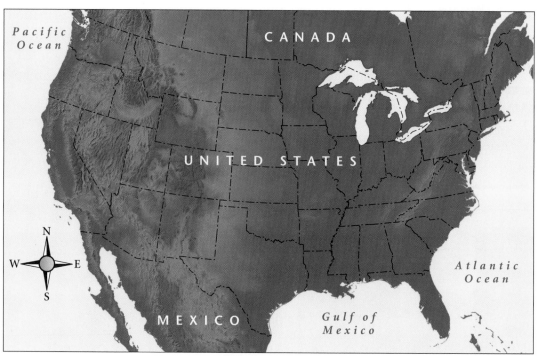

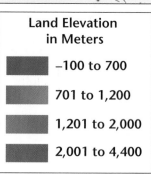

Land Elevation in Meters

	−100 to 700
	701 to 1,200
	1,201 to 2,000
	2,001 to 4,400

Compass rose

Part of a map that shows the major compass directions

Did You Know?

The oldest known maps are about 4,300 years old. They were drawn on clay tablets in Babylon, an ancient city in Asia. Ancient American Indians drew maps on skin, bone, and wood.

Compass Directions

OK, where's north? This is the first question someone might ask when looking at a map. For a map to make sense, you have to know the map's compass directions: north, south, east, and west.

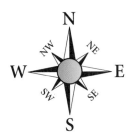

A way of showing direction is usually given on a map. Some maps show direction by using a **compass rose**, like the one shown here. This symbol shows the four major points of direction. It also shows combined points of direction: northeast, southeast, southwest, and northwest. Notice that northeast is between north and east. Between what two major direction points is southwest?

Find the compass rose on the map on page 10. In what direction would you have to travel to get from Portland to Augusta?

The compass rose on some maps gives only the four major direction points. Other maps may not have a compass rose at all. Instead, they show direction by using a single arrow with the letter *N*. The arrow shows the direction of north. From that information, you can tell where south, east, and west are located.

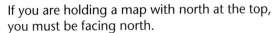

Science Myth

If you are holding a map with north at the top, you must be facing north.

Fact: The compass rose on a map does not tell you the direction you are facing as you hold the map. You could hold a map with north at the top, but be facing south. The compass rose shows only the directions within the map itself.

Map Scales

Scale

Part of a map that shows the relationship between map distance and actual distance

Another part of a map is the **scale**. A scale is a comparison between the distances on a map and the actual distances on the earth. Using a scale, you can find actual distances between different points on a map.

There are three common kinds of map scales. One kind is a bar scale. It is a line or a bar divided into equal parts and labeled with a unit of length, such as kilometers. One kilometer on the scale represents 1 kilometer on the earth. To find the distance between two points on the earth, use a ruler to measure the distance between those points on a map. Then hold the ruler against the bar scale and compare your measurement with the scale.

For example, you can use the map of Maine below to find out how far Portland is from Augusta. First, measure the distance between these cities with a ruler. On this map, they are a little more than 5 centimeters apart. Next, measure the bar scale that represents 80 kilometers. Compare these two measurements. You can tell that Portland and Augusta must be a little more than 80 kilometers apart (83 to be exact).

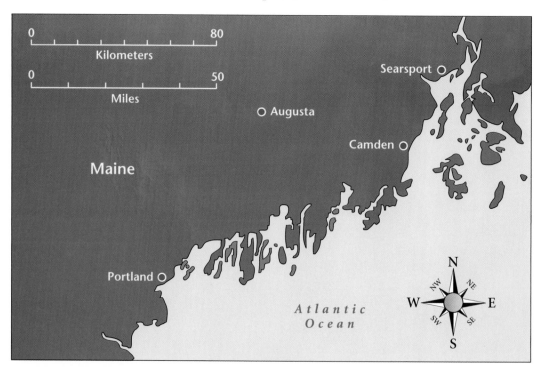

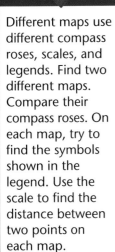

Different maps use different compass roses, scales, and legends. Find two different maps. Compare their compass roses. On each map, try to find the symbols shown in the legend. Use the scale to find the distance between two points on each map.

Another kind of map scale is an equivalence scale. It uses two distances and an equal sign to make a comparison. For example,

1 centimeter = 2 kilometers

This scale tells you that 1 centimeter on the map stands for an actual distance of 2 kilometers on the earth. So if two points on the map are 8 centimeters apart, they are 16 kilometers apart on the earth's surface (8 × 2 = 16). How far apart would two cities be if they were 3 centimeters apart on the map?

The third kind of map scale is a ratio. A ratio may be written as follows.

1:100,000

This ratio tells you that one unit on the map equals 100,000 of the same units on the earth's surface. For example, if the measured distance on the map is 1 centimeter, then the actual distance is equal to 100,000 centimeters.

A centimeter is not a convenient unit for expressing actual distances. You will usually want to change the distances that you calculate in centimeters into meters or kilometers. Here is how you can do this.

EXAMPLE
distance in centimeters ÷ 100 = distance in meters
100,000 centimeters ÷ 100 = 1,000 meters

distance in meters ÷ 1,000 = distance in kilometers
1,000 meters ÷ 1,000 = 1 kilometer

You have learned about three main parts of a map: the legend, compass directions, and the scale. By understanding these parts, you can read almost any map.

Write your answers to these questions on a sheet of paper.

1. What is a map?

2. What is a map legend?

3. Why is it helpful to have a compass rose on a map?

4. What are three kinds of map scales?

5. If a map scale reads "1 centimeter = 5 kilometers," how many kilometers does 3 centimeters represent?

▼◄▲▼◄▲▼◄▲▼◄▲▼◄▲▼◄▲▼◄▲▼◄▲▼◄▲▼◄▲▼◄▲▼◄▲▼◄▲▼◄▲▼◄▲▼◄▲▼◄▲▼

Science at Work

Cartographer

Cartographers create maps that describe features of the earth's surface. They also create graphs and other visual ways to present data. Tools used by cartographers include land surveys, aerial photos, satellite images, and computers.

To make a map, cartographers first research and collect data about the area to be mapped. Large computer systems store and organize the data. Such systems can also change the data into models and maps. For example, cartographers often use a geographic information system. This changes computer information into three-dimensional maps. These maps are laid on top of one another and combined into one image. These three-dimensional images are helpful to city planners and meteorologists.

Most cartographers have a bachelor's degree in engineering, forestry, geography, or physical science. They need to be detail-oriented and have strong computer and math skills. Good communication and organization skills are helpful.

Making a Map

Purpose

How would you make a map of the room you're in? In this investigation, you will construct a map using a map scale and legend.

Procedure

1. Copy the data table on a sheet of paper.

Name of area to be mapped _____
Actual length and width _____
Map scale _____

Object	Symbol	Location Measurements

2. Select a familiar area to map, such as your classroom.

3. Use the meterstick to measure the length and width of the area that your map will show. Record your measurements in the data table. Remember to include units.

4. Decide on a scale for your map. Pick a scale that will allow your map to fit on a sheet of paper. Then write this scale in your data table and at the bottom of a new sheet of paper. This is the start of your map.

5. Use the scale and the measurements from step 3 to draw the outer boundaries of your map.

6. Choose several objects in the area to include on your map. The example classroom map on the next page shows some objects you might include.

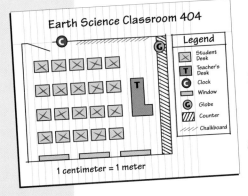

Earth Science Classroom 404

Legend

⊠	Student Desk
T	Teacher's Desk
C	Clock
▭	Window
G	Globe
▨	Counter
⁄⁄⁄⁄	Chalkboard

1 centimeter = 1 meter

Record these objects in your data table. Design symbols for the objects and draw them in the table, too.

7. Use your meterstick to measure where these objects are in relation to nearby walls or other objects. Record these location measurements.

8. Refer to these measurements and your scale. Then draw the symbols in the correct places on your map.

9. Add a legend and compass rose to your map.

Questions and Conclusions

1. Explain why you chose the symbols you used on your map.

2. How might you change your scale if you wanted to make this map twice as large?

3. Exchange maps with a partner. Use your partner's map and scale to find the actual distance between two points on the map. Then use a meterstick to measure this distance in the room. Was your partner's map accurate?

4. How are your map and your partner's map alike? How are they different?

Explore Further

Choose an area outside your home or school and make a map of it. To measure distance, use a meterstick, a tape measure, or the length of your foot. Include a legend, compass rose, and scale.

Objectives

After reading this lesson, you should be able to

◆ explain how contour lines show shape and elevation.

◆ visualize the landscape by looking at a topographic map.

Topographic map

Map that shows the shape and elevation of the land surface

Contour line

Line on a map that connects points of equal elevation

If you want to explore the earth's surface, one of the most helpful tools you can have is a **topographic map**. A topographic map shows the shape and elevation of the land surface. For example, a road map might mark the location of a mountain with a dot. But a topographic map shows the shape and elevation of the mountain in addition to its location.

Contour Lines and Intervals

A topographic map uses **contour lines** to show shape and elevation. A contour line is a line on a map that connects all points of equal elevation. To understand contour lines, study the figure below. The top part shows an island with contour lines wrapped around it. The bottom part shows how those contour lines look on a flat map.

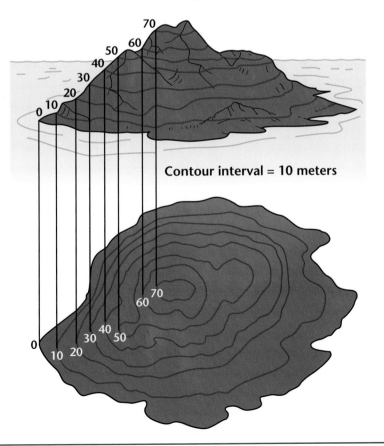

Contour interval = 10 meters

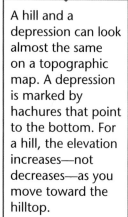

A hill and a depression can look almost the same on a topographic map. A depression is marked by hachures that point to the bottom. For a hill, the elevation increases—not decreases—as you move toward the hilltop.

Every point located on the zero contour line is at sea level. Every point located on the next contour line is 10 meters above sea level. The next contour line is 20 meters above sea level, and so on.

Notice that each contour line of the island is 10 meters higher than the one below it. This up-and-down distance between contour lines is the **contour interval**. The contour interval can be different from one map to another. The interval might be 5 meters on a map that shows mostly flat land. It might be 50 meters on a map that shows mostly mountains.

If you wanted to climb most easily to the top of the island, which side would you choose? The map tells you. One side of the island has a gentle slope and the other side has a steep slope. The topographic map shows this difference by the closeness of the contour lines. The closer the contour lines are to each other, the steeper the slope is.

What is the elevation of the highest point of this island? The highest contour line is 70 meters, so the island is at least that high. There is no 80-meter contour line, so the highest point is between 70 and 80 meters above sea level.

Using Topographic Maps

Look at the topographic map on the next page. It shows several land features. Try to find them as they are described below.

A series of closed loops shows a hill or mountain. The elevations of these contour lines increase toward the center. Find the contour lines that show Bear Mountain.

Closed loops may also show a depression, such as a watering hole or a pit. In this case, the elevations decrease toward the center. Short lines, called **hachures**, point into the depression. Find a depression in the southwest corner of the map.

Notice that some of the contour lines are bent into a V. Contour lines form a V on a map when they cross a valley. The V points up the valley. So if a river is flowing in the valley, the V points upstream. This is the direction from which the water is coming. In which direction does Beaver Creek flow?

Here are some other things to remember about contour lines.

- ◆ All contour lines eventually close, either on the map or beyond its borders.
- ◆ Contour lines never cross each other because one point cannot have more than one elevation.
- ◆ On most topographic maps, every fifth contour line is labeled with an elevation value.

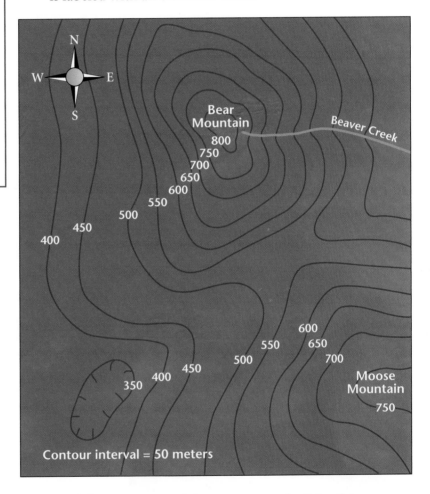

Topographic maps are useful to many people. Scientists use them to study land features and to plan expeditions. Engineers use them to plan highways and pipelines. Hikers use detailed topographic maps to locate trails, cliffs, ponds, hills, and rivers.

Write your answers to these questions on a sheet of paper.

1. What is a topographic map?

2. What is a contour interval?

3. How do contour lines show a steep slope?

4. On a topographic map, how can you tell where a valley is located?

5. On the map on page 17, which mountain is higher?

Science in Your Life

Mapping a Park

Which state park or national park is closest to where you live? You can find out by looking at a state map that shows all of these parks. Obtain a topographic map for a nearby park. Study the topographic map. What does the map show you about the surface features of the park? Pick out an interesting landmark or surface feature on the map. Then visit the park with a friend. Use the map to reach the landmark on foot. Take a hand compass with you to make sure you are facing the right direction as you read the map.

Reading a Topographic Map

Purpose

How might you use a topographic map? In this investigation, you will practice reading such a map.

Procedure

Answer the following questions about the map shown below.

1. What is the contour interval of this map?

2. How far is the top of Spruce Hill from the top of Castle Rock?

3. In which direction does the Meadow River flow?

Materials
◆ map shown below

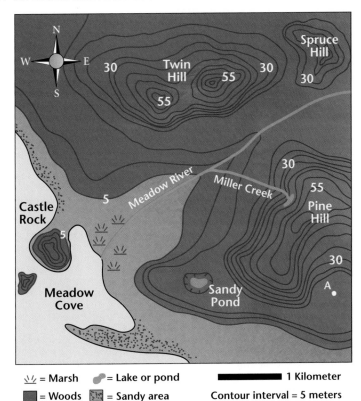

= Marsh   = Lake or pond   ▬▬▬ 1 Kilometer

= Woods   = Sandy area   Contour interval = 5 meters

4. Which side of Twin Hill is the steepest?

5. If you were standing at Point A near Pine Hill, would you be able to see Spruce Hill? Why or why not?

6. What covers most of the hills?

7. Which hill on the map is the highest?

8. About how high is Pine Hill?

Questions and Conclusions

1. How would this map look different if the contour interval was changed to 1 meter?

2. Give a specific example of how someone might use this map.

Explore Further

The United States Geological Survey (USGS) is a government agency that collects and provides earth science information. Its goal is to help solve natural resource problems. Providing accurate maps is an important task of this agency.

Use the library or the Internet to find an example of a USGS topographic map. Find the contour interval on the map. What land features do you see?

Chapter 1 SUMMARY

- Earth science is the study of the earth's land, water, and air, and outer space.

- Earth science includes four main fields: geology, oceanography, meteorology, and astronomy.

- Scientists use many tools to study the earth. Some tools are simple; some are complex.

- Scientists around the world use the metric system for measuring.

- Studying the earth provides knowledge that improves people's lives. You can use your own knowledge of earth science to make wise decisions.

- A map is a drawing that shows part of the earth's surface as seen from above.

- A map legend explains the symbols used on the map.

- Compass directions are shown on a map in different ways.

- A map scale is a comparison between distance on the map and actual distance on the earth.

- There are three common kinds of map scales: bar scales, equivalence scales, and ratios.

- Topographic maps are especially useful in earth science because they show the shape and elevation of the land surface.

- Topographic maps have contour lines, which connect points of equal elevation.

- The vertical distance between contour lines on a map is the contour interval.

- Certain patterns of contour lines show certain land features, such as hills, depressions, and valleys.

Science Words

astronomer, 4	geologist, 3	meteorology, 2	topographic
astronomy, 2	geology, 2	metric system, 3	map, 15
compass rose, 9	hachure, 16	oceanographer, 4	unit, 3
contour interval, 16	legend, 8	oceanography, 2	
contour line, 15	map, 7	scale, 10	
earth science, 2	meteorologist, 4	submersible, 4	

Chapter 1 R E V I E W

Word Bank

compass rose

contour interval

contour line

earth science

hachures

legend

scale

submersibles

topographic map

unit

Vocabulary Review

Choose the word or phrase from the Word Bank that best completes each sentence. Write the answer on your paper.

1. To find directions on a map, you would look for a(n) _____.

2. An example of a(n) _____ would be 1:10,000.

3. A known amount used for measuring is a(n) _____.

4. A map's _____ shows the meaning of the map's symbols.

5. A(n) _____ shows the shape and elevation of the earth's surface.

6. The study of land, water, and air is part of _____.

7. Scientists travel to the ocean floor in _____.

8. On a topographic map, points with the same elevation are connected by a(n) _____.

9. A depression would be shown by _____ connected to contour lines on a topographic map.

10. The vertical distance between contour lines on a topographic map is the _____.

Concept Review

Choose the word or phrase that best completes each sentence. Write the letter of the answer on your paper.

11. An earth scientist who studies weather is a(n) _____.
  A geologist   **C** astronomer
  B meteorologist   **D** oceanographer

12. A scientist who studies the stars is a(n) _____.
  A geologist   **C** meteorologist
  B oceanographer   **D** astronomer

13. A contour line that crosses a river makes a _____.

    A straight line   **B** V   **C** circle   **D** hachure

14. Several contour lines far apart on a map indicate a _____.

    A steep slope   **C** gentle slope

    B river   **D** flat area

15. If a map scale is 1:24,000, 1 centimeter on the map equals _____ on the earth's surface.

    A 24,000 centimeters   **C** 1 centimeter

    B 24,000 meters   **D** 24,000 feet

16. Scientists use the _____ system for measuring quantities and distances.

    A decimal   **B** metric   **C** inches   **D** customary

17. A(n) _____ is a metric unit of length.

    A inch   **B** foot   **C** centimeter   **D** mile

Critical Thinking

Write the answer to each of the following questions.

18. Look at the lettered illustrations. Name the land feature that each contour pattern represents.

19. You are given two maps, both of which are 10 centimeters wide by 10 centimeters long. One has a scale of 1 centimeter = 2 kilometers, and the other has a scale of 1 centimeter = 3 kilometers. Which map shows a larger part of the earth? Explain your answer.

20. Which contour interval would be better on a topographic map of a mountainous area: 5 meters or 30 meters? Why?

Test-Taking Tip If you have to choose the correct term to complete a sentence, read the sentence using each of the terms. Then choose the one that best fits the sentence.

2 Describing the Earth

I f you looked down on the earth from space, what would you see? This photo was taken from the space shuttle *Atlantis*. It shows a mountain range in Southeast Asia. It shows ocean water and a coastline. There is smoke from a forest fire. The photo was placed on top of a map of the same area. What does the map have that the photo doesn't? Besides contour lines, the map has straight lines that intersect. In Chapter 2, you will learn about this grid system and other ways to describe the earth.

Organize Your Thoughts

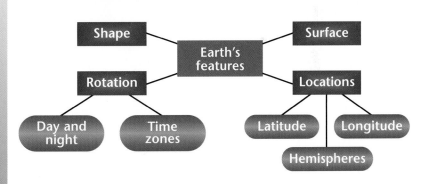

Goals for Learning

◆ To describe the earth's shape, continents, and oceans

◆ To explain what causes day and night

◆ To explain the earth's time zones

◆ To interpret a block grid on a map

◆ To use latitude and longitude to locate points on the earth

Objectives

After reading this lesson, you should be able to

◆ describe the earth's shape.

◆ locate the seven continents.

◆ name the four major oceans.

◆ explain rotation.

At one time, many people believed that the earth was flat. They thought that if they walked past its edge, they would fall off the earth! Of course, the earth is not flat and you cannot fall off.

The Earth's Shape

If you could view the earth from the moon, you would see that it has a shape like a ball. Most balls are perfectly round. If you measured the distance around the widest part of a ball in any direction, you would find that all the measurements would be equal. Compare the shape of the earth with the perfect circle below. You can see that the earth is not perfectly round. The distance around the earth in two different directions is given below. How do the measurements compare?

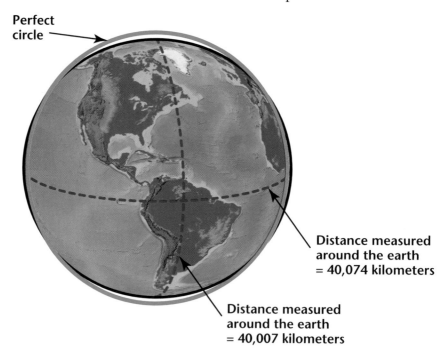

Perfect circle

Distance measured around the earth = 40,074 kilometers

Distance measured around the earth = 40,007 kilometers

The Earth's Surface

The earth's surface includes areas of land and water. The land areas make up about 30 percent of the earth's surface. Look at the circle graph. How much of the earth's surface is water?

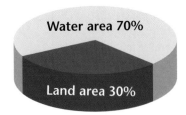

The land on the earth's surface is divided into seven major areas called **continents**. Find the continents of the earth on the map. Which continent do you think is the largest? Which is the smallest? Check your answers in the table below.

> **Continent**
>
> *One of the seven major land areas of the earth*

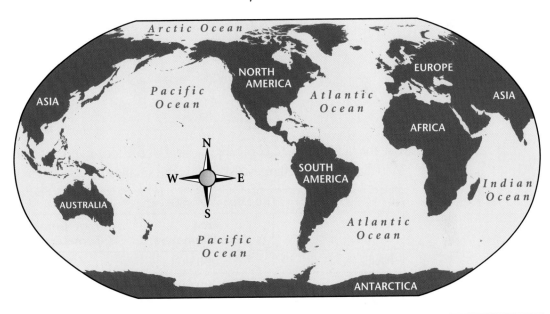

The Seven Continents		
Continent	Area (square kilometers)	Percent of Earth's Land Area
Asia	44,614,000	29.9
Africa	30,355,000	20.3
North America	24,208,000	16.2
South America	17,819,000	11.9
Antarctica	14,200,000	9.5
Europe	10,498,000	7.0
Australia	7,682,000	5.2

Look again at the map on page 27. The major areas of water connect with each other and form one huge, continuous ocean. The earth's ocean, however, is usually divided into four major bodies of water: the Pacific Ocean, Atlantic Ocean, Indian Ocean, and Arctic Ocean. Locate each of these on the map. There are smaller bodies of water, too. Among them are lakes, bays, gulfs, and seas. Oceans are much larger than any of these.

You cannot see across an ocean to land on the other side. The diagram shows why. Just like you cannot see around a ball, the earth's curve keeps you from seeing across an ocean.

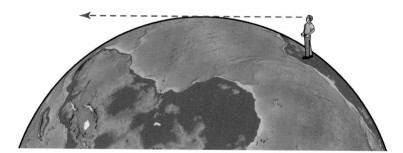

Use the table below to compare the sizes of the four major oceans. Which ocean is the largest? Which is the smallest?

The Four Major Oceans		
Ocean	Area (square kilometers)	Average Depth (kilometers)
Pacific	166,000,000	4.2
Atlantic	82,000,000	3.7
Indian	73,000,000	3.9
Arctic	14,000,000	1.2

To find out more about the earth's land and water, look at Appendixes G and H. Appendix G is a map showing the countries that make up the earth's continents. It also shows major seas, gulfs, and bays of the world. Appendix H is a map of North America.

The Earth's Rotation

If you spin a top, at first it stands upright, turning around and around. After a while, friction slows down the top. It begins to wobble and stops spinning. Like a top, the earth also spins around. But unlike a top, the earth does not stop—it keeps on spinning. The spinning of the earth is called **rotation**.

As shown below, the earth spins, or rotates, from west to east around an imaginary line that passes through the center of the earth. This line is called the **axis** of the earth. The axis passes through two points called poles. The **North Pole** is the point farthest to the north on the earth. The **South Pole** is the point farthest to the south.

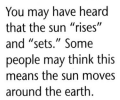

Science Myth

You may have heard that the sun "rises" and "sets." Some people may think this means the sun moves around the earth.

Fact: The sun does not move around the earth "rising" and "setting." Day and night occur because the earth rotates on its axis. As it rotates, one part of the earth moves into the sun's light. As this happens, another part of the earth turns away from the sun's light.

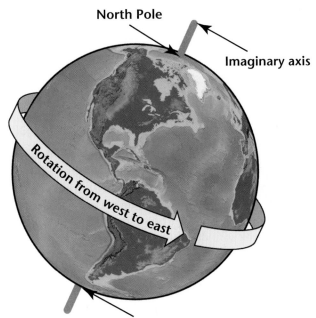

North Pole

Imaginary axis

Rotation from west to east

South Pole (not visible)

Write your answers to these questions on a sheet of paper.

1. Describe the earth's shape.

2. What are the seven continents?

3. What are the four major oceans?

4. What is rotation?

5. Use compass directions to describe how the earth rotates.

Achievements in Science

A Trip Around the World

In July 2002, Steve Fossett, an athlete and adventurer, achieved what no other human had ever done alone. After four failed attempts, he flew a hot-air balloon completely around the earth. The successful trip took Fossett about 14 days and 20 hours.

Fossett's balloon, the *Spirit of Freedom*, contained about 165,000 cubic meters of helium and 30,000 cubic meters of hot air. The capsule Fossett traveled in during the flight was just big enough for him to stretch out. There was also a special heating system to keep him warm.

Fossett navigated the flight using a global positioning system (GPS). During the trip, he used a laptop computer and satellite e-mail to communicate with his control center in St. Louis, Missouri.

The *Spirit of Freedom* started its flight in Australia. It flew east across the South Pacific Ocean, the tip of South America, across the Atlantic and Indian Oceans, then back to Australia. That's 34,000 kilometers! Trace this trip on the map on page 27. Why was Fossett's trip shorter than the distances shown on page 26?

What determines when you go to school, eat lunch, or get ready for bed? More than likely, what you are doing depends on what time of day it is. The time of day depends on the earth's rotation.

Day and Night

You have learned that the earth rotates on its axis. The earth takes 24 hours, or 1 day, to rotate once on its axis. Notice in the diagram how the sun shines on the earth as the earth rotates. The sun can shine on only one side at a time. As a result, one side of the earth is light and has daytime. The opposite side is dark and has nighttime.

Sunlight

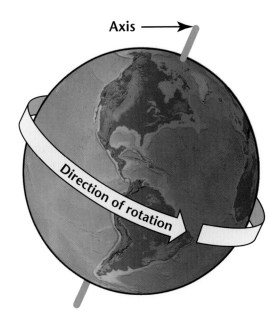

Axis

Direction of rotation

Because the earth continues to rotate, the places on the earth that have daytime keep changing. In other words, the time of day keeps changing everywhere on the earth. The time of day depends on where the sun appears to be in the sky. The sun does not really move across the sky, but the rotating earth makes the sun appear to move. As the earth turns from west to east, the sun appears to rise in the east in the morning. Then it appears to move across the sky and set in the west at night.

Standard Time Zones

Compare the diagram on page 31 with the one below. Both show areas of daytime and nighttime. The diagram below shows the earth as seen from above the North Pole. Notice how time varies around the earth.

Standard time zone

Area that has the same clock time

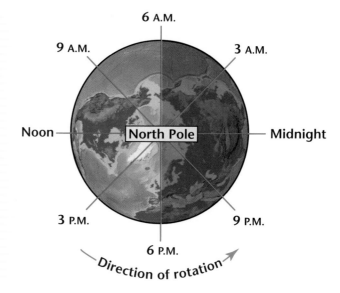

Sunlight

6 A.M.

9 A.M.

3 A.M.

Noon — North Pole — Midnight

3 P.M.

9 P.M.

6 P.M.

Direction of rotation

Did You Know?

Standard time zones were set up in 1883. Until then, most places set their own time zones. For example, Philadelphia's clocks were 5 minutes behind New York's and 19 minutes ahead of Pittsburgh's. Confusing to travelers? You bet.

When it is noon at one point on the earth, it is midnight at a point that is halfway around the earth. The remaining hours of the day are equally spread around the earth between noon and midnight.

All 24 hours in the day are occurring somewhere on the earth right now. The earth has been divided into 24 **standard time zones,** one for each hour of the day. A standard time zone is an area of the earth that has the same clock time.

The map below shows the world's standard time zones. The boundaries of the time zones do not exactly follow straight lines. Over land areas, the zones usually follow borders of countries, states, counties, and towns. How many time zones are there across North America?

Find the **international date line** on the map. It is an imaginary line that defines the start of a day. When you cross it going west, you move to the next calendar day. When you cross it going east, you move to the previous calendar day.

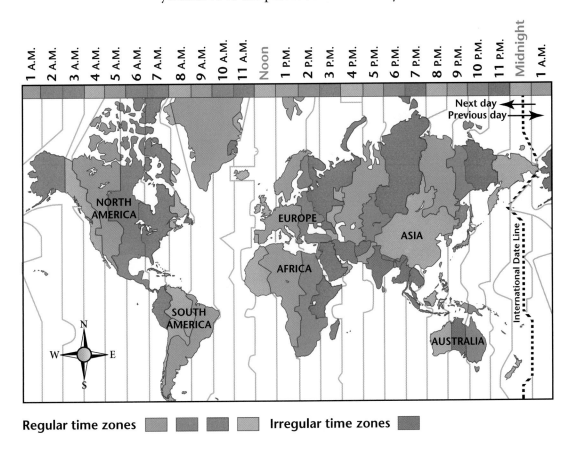

Regular time zones ▢ ▢ ▢   Irregular time zones ▢

The map below shows the time zones for Hawaii and parts of North America. Notice that the time on the West Coast of the United States is 3 hours earlier than on the East Coast. So the time gets earlier as you travel westward.

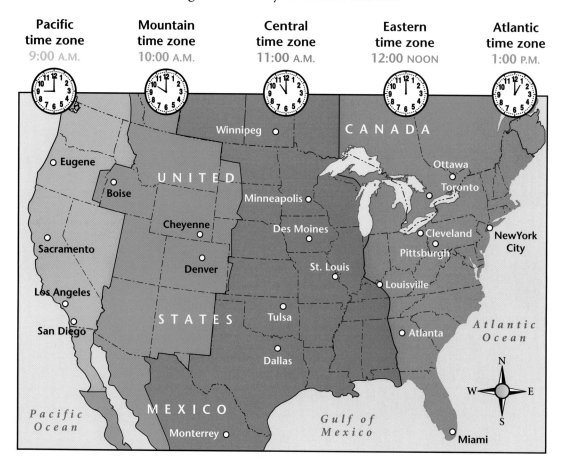

Pacific time zone
9:00 A.M.

Mountain time zone
10:00 A.M.

Central time zone
11:00 A.M.

Eastern time zone
12:00 NOON

Atlantic time zone
1:00 P.M.

Hawaii-Aleutian time zone
7:00 A.M.

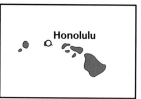

Honolulu

Alaska time zone
8:00 A.M.

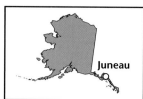

Juneau

Use the map on page 34 to answer these questions on a sheet of paper.

1. In what time zone is your home located? What time zone is 1 hour ahead of yours?

2. If it is 10:00 A.M. in Tulsa, what time would it be in Juneau?

3. If it is noon in New York City, what time would it be in Monterrey?

4. If it is 11:00 P.M. in Sacramento, what time would it be in Honolulu?

5. If you were to travel from Toronto to Eugene, would you move your watch forward or backward?

Science in Your Life

New York   Tokyo

Local

Zurich   London

Time Zones

You deal with time zones in your daily life. You may have noticed that when a TV show is advertised, more than one time is given for its airing. For example, a show might air at 8:00 P.M. Eastern Standard Time (EST) and 7:00 P.M. Central Standard Time (CST).

Let's say you live on the East Coast of the United States and want to call someone on the West Coast. Think about time zones before you place the call. If you call at 9:00 A.M. your time, it's only 6:00 A.M. on the West Coast. The person you called may still be asleep!

Now consider different time zones around the world. Find your time zone on the map on page 33. Then count 12 time zones to the right to see what time zone is a half day (exactly 12 hours) ahead of your time. What continent is shown within that time zone? What might people there be doing now?

International airports often have clocks showing the time in different cities or zones. Travelers use them to set their watches. Suppose you are catching a flight to London. You could look at the clocks shown here and set your watch from local time to London time, which is 8 hours ahead.

Modeling the Earth's Rotation

Purpose

How would you create a model explaining day and night? In this investigation, you will model the earth's rotation.

Materials

◆ globe
◆ masking tape
◆ flashlight

Procedure

1. Work with a partner in this investigation. Copy the data table on your paper.

Step 5 Observations	Step 7 Observations

2. On the globe, find the approximate spot where your home is located. Place a piece of masking tape over the spot.

3. On the globe, find the North and South Poles. Imagine that the globe is the earth and that its axis runs through the poles. Place the globe on a table, with the South Pole toward the table. Practice rotating it slowly on its axis. Remember to rotate it from west to east (or counterclockwise, as seen from above the North Pole).

4. Darken the room. Have your partner hold the flashlight and stand at one end of the table. The flashlight represents the sun. Have your partner turn on the flashlight and shine it at the globe. Position the globe so that the masking tape is facing the flashlight. **Safety Alert: Do not shine the flashlight into the eyes of others.**

5. Observe what part of the globe is in light and what part is in shadow. Record your observations in the data table, noting the position of the masking tape.

6. Slowly rotate the globe on its axis from west to east. Stop when the masking tape has moved halfway around the globe.

7. Repeat step 5.

8. Switch places with your partner and repeat steps 4 through 7.

Questions and Conclusions

1. In which step did you model daytime at your home?

2. In which step did you model nighttime at your home?

3. Describe how daytime becomes nighttime at any spot on the earth.

Explore Further

Use the globe and flashlight to model how the earth turns during one 24-hour day. Describe how the position of your home changes during that time. Describe the sunlight you receive during the 24-hour period.

Objectives

After reading this lesson, you should be able to

◆ explain what a block grid is.

◆ use a block grid to locate a point on a map.

Grid

Set of horizontal and vertical lines on a map

Locating places on a small, simple map is quick and easy. You simply search the map for the place name. Searching for places on a large, complex map, like a state or world map, is not as quick or easy. A better way to locate places on a complex map is to use a **grid**. A map grid is a set of horizontal and vertical lines drawn on a map.

The map below shows an example of one kind of grid called a block grid. The lines on a block grid divide a map into blocks. Each block is numbered and lettered. The numbers and letters help you to quickly locate the blocks and the places inside them.

Notice in the map that each letter represents a row and each number represents a column. Block C3 is highlighted in gray. It is located in row C and column 3. To find block C3, look across row C and down column 3. The city of Morris is in this block.

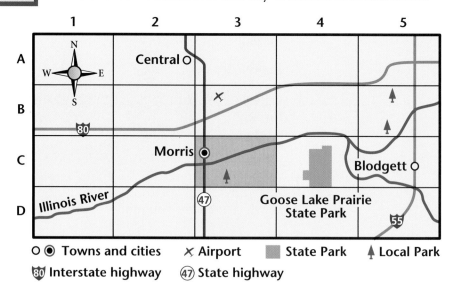

Now, use the same method to locate block B3 on the map. Look across row B and down column 3. What features are located in block B3? Refer to the map legend. If you said highways and an airport, you are correct.

Lesson 3 R E V I E W

Use the map on page 38 to answer these questions on a sheet of paper.

1. Which highway is located in column 5?

2. In which block is Central located?

3. In which block does Highway 80 cross Highway 55?

4. Which block includes two parks?

5. In which block is Goose Lake Prairie State Park located?

Achievements in Science

Global Positioning Systems

Global positioning systems (GPSs) are computers that can tell you exactly where you are. GPSs use signals from satellites to locate objects on the earth's surface. These tools were first used by astronauts and airline pilots to help them steer, or navigate. Today GPSs are used in a variety of ways. They are even found in many current-model cars.

Imagine getting into your car, fastening your seatbelt, starting the engine, and then entering an address into your car's GPS. A friendly voice guides you to your destination. It tells you when to turn right or left. You can even watch your progress on a colorful, on-screen map. If you miss a turn, the GPS figures out a new route for you to take.

Some GPS models are equipped with voice recognition. If you need help but cannot take your eyes off the road, you can simply talk to the GPS and it will respond.

Materials

◆ 2 round balloons

◆ marker

Describing Location on a Round Surface

Purpose

Can you think of a good way to describe a certain location on a round balloon? In this investigation, you will explore ways to describe a location on a round surface.

Procedure

1. Copy the data table on your paper.

Location of the X	Method for Locating the X

2. Blow up two balloons until they have a rounded shape. They should also be the same size. With the marker, make a small **X** on one of the balloons. **Safety Alert: Do not overfill balloons. They can burst and cause injury.**

3. In the data table, describe the location of the **X** on the balloon. Be as accurate and clear as possible.

4. Set aside the marked balloon. Show your description to another student. Then have the student point to the location on the unmarked balloon. See if he or she can use your description to tell where the **X** is.

5. Think about how you might improve your description. Then think of the best method you can for clearly describing the location of the **X**. In the data table, write the steps for your method. If possible, include diagrams.

6. To test your method, trade methods with another student. See how well you can follow each other's steps and how well each method works.

7. If necessary, rewrite your steps.

Questions and Conclusions

1. Was describing the location of the **X** difficult or easy? Explain your answer.

2. How is the earth like the balloon?

3. How well did your method work? What would you change about it?

Explore Further

Look at a globe and a world map. What differences do you see? Compare the size and shape of the continents, especially Antarctica. Some maps distort the relative size of features close to the poles. Why do you think this happens?

Objectives

After reading this lesson, you should be able to

◆ explain what a global grid is.

◆ define latitude.

◆ estimate a point's latitude.

Latitude

Angle that describes the distance north or south of the equator

Equator

Line of 0° latitude halfway between the poles

Parallel

Line of latitude

Degree

Unit for measuring angles in a circle or sphere

In Investigation 2-2, you may have discovered that a grid can be laid over a round object to locate points on the object. This grid is a global grid. Like other grids, it consists of two sets of lines. The first set of lines are lines of **latitude**. These are imaginary lines that run in an east-west direction around the earth. Latitude describes the distance north or south of the **equator**. The equator is the line of latitude halfway between the North and South Poles. Find the lines of latitude on the map on page 43. Lines of latitude are also called **parallels**.

Notice the two parallels called the tropic of Cancer and the tropic of Capricorn. The sun is directly over the tropic of Cancer on the first day of summer north of the equator. It is directly over the tropic of Capricorn on the first day of summer south of the equator. You will learn more about these parallels and the seasons in Chapter 3.

On the map, you can see that parallels are numbered, beginning at the equator and ending at each of the poles. The parallels are numbered in **degrees**. Degrees are used to measure angles in circles and spheres. A complete circle has 360 degrees. The symbol for degrees is a small circle. For example, 90 degrees is written as 90°.

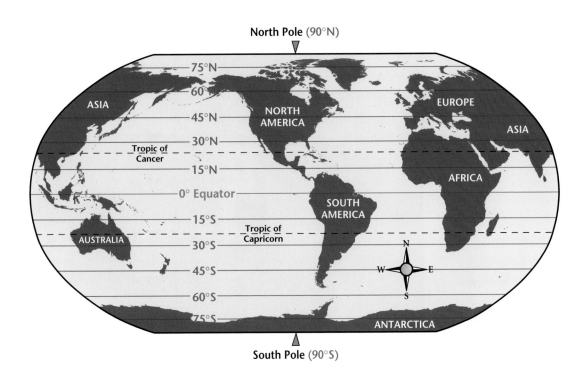

North Pole (90°N)

75°N
60°N
ASIA
45°N
NORTH
AMERICA
30°N
Tropic of
Cancer
15°N
EUROPE
ASIA
0° Equator
AFRICA
15°S
SOUTH
AMERICA
Tropic of
Capricorn
AUSTRALIA
30°S
45°S
N
W   E
S
60°S
75°S
ANTARCTICA

South Pole (90°S)

A *degree* can refer to two very different measurement units in science. Degrees are used to measure angles in a circle or sphere. Latitude is an example of this. Degrees are also used to measure temperature. For example, water freezes at 0°C. Both of these measurement units have the same symbol. But they are not related at all.

Notice that the latitude numbers begin at 0° at the equator and increase to 90° at the North Pole. All latitude numbers north of the equator are followed by the letter *N*.

The latitude numbers also begin at 0° at the equator and increase to 90° at the South Pole. South of the equator, all latitude numbers are followed by the letter *S*.

No line of latitude is greater than 90°. What happens if you try to go to a latitude that is higher than 90°N or 90°S? Trace an imaginary trip on a globe. Start at the equator and go north. From the equator to the North Pole, the number of degrees of latitude increases. If you continue your path past the pole, you will find yourself on the other side of the earth. You will be heading back toward the equator, and the number of degrees of latitude will be decreasing.

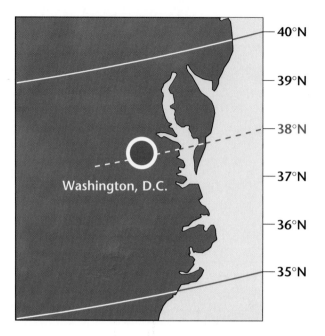

When a map, such as the one above, does not show every parallel, the person using the map must estimate the parallels that are not shown. To do that, the person must divide the space that is between the parallels that are shown. The divisions should be equal.

To find the latitude of Washington, D.C., on the map, use the following procedure.

1. Find the two parallels on either side of Washington, D.C. (35°N and 40°N).

2. In your mind or on paper, put in the latitude lines between 35°N and 40°N that are missing (36°, 37°, 38°, and 39°). Divide the space equally.

3. Use the divisions you added to estimate the latitude of Washington, D.C., to the nearest degree. The correct latitude is 38°N.

Use the map on page 43 to answer these questions on a sheet of paper.

1. What is the latitude of the equator?

2. What is the latitude of the South Pole?

3. Which two continents extend both north and south of 0° latitude?

4. Estimate the latitude of the northern tip of South America.

5. Estimate the latitude where you live.

Science at Work

Air-Traffic Controller

Air-traffic controllers are responsible for directing millions of aircraft flights around the world. Their job is to keep the sky safe by preventing aircraft collisions. To do this, they communicate with pilots using a radio. They tell pilots how high to fly and when and where to land or take off. They use special maps to keep track of the positions of aircraft.

To apply for the position of air-traffic controller, a person must have a degree from a 4-year college or at least 3 years of related work experience. The applicant must also pass a written test.

Good air-traffic controllers are calm and able to make snap decisions in emergencies. They must have excellent vision and hearing. For example, in a single glance, they must memorize the positions of several aircraft. Air-traffic controllers must have another special skill. Since their air-traffic maps are flat, they must be able to visualize this information in three dimensions.

Where can you find an air-traffic controller? Every airport that has regularly scheduled flights has an air-traffic control tower where controllers work. From this tower, they can see planes coming in and taking off. Look for the air-traffic control tower the next time you visit an airport.

Longitude

Angle that describes the distance east or west of the prime meridian

Meridian

Line of longitude

Prime meridian

Line of 0° longitude

You have learned about global grid lines of latitude, which run east and west. The second set of lines making up a global grid are lines of **longitude**. These are imaginary lines that run in a north-south direction from pole to pole. Longitude lines are also called **meridians**. Longitude describes the distance east or west of the **prime meridian**. The prime meridian is the line of 0° longitude. It is sometimes called the Greenwich meridian because it passes through the town of Greenwich, England.

Like parallels, meridians are numbered in degrees. Numbering begins with 0° at the prime meridian and ends at 180°. The 180° line is on the opposite side of the earth from the prime meridian. Numbers east of the prime meridian are followed by the letter *E*. Numbers west of the prime meridian are followed by a *W*. The line that is 180°W is also 180°E. As you can see on the map below, meridians are not spaced equally at all points. They come together at the poles and are farthest apart at the equator.

Do you remember the steps used to estimate the latitude of Washington, D.C.? Review page 44. To estimate meridians that are not shown on a map, follow a similar procedure.

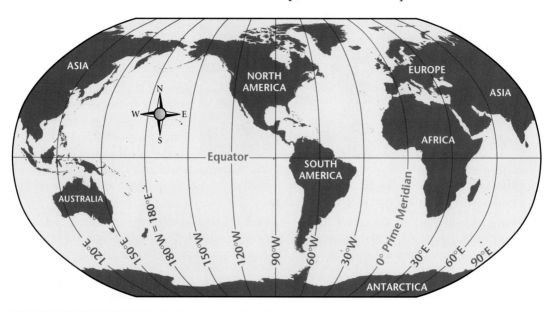

Use the map on page 46 to answer these questions on a sheet of paper.

1. What is the longitude of the prime meridian?

2. What is the highest numbered meridian?

3. Estimate the longitude of the eastern edge of South America.

4. Estimate the longitude where you live.

5. Compare latitude and longitude lines. How are they different?

Technology Note

Mercator projection

Orthographic projection

Robinson projection

Through history, mapmakers, or cartographers, have used a variety of tools to create maps. Today cartographers use mathematics, computers, and photos taken from aircraft or satellites.

Imagine cutting open a hollow ball and taping it on a flat piece of paper. That's a bit like what cartographers do to make a map of the world. The result is called a map projection. There are many kinds. Three map projections are shown here.

A Mercator projection is a rectangle-shaped map. Its lines of latitude and longitude are equally spaced. These projections are useful for navigating the oceans. However, the true area of water and land near the poles is distorted on a Mercator projection.

An orthographic projection shows the earth as it might look from space. Because this kind of map is a globe shape, it can only show one half of the earth at a time. Areas at the edge of the map are distorted.

Robinson projections are frequently used for world maps. These kinds of maps are oval shaped. Lines of latitude appear as straight lines. Lines of longitude increase in curvature from the center of the map to the outer edges. Area near the poles is still distorted, but less than on a Mercator projection.

Look at the world maps in this chapter. What kinds of map projections are used?

Technology Note

Photogrammetry is a process used to make accurate maps. First, photos of the area to be mapped are taken from two locations above the earth. Then a computer called a stereoplotter creates a three-dimensional image using the photos.

Intersecting parallels and meridians form a global grid for the entire earth. Two intersecting lines meet only at one point. So intersecting parallels and meridians make it possible for you to locate a single point anywhere on the earth.

Locating Points by Latitude and Longitude

To locate any point on the surface of the earth, you need to know both the latitude and longitude of that point. When stating any point's location, the latitude is written before the longitude. For example, find point A on the map below. Point A lies on the 45°N parallel and the 30°W meridian. Its location is written as 45°N, 30°W. This means point A is 45° north of the equator and 30° west of the prime meridian.

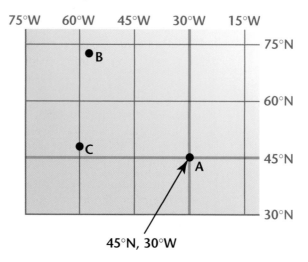

By estimating the position of any missing grid lines, you should be able to locate point C at about 48°N, 60°W. What is the location of point B? It is about 72°N, 57°W.

Hemispheres

The equator is the line of latitude halfway between the North and South Poles. This line divides the earth into two **hemispheres**. A hemisphere is half of the earth. Two equal-sized hemispheres make up the whole earth. The half of the earth north of the equator is called the Northern Hemisphere. The half south of the equator is the Southern Hemisphere. In which of these hemispheres do you live?

If the earth were cut in half through the prime meridian, it would be divided into another set of hemispheres. These two halves are known as the Eastern Hemisphere and the Western Hemisphere. Which hemisphere includes most of Africa?

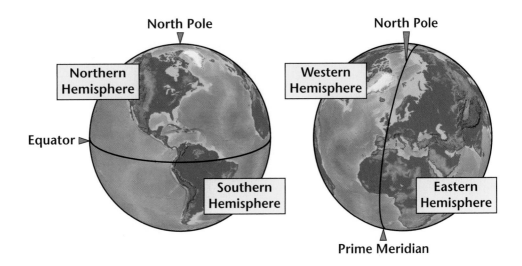

Use the map below to answer these questions on a sheet of paper.

1. What city is located at 30°N, 90°W?

2. What city is located at 40°N, 76°W?

3. What city is located at 39°N, 105°W?

4. What is the latitude and longitude of Helena?

5. What is the latitude and longitude of Winnipeg?

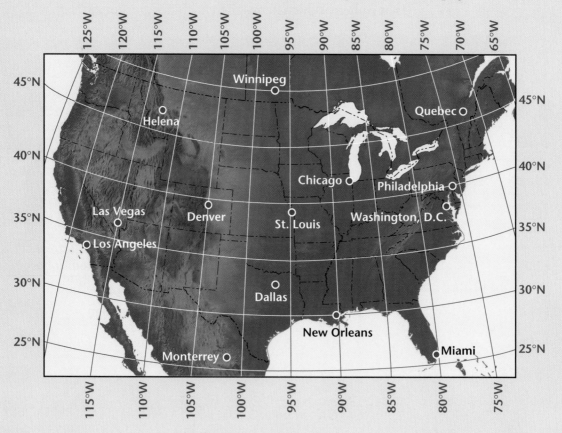

- The earth has a rounded shape, but it is not perfectly round.

- About 30 percent of the earth's surface is land, which is broken up into seven continents.

- About 70 percent of the earth's surface is water, most of which is divided into four oceans.

- Rotation is the spinning of the earth on its axis. The earth rotates from west to east.

- The turning of the earth on its axis results in day and night.

- The earth is divided into 24 standard time zones. Within a given zone, the clock time is the same.

- A grid is a set of horizontal and vertical lines on a map. A grid is used to locate places on a map.

- Latitude lines are imaginary lines that run east and west around the earth. Latitude lines are called parallels.

- Latitude is an angle that describes the distance from the equator.

- Longitude lines are imaginary lines that run north and south from pole to pole. Longitude lines are called meridians.

- Longitude is an angle that describes the distance from the prime meridian.

- Intersecting parallels and meridians make it possible to locate a single point anywhere on the earth.

- A hemisphere is half of the earth.

- The equator divides the earth into the Northern and Southern Hemispheres. The prime meridian divides the earth into the Western and Eastern Hemispheres.

Science Words

axis, 29	hemisphere, 49	meridian, 46	South Pole, 29
continent, 27	international date	North Pole, 29	standard time
degree, 42	line, 33	parallel, 42	zone, 32
equator, 42	latitude, 42	prime meridian, 46	
grid, 38	longitude, 46	rotation, 29	

Chapter 2 R E V I E W

Word Bank

axis
continents
equator
grid
hemisphere
longitude
parallel
prime meridian
rotation
standard time zone

Vocabulary Review

Choose the word or phrase from the Word Bank that best completes each sentence. Write the answer on your paper.

1. The set of horizontal and vertical lines on a map is its _____.

2. One half of the earth is a(n) _____.

3. The line of 0° longitude is the _____.

4. An area that has the same clock time is a(n) _____.

5. The imaginary line through the earth connecting the North and South Poles is the _____.

6. A line of latitude is a(n) _____.

7. The seven major land areas of the earth are _____.

8. The spinning of the earth is _____.

9. The line of latitude halfway between the North and South Poles is the _____.

10. The angle that describes the distance east or west of the prime meridian is _____.

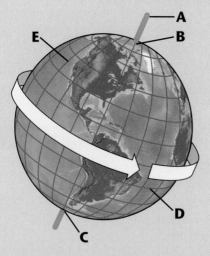

Concept Review

Write the answer to each of the following questions.

11. Name each of the lettered features in the diagram.

12. Describe the shape of the earth.

13. What percentage of the earth's surface do the continents represent?

14. When it is midnight at one point on the earth, what time is it at a point exactly halfway around the earth?

15. What is the measurement unit for latitude and longitude?

16. What is the line of 0° latitude called?

17. On which line of longitude does a point at 31°S, 92°W lie?

18. Which hemispheres lie on either side of the prime meridian?

Choose the word or phrase that best completes each sentence. Write the letter of the answer on your paper.

19. The earth rotates from _____.
   A east to west   **C** west to east
   B north to south   **D** south to north

20. The earth rotates once every _____.
   A day   **B** week   **C** month   **D** year

21. The time in Europe is _____ the time in North America.
   A behind   **C** the same as
   B ahead of   **D** 1 hour different from

22. A point at 80°N latitude is located near the _____.
   A equator   **C** tropic of Capricorn
   B South Pole   **D** North Pole

23. The entire continent of Antarctica is located in the _____ Hemisphere.
   A Northern   **B** Eastern   **C** Western   **D** Southern

Critical Thinking

Write the answer to each of the following questions.

24. How are latitude and longitude alike and different?

25. How would day and night be different if the earth did not rotate?

Test-Taking Tip   Answer all questions you are sure of first, then go back and answer the others.

3

The Earth and Moon System

Looking up at a full moon on a clear night, it might be hard to believe that the moon is about 400,000 kilometers away from us. It seems closer! Even though the earth and moon are far apart, they affect each other in many ways. Ocean tides, lunar eclipses, the phases of the moon—these all happen because of the interaction between the earth and moon. In Chapter 3, you will find out about the earth and moon system.

Organize Your Thoughts

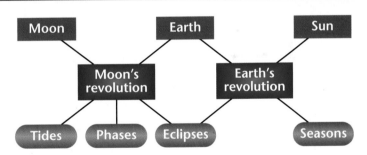

Goals for Learning

◆ To define gravity and understand its effects

◆ To describe how the earth and moon move in space

◆ To explain how the earth's revolution and the tilt of its axis cause seasons

◆ To describe the four major phases of the moon

◆ To explain how an eclipse happens

◆ To explain how the moon causes tides

◆ To describe features of the moon's surface

Gravity

Force of attraction between any two objects

Mass

Amount of matter that an object contains

Orbit

Curved path that an object follows as it revolves around another object

When you throw a ball into the air, it eventually falls. It falls because of **gravity**. Gravity is a force of attraction between any two objects, caused by those objects pulling on each other. The strength of this force depends on two factors:

◆ The distance between the two objects
◆ The **mass** of each object, or how much matter each object contains

The closer the objects are to each other, the stronger the gravity between them. Objects with greater mass have greater gravitational pull. For example, when you throw a ball, the ball and the earth pull on each other. The earth and the ball are very close to each other, and the earth's mass is much greater than the ball's mass. Therefore, the earth's gravitational pull brings the ball back toward the earth, and the ball falls.

The diagram shows how gravity affects the earth and moon. The earth has more mass than the moon. So the gravity between the earth and moon pulls the moon into a curved path around the earth. This curved path is an **orbit**. The sun has more mass than the earth. Gravity pulls the earth, with its moon, into an orbit around the sun. Notice that the shape of an orbit is not an exact circle. It is an ellipse, which is an oval shape.

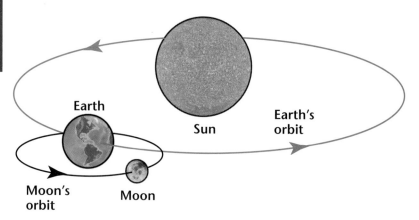

Earth

Sun

Earth's orbit

Moon's orbit

Moon

Write your answers to these questions on a sheet of paper.

1. What is gravity?

2. What factors affect the strength of gravity?

3. What is an orbit?

4. How does gravity affect the motion of the earth?

5. Explain the relationships between the earth, moon, and sun in terms of orbits.

Achievements in Science

Almanacs

An almanac is a book of information organized by the days of a year. Almanacs are updated and published each year. They predict moon phases, times of sunrise and sunset, weather, and much more. These predictions are based on carefully recorded facts from previous years.

In 1476, a German astronomer wrote one of the first almanacs to be printed on a printing press. Almanacs became important resources, especially for farmers and ship navigators. The early almanacs were often one of the few books in a home.

The most famous almanac in the American colonies was *Poor Richard's Almanack*. Benjamin Franklin wrote and published this almanac from 1732 to 1757. He did all of his own calculations for the data in his almanacs. Benjamin Banneker was another American inventor who wrote almanacs. He started studying math and astronomy when he was 40. By teaching himself, he accurately predicted solar eclipses, tides, and weather. He published his almanac from 1792 to 1802.

In 1886, Joseph Pulitzer began publishing *The World Almanac*. This was the first almanac to include a wider range of topics, such as sports records and facts about countries. During World War II, copies of *The World Almanac* were given to soldiers overseas. It is still produced every year, but now it is called *The World Almanac and Book of Facts*.

There are many kinds of almanacs published today. The next time you visit a library, look in the reference section. Find an almanac and page through this handy book.

INVESTIGATION

Materials

- sheet of paper
- piece of corrugated cardboard
- safety glasses
- 2 pushpins
- centimeter ruler
- scissors
- string

Making a Model of an Orbit

Purpose

How might you model an orbit? In this investigation, you will construct a device that helps you draw an ellipse.

Procedure

1. Place the sheet of paper over the piece of cardboard.

2. **Safety Alert: Put on safety glasses.**

3. Stick two pins near the center of the paper so they are 7 centimeters apart. Stick the pins through both the paper and the cardboard. **Safety Alert: Use care with pins. The points are sharp.**

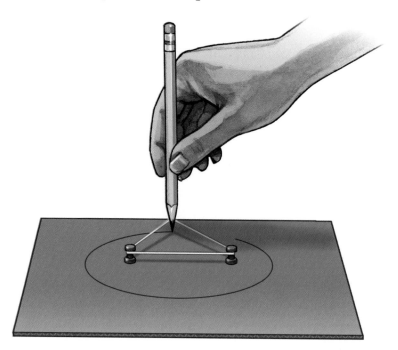

4. Cut a piece of string about 25 centimeters long. Tie the ends together to form a loop. Place the loop of string over both pins. The loop should be about 5 centimeters longer than the distance between the pins.

5. Place a pencil inside the loop and pull it gently away from the pins so the string straightens out.

6. Keeping the string fairly tight, draw a curving line all the way around both pins. **Safety Alert: Avoid pulling the string too tight and pulling out the pins.**

7. Remove the pins and place them a little farther apart. Repeat steps 5 and 6.

Questions and Conclusions

1. The shapes that you drew are ellipses. How would you describe an ellipse?

2. What is the difference between the first ellipse and the second ellipse you drew?

3. What do you think would happen if you drew an ellipse with the pins closer together instead of farther apart? Try it.

Explore Further

Design an experiment to find the relationship between ellipse size and the distance between the pins. Use a ruler. Make a data table for recording different pin distances and the resulting ellipse width and length. What patterns do you see in your data? What happens when the distance between the pins is zero?

Why is a year about 365 days? Why do seasons change throughout the year? You can answer these questions once you know how the earth moves in space.

Revolution and Rotation

The movement of the earth in its orbit around the sun is the earth's **revolution**. A single revolution of the earth takes about 365 days, which is one year.

While the earth is revolving around the sun, it is also rotating on its axis. As discussed in Chapter 2, the earth rotates once every day, or every 24 hours.

Seasons

Revolution
_____
Movement of one object in its orbit around another object in space

As the earth revolves around the sun, the earth's axis always stays tilted at $23\frac{1}{2}°$, as shown below. The tilt causes sunlight to fall more directly on different parts of the earth throughout its orbit. The diagram on the next page shows how this causes seasons. Notice that when it is summer in the Northern Hemisphere, that hemisphere is tilted toward the sun. When it is winter in the Northern Hemisphere, that hemisphere is tilted away from the sun.

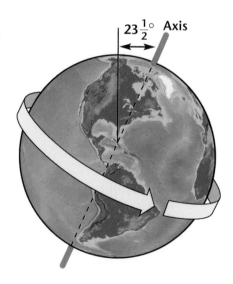

$23\frac{1}{2}°$ **Axis**

When it is summer in the Northern Hemisphere, it is winter in the Southern Hemisphere. For example, July is a summer month in the United States, but it is a winter month in Argentina. In the Northern Hemisphere, October is a fall month. In the Southern Hemisphere, October is in springtime.

No matter where you live, in the summer, the noontime sun appears at its highest in the sky. During the winter, it appears at its lowest. The sun's rays strike the earth more directly in the summer than in the winter. The more direct the sunlight is, the more it heats up the ground. Thus, it is warmer in the summer than it is in the winter.

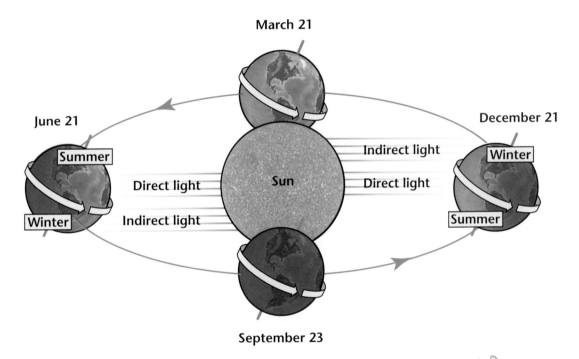

Science Myth

You may think it is warmer in summer because the earth is closer to the sun.

Fact: Actually, in the Northern Hemisphere, the distance between the earth and the sun is slightly greater during the summer months. It is the tilt of the earth toward the sun that causes summer sunlight to hit the earth directly. This results in the warmer temperatures of summer.

Write your answers to these questions on a sheet of paper.

1. Why is a year about 365 days long?

2. How far is the earth tilted on its axis?

3. When the Northern Hemisphere is tilted toward the sun, what season is it in that hemisphere?

4. When it is spring in the Northern Hemisphere, what season is it in the Southern Hemisphere?

5. Explain the difference between indirect and direct sunlight.

▼◀▲▼◀▲▼◀▲▼◀▲▼◀▲▼◀▲▼◀▲▼◀▲▼◀▲▼◀▲▼◀▲▼◀▲▼◀▲▼◀▲▼◀▲▼◀▲▼◀▲▼◀▲▼

Science at Work

Space Shuttle and International Space Station Crews

The International Space Station (ISS) is a big research laboratory orbiting the earth. Many countries, including the United States, Canada, and Russia, use and contribute to the ISS. Space shuttles are launchable spacecraft designed to shuttle, or go back and forth, between the earth and the ISS.

Space shuttle crew members fly shuttle missions to maintain and supply the ISS. Astronaut and pilot Pamela Ann Melroy was part of a 2002 crew that carried equipment to the ISS and installed it. The entire mission took 11 days.

In addition to space shuttle crews, there are ISS crews. They live and work on the ISS for months at a time.

Space shuttle and ISS crew members help construct, maintain, and repair the ISS. Sometimes crew members go on space walks to perform these tasks. Crew members also perform scientific experiments to test the effects of the space environment on human beings, animals, and diseases. Some experiments test properties of matter in space.

Space shuttle and ISS crew members come from several countries. They must have a bachelor's degree in engineering, biological science, physical science, or mathematics. At least three years of related job experience is also required. An applicant must pass a physical exam that tests vision and blood pressure, among other things. An astronaut must have strong science and math skills and be physically strong and healthy.

Exploring Light Angle

Purpose

How does the angle of a light affect its brightness on an object? In this investigation, you will model how the angle of sunlight affects its strength.

Procedure

1. Copy the data table on your paper.

Light Spot	Number of Squares Lit
1	
2	

2. Place a sheet of graph paper on a flat surface.

3. Holding the flashlight 20 centimeters directly above the paper, shine the light on the paper, as shown. Trace the spot of light. Label it Spot 1. **Safety Alert: Do not shine the flashlight into the eyes of others.**

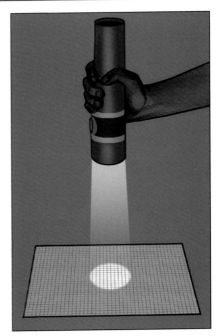

Materials

- ◆ two sheets of graph paper
- ◆ flashlight
- ◆ centimeter ruler

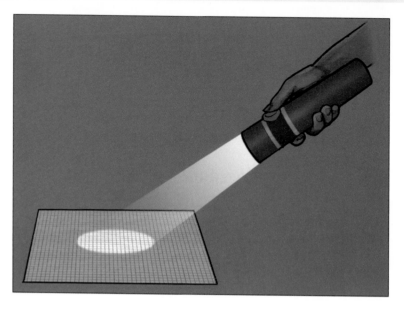

4. Now use a second sheet of graph paper. Hold the flashlight at the same distance from the paper, but at an angle, as shown. Trace the spot of light. Label it Spot 2.

5. Count the whole graph squares in each spot you traced. Record your data.

Questions and Conclusions

1. Which light spot seemed brighter?

2. Which spot represents sunlight during the summer season? Why?

Explore Further

Design an experiment to compare the temperature of direct light with the temperature of angled light. Use a thermometer and a flashlight. You may have to leave the light shining for several minutes to get an accurate measurement. What differences do you observe?

Did You Know?

The first photos of the far side of the moon were taken by robotic spacecraft in 1959. Astronauts saw the far side of the moon for the first time during the Apollo flights of the late 1960s.

Revolution and Rotation

It takes the moon about 29 days to complete its revolution around the earth. From the earth, we can see only one side of the moon as it travels around us. The moon always keeps the same side toward the earth.

You might think that the moon does not rotate on its axis. It does rotate, but the rotation is unusual. It takes the moon the same amount of time to rotate once as it takes to revolve once around the earth. If the moon rotated slower or faster, you would be able to see its other side, too.

The figure below shows how you can make a model of the moon's movement. Hold your left fist in front of you. This is the earth. Hold your right fist at its side. This is the moon. Move the "moon" in a half circle around the "earth." Do not change the position of your right fist. Notice how you can see different parts of your right fist as it orbits your left fist. You did not rotate your right fist. Now move the "moon" again. This time, keep the same part of your right fist facing your left fist, as shown. In order to do that, you have to rotate your right fist.

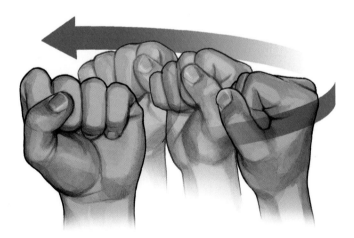

The Phases of the Moon

Phases of the moon

Changes in the moon's appearance as it orbits the earth

Full moon

Phase of the moon when the earth is between the sun and the moon

New moon

Phase of the moon when the moon is between the sun and the earth

The moon is the brightest object in the night sky. It shines by reflecting light from the sun. The side of the moon facing the sun is always lit up. Notice in the diagram below that not all of the sunlit side can be seen from the earth at all times. For this reason, the moon's appearance changes as it orbits the earth. These changes are known as the **phases of the moon**.

The bottom diagram shows how each phase looks from the earth. When the earth is between the sun and the moon, the side of the moon facing the earth is completely lit. You see a **full moon**. When the moon is between the earth and the sun, the side of the moon facing the earth is dark and cannot be seen. This is called the **new moon** phase. As the moon moves around the earth from phase to phase, you can see different amounts of the sunlit side. The full moon and the new moon phases are about two weeks apart.

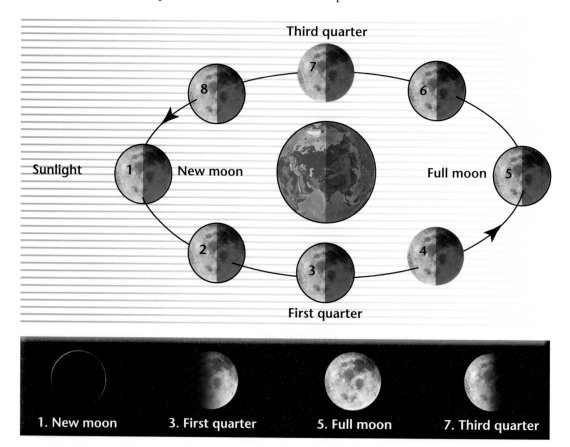

1. New moon 3. First quarter 5. Full moon 7. Third quarter

Eclipses

Sometimes the earth, the moon, and the sun line up together. When they line up exactly, there is an eclipse. An eclipse is either the earth blocking sunlight from reaching the moon or the moon blocking sunlight from reaching part of the earth.

A **lunar eclipse** happens when the earth is between the moon and the sun. The earth casts a shadow on the moon, as shown in the diagram below. As the earth moves between the sun and the moon, the moon darkens. A total lunar eclipse occurs when the shadow covers the entire surface of the moon. If the shadow does not cover the moon completely, then there is a partial lunar eclipse.

When the moon is between the earth and the sun, there is a **solar eclipse**. The moon casts a shadow on the earth, as shown below. People in the dark, central part of the moon's shadow cannot see the sun. For those people, the moon is in just the right position to hide the sun completely. They are seeing a total solar eclipse. Viewers who are in the outer part of the shadow see a partial eclipse. People who are outside the shadow do not see a solar eclipse at all.

Looking directly at the sun is dangerous, even during an eclipse. The sun's rays can burn the retina of the eye. To look at a solar eclipse safely, you need to use an eclipse viewer. You can make an eclipse viewer yourself. Simply make a pinhole in a small sheet of paper and hold it about 15 centimeters in front of a larger sheet of paper. First, face away from the eclipse. Next, line up the two sheets of paper until you can see the outline of the eclipse on the larger sheet.

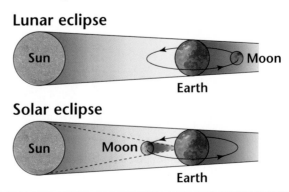

Lunar eclipse

Sun | Moon | Earth

Solar eclipse

Sun | Moon | Earth

Other factors besides gravity affect tides. Some of these factors are wind, ocean temperature, and rainfall or river water flowing into an ocean.

Tides

Recall from Lesson 1 that the gravity between the earth and moon pulls on the moon, keeping it in its orbit.

As the earth pulls on the moon, the moon also pulls on the earth. The moon pulls on the land and the water. The continents are too solid for the moon's pull to move them very much. But the pull on the earth's oceans is noticeable. This pull is the main cause of **tides**. Tides are the regular rising and falling of the major bodies of water on the earth.

Look at the diagram below. The moon's pull causes ocean water to pile up on the side of the earth facing the moon. The water also piles up on the side opposite the moon. These bulges are high tides. Low tides happen between the bulges. What is the difference between high tides and low tides? Compare the photos to find out.

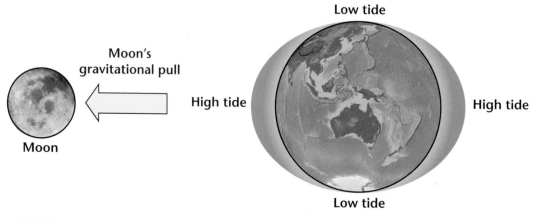

Low tide

Moon's gravitational pull

High tide

High tide

Moon

Low tide

The difference between high and low tide can be 16 meters in the Bay of Fundy in New Brunswick, Canada.

Lesson 3   R E V I E W

Write your answers to these questions on a sheet of paper.

1. Why do we see the same side of the moon?

2. Why does the moon shine?

3. Describe the phases of the moon.

4. How is a solar eclipse different from a lunar eclipse?

5. What is the main cause of tides?

Science in Your Life

Natural and Artificial Satellites

A natural satellite is a naturally occurring object that revolves around a larger object, usually a planet. The moon is the earth's only natural satellite.

There are artificial satellites, too. These are human-made objects that are sent into space, then continuously orbit. Some artificial satellites orbit the earth, the moon, or another planet.

Many forms of communication rely on signals from artificial satellites. These signals are received by satellite dishes. Cable television and cellular telephones require artificial satellites. Global positioning systems track and locate people and things by using satellite signals. Emergency radio signals given off by lost ships are transmitted by artificial satellites. Weather information is gathered using instruments on satellites. Then this information is sent by way of satellite across the world. Meteorologists use this information to prepare weather forecasts. You probably rely on artificial satellites more than you think!

Objectives

After reading this lesson, you should be able to

◆ describe physical features of the moon.

◆ tell when astronauts visited the moon and what their missions accomplished.

Telescope

Instrument that collects light, making faint objects easier to see and enlarging distant objects

Maria

Low, flat plains on the moon's surface that appear as dark areas

Crater

Circular low area surrounded by a rim, usually caused by an object hitting the ground

Meteorite

Piece of rock that hits the surface of a planet or moon after traveling through space

For hundreds of years, scientists could only study the moon by using **telescopes**. A telescope is an instrument that makes the moon and stars appear much brighter. Telescopes can also make objects look closer and larger.

Maria and Craters

If you look at the moon without using a telescope, among the first things you may notice are the light and dark areas of the moon's surface. The dark areas of the moon are low, flat plains called **maria**. *Maria* is the Latin word for "seas." But the moon does not have water. The maria are places where melted rock flowed onto the surface and hardened billions of years ago. The lighter areas are mountains and other highlands.

The surface of the moon is covered with craters and plains called maria.

If you use binoculars or a telescope to look at the moon, you will see many **craters**. The craters are circular areas with rims around them. These rims form many of the mountains on the moon.

Craters are caused by rocks called **meteorites**. A meteorite is a piece of rock traveling through space that hits the surface of a planet or moon. A meteorite may be as small as a sand grain or as large as a boulder. The impact of a meteorite causes an explosion. Rocky material is blasted away, forming a crater. Most of the rocky material settles around the crater, forming a rim. You can make a model of a moon crater by dropping a marble onto a pile of sand or mud.

Did You Know?

Astronauts left behind on the moon an American flag, pieces of equipment, four mirrors, and a camera.

Apollo Missions

After a decade of space flights in the 1960s, people were finally able to study the moon "up close." On July 20, 1969, *Apollo 11* astronauts Neil Armstrong and Buzz Aldrin became the first people to walk on the moon.

Between 1969 and 1972, six more Apollo missions carried astronauts almost 400,000 kilometers to the moon. They took thousands of photographs and brought back nearly 400 kilograms of rocks to study. The astronauts also set up equipment to carry out many scientific experiments.

Some equipment left on the moon measured moonquakes, which are like earthquakes. Other equipment was used to learn about the inside of the moon and the environment on the surface of the moon. By studying moon rocks, scientists discovered that the moon is about 4.6 billion years old, the same as the earth. They also learned that the moon rocks were melted at one time, erupting through volcanoes. The moon's rocks and dust have even provided information about the sun's history.

In 1972, Apollo 17 *astronauts Eugene Cernan, above, and Harrison Schmitt were the last to walk on the moon.*

Write your answers to these questions on a sheet of paper.

1. What are the dark and light areas on the moon's surface?

2. How are craters formed on the moon?

3. When did the first person walk on the moon?

4. About how far away is the moon from the earth?

5. What did the Apollo space missions accomplish?

Technology Note

There are two kinds of telescopes: refracting and reflecting. Most telescopes used by astronomers are reflecting telescopes.

In a refracting telescope, light enters the telescope, is bent by a convex lens, and then forms an image. A second lens in the eyepiece makes the image appear larger when you look through the telescope. A convex lens is a glass lens that is thicker in the middle. Most refracting telescopes are used for observing small areas in space.

In a reflecting telescope, light enters the telescope, is reflected off a concave mirror, and then is reflected off a flat mirror to the eyepiece lens. A concave mirror is curved inward like a bowl. Reflecting telescopes tend to be larger than refracting telescopes and can collect more light. They are used to look far into space.

- Gravity is a force of attraction between any two objects, caused by those objects pulling on each other.

- Gravity between the earth and moon pulls the moon into an orbit around the earth.

- The earth revolves around the sun once about every 365 days.

- The tilt of the earth's axis causes sunlight to fall more directly on different parts of the earth throughout its orbit. This causes seasons.

- The moon revolves around the earth once about every 29 days.

- Because it takes the moon the same amount of time to rotate as it does to orbit the earth, we always see the same side of the moon.

- The changes in the moon's appearance are the phases of the moon.

- A lunar eclipse happens when the earth is between the moon and the sun. The moon passes through the earth's shadow.

- A solar eclipse happens when the moon is between the earth and the sun. The moon's shadow falls on the earth and blocks out part or all of the sun.

- Gravity between the earth and moon is the main cause of tides on the earth. Tides are the regular rising and falling of major bodies of water.

- The moon's surface has dark areas called maria and light areas that are highlands.

- The highlands are mountainous areas including the rims of craters. Craters are caused by rocks, such as meteorites, hitting the moon's surface.

- During the 1960s and 1970s, astronauts walked on the moon, collecting information about it.

Science Words

crater, 70	maria, 70	orbit, 56	solar eclipse, 67
full moon, 66	mass, 56	phases of the	telescope, 70
gravity, 56	meteorite, 70	moon, 66	tides, 68
lunar eclipse, 67	new moon, 66	revolution, 60	

Chapter 3 R E V I E W

Word Bank

crater

gravity

lunar eclipse

maria

mass

meteorite

orbit

revolution

solar eclipse

tides

Vocabulary Review

Choose the word or phrase from the Word Bank that best completes each sentence. Write the answer on your paper.

1. The movement of the earth in its path around the sun is the earth's _____.

2. The amount of matter in an object is its _____.

3. When the moon casts a shadow on the earth, there is a(n) _____.

4. The moon stays in its orbit because of _____.

5. The earth's oceans rise and fall because of _____.

6. A(n) _____ is caused by the impact of a meteorite.

7. The curved path of the moon around the earth is called its _____.

8. A piece of rock that hits a moon or planet after traveling through space is called a(n) _____.

9. When the earth casts a shadow on the moon, there is a(n) _____.

10. The dark areas on the moon's surface are low, flat plains called _____.

Concept Review

Follow the directions for each of the questions below.

11. Explain the difference between the earth's rotation and the earth's revolution.

12. Which of the following spins on its axis faster: the earth or the moon?

13. Identify each lettered phase of the moon shown in the photos on the left.

14. What was the name of the missions to the moon in the 1960s and 1970s?

A

B

C

D

Choose the phrase that best answers each question. Write the letter of the answer on your paper.

15. What is the main cause of the earth's seasons?
   A the earth's tilt
   B the earth's tides
   C the moon's revolution around the earth
   D the gravity between the moon and earth

16. What is the main cause of ocean tides?
   A the earth's tilt
   B the earth's revolution around the sun
   C the moon's revolution around the earth
   D the moon's gravitational pull

17. If it is winter in the Northern Hemisphere, which statement is true?
   A The noontime sun is high in the sky there.
   B It is winter in the Southern Hemisphere.
   C It is summer in the Southern Hemisphere.
   D The Northern Hemisphere is tilted toward the sun.

Critical Thinking

Write the answer to each of the following questions.

18. The far side of the moon has more craters than the near side has. Why?

19. The moon looks dark during a lunar eclipse. The moon also looks dark during a new moon. What is the difference? You may make a drawing to help explain.

20. If the force of gravity between the earth and moon were reduced, how might the moon's orbit change?

Test-Taking Tip When studying for a test, use a marker to highlight important facts and concepts in your notes. For a final review, read what you highlighted.

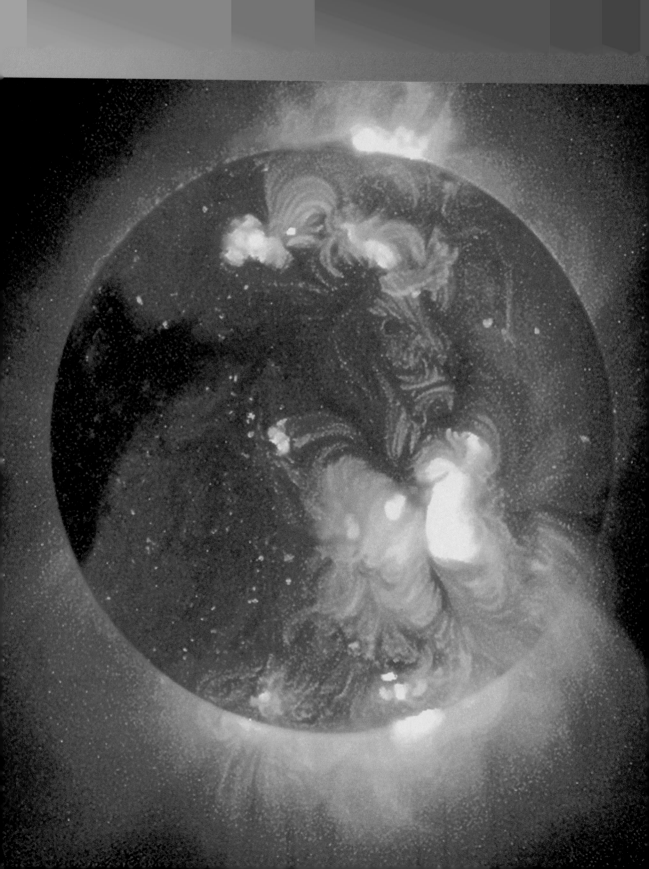

The Solar System

The center of the solar system is the sun. Even though it is 150 million kilometers away, the sun affects us in many ways. For example, huge explosions, called solar flares, sometimes move outward from the sun's surface. Solar flares send electrically charged particles into space. Some of these particles reach the earth and cause static on radios. The particles can also change the amount of power in electric lines. In Chapter 4, you will learn more about the sun, planets, and other objects in the solar system.

Organize Your Thoughts

```
                    Solar system
   ┌──────┬──────────┬──────────────┬──────────┬────────┐
  Sun    Inner      Asteroids       Outer      Comets
        planets     and meteors     planets
```

Goals for Learning

◆ To explain what the solar system is

◆ To identify the four inner planets

◆ To identify the five outer planets

◆ To tell something about each planet

◆ To describe the motions and positions of the planets

◆ To compare comets and asteroids

Stars, Planets, and Moons

If you stand outside on a clear night, away from bright city lights, you should be able to see hundreds of shining objects in the sky. Most of the objects are **stars**. These glowing balls of hot gas shine because they make their own light. A few of the objects you might see are **planets**. Planets are large objects in space that orbit the sun. You will likely see the earth's **moon**, although there are other moons in space. A moon is an object that orbits a planet. Another name for a moon is a satellite. Later you will read about some moons of other planets.

Planets and moons do not make their own light. They shine because they reflect the light of the sun, our closest star. Stars are the source of light for all objects in space. The diagram shows how a star like the sun can cause a planet to shine. You can see the ball because it reflects light from the flashlight. You can see a planet or moon because it reflects light from the sun.

Star

Glowing ball of hot gas that makes its own energy and light

Planet

Large object in space that orbits a star such as the sun

Moon

Natural satellite that orbits a planet

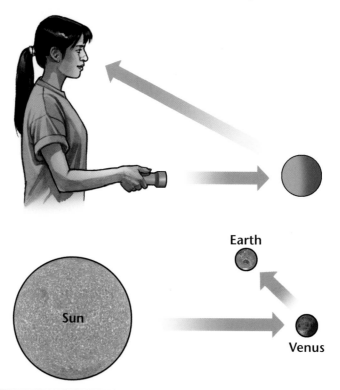

Earth

Sun

Venus

The stars, planets, and moons in the sky are moving. The word *planet* comes from a Greek word meaning "wanderer." Because planets change their position in the sky from day to day, ancient stargazers thought of planets as wandering stars.

In Chapter 3, you read about the movement of the earth and its moon. Planets, with their moons, revolve around the sun in what is known as the **solar system**. *Solar* refers to the star in the center of the system: the sun.

The stars in the night sky are not part of the solar system. But they do move. Planets seem to move across the sky faster than stars do. Why? Think about riding in a car and looking out the window. Have you ever noticed that objects closer to the car seem to go by faster than objects farther away? The more distant something is, the more slowly it seems to move. Stars are much, much farther away from the earth than the planets are. Therefore, stars appear to move very slowly in the sky.

The motion of the solar system has a regular pattern to it. This means you can predict where in space a planet will be on your next birthday! You can even predict where it will be several years from now.

Objects in the Solar System

The solar system contains many objects. Nine of these objects are planets. Each planet travels in a fixed orbit around the sun. Look at the diagram to find the name and path of each planet. Most of the planets do not orbit in an exact circle, but in an ellipse.

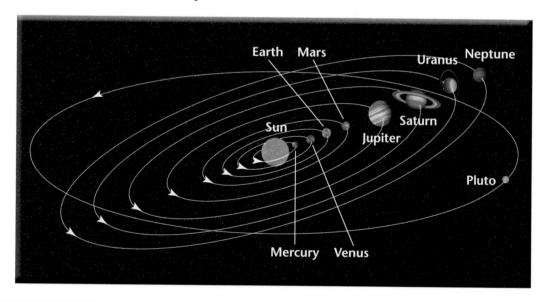

Imagine tracing the paths of these nine planets in space. You would see that most of the orbits could be traced on a flat plane or on a giant piece of paper. One planet orbits a little outside of this flat plane. Look at the diagram on page 79 to see which one it is.

All of the planets move around the sun in the same direction. However, the planets don't orbit together as a group. Each planet moves along its path at its own speed. Mercury orbits the fastest. In general, the farther away a planet is from the sun, the bigger its orbit and the slower its speed. Besides planets, smaller objects in space orbit the sun, too.

The entire solar system holds together because of gravity. There is gravity between every object in the solar system, attracting these objects to each other. Because the sun has much more mass than the objects orbiting it, the objects are pulled toward the sun. This pull of gravity is balanced by the speed and motion of the objects. This balance keeps the objects in orbit. Without this perfect balance, an orbiting planet could fly off in a straight line or fall toward the sun.

Science Myth

Since astronauts float in outer space, some people may think this means that there is no gravity there.

Fact: Gravity is everywhere. It holds our solar system together. Astronauts appear to float because they are in orbit. The orbital force pulling them away from the earth is balanced by the force of gravity pulling them toward the earth. Because of this, astronauts weigh less in space than at home.

The Sun

The largest object in the solar system is the sun. In fact, the sun is larger than all of the planets put together. Its mass, the amount of matter it contains, is 99 percent of the entire solar system. So 99 percent of the "stuff" in the solar system is in the sun! The diagram compares the size of the earth and the sun.

The sun is made mostly of two gases: hydrogen and helium. The sun also contains very small amounts of the elements found on the earth. Because the sun is mostly gas, it has no solid surface.

The sun is not fixed in space. It rotates on an axis like a planet. Because it is mostly gas, parts of the sun rotate at different rates. On average, the sun rotates once a month.

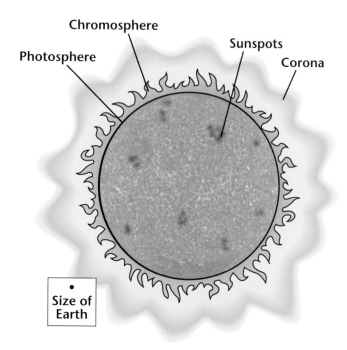

Chromosphere

Photosphere

Sunspots

Corona

Size of Earth

The outer temperature of the sun is about 5,500°C. This high temperature is caused by nuclear reactions inside the sun. In the sun's center, temperatures of 15,000,000°C cause hydrogen particles to fuse and form helium. These nuclear reactions produce energy that we see as light and feel as heat. Later you will learn how the sun's energy is important for many processes on the earth, such as wind and rainfall.

The only part of the sun that can be seen is its **atmosphere**. An atmosphere is an envelope of gas surrounding an object in space. The sun's atmosphere consists of three layers, as shown in the diagram on page 81. The inner layer is called the photosphere. This is the layer of gas that gives off light. Just outside of this layer is another layer of gas called the chromosphere. The gas of the chromosphere can sometimes be seen during a total solar eclipse, when the photosphere is blocked. The outer layer of the sun's atmosphere is the corona. It is a layer of gas thicker than the chromosphere. The corona can also be seen during a solar eclipse.

Notice in the diagram that the photosphere contains dark areas called **sunspots**. Sunspots give off less energy and are, therefore, cooler than the rest of the sun. But they are still about 4,000°C. Sunspots move in groups across the face of the sun. This shows that the sun rotates.

Many spacecraft and satellites have photographed the sun and measured its surface activity. The satellite SOHO was launched in 1995 to study the sun. It contains 12 instruments. Besides taking photos, it measures corona activity, vibrations in the sun, and space conditions. SOHO stands for Solar and Heliospheric Observatory.

Lesson 1 **REVIEW**

Write your answers to these questions on a sheet of paper.

1. What is the difference between a star and a planet?

2. Why do the moon and planets shine in the night sky?

3. What makes up our solar system? What holds it together?

4. Compare the sun and the earth in terms of size, makeup, and temperature.

5. Describe the layers of the sun's atmosphere.

Science in Your Life

A Solar House

The sun not only warms our planet, but it also provides us with energy. Solar energy is energy that comes from the sun.

Solar energy can be used in many ways. For example, a solar house is specially built to capture solar energy. Solar panels are mounted on the roof of the house. The panels collect radiant energy from the sun and change it to heat energy. This heat energy is used to run electric appliances and heat water.

The main benefit of using solar energy is that it saves our natural resources. Oil, gas, and coal are natural resources that are burned for energy. These resources are limited and will run out someday. But the sun's energy is unlimited. The sun will keep producing energy for about another 5 billion years.

Are there any solar houses or solar panels in your neighborhood? To learn about other ways to save our natural resources, read Appendix B: Alternative Energy Sources.

INVESTIGATION

Materials

- telescope or binoculars
- clipboard

Observing Sunspots

Purpose

What does a telescope image of the sun look like? In this investigation, you will observe sunspots.

Procedure

1. Work with a partner in this investigation. Set up a telescope aimed in the direction of the morning sun. If you use binoculars, cover one of the large lenses. **Safety Alert: Never look at the sun, especially through a telescope or binoculars.**

2. Place a sheet of paper on the clipboard and position it 20 to 30 centimeters behind the eyepiece of the telescope. Without looking through the telescope, aim the telescope so that the sun causes a light spot to appear on the paper.

3. Move the clipboard back and forth behind the eyepiece until the light spot is brightest. This is the sun's image.

4. While your partner holds the clipboard steady, trace the outline of the sun's image. Trace any spots you see on the image. These are sunspots.

5. Write the date and the time at the top of the paper.

6. Repeat the procedure on the next four mornings. Each time, take turns tracing the sun's image.

Questions and Conclusions

1. Can you see the same sunspot two days in a row? How do you know?

2. Does the position of a sunspot change? If so, in what direction does the sunspot seem to move?

Explore Further

Try tracking sunspot changes over a longer period of time. Repeat this investigation for a week or longer. Keep a record of the sunspot changes you observe. What patterns do you see?

Objectives

After reading this lesson, you should be able to

◆ identify the four inner planets.

◆ describe the four inner planets.

◆ explain what the greenhouse effect is and how it affects Venus.

The planets of the solar system are divided into two groups: the inner planets and the outer planets. The inner planets are the ones that are closest to the sun. They are Mercury, Venus, Earth, and Mars. All of the inner planets are solid and similar in size. But these rocky worlds are also very different from one another. Read about each one below. Then look at Appendix C to learn more facts about the planets.

Mercury

The planet closest to the sun is Mercury. Because it is so close to the sun, Mercury is not easy to see in the sky. Named after the Roman god of speed, Mercury is the fastest-moving planet. Its average speed as it orbits the sun is about 50 kilometers per second. Mercury completes an entire revolution of the sun in 88 Earth days. It rotates slowly though. One day on Mercury lasts about 59 Earth days.

In 1974 and 1975, a spacecraft called *Mariner 10* passed close by Mercury three times. It photographed about half of its surface. These photos show that Mercury is covered with craters and flat areas, like those on the moon.

Of all the planets, Mercury's surface temperature changes the most. This is because Mercury has almost no atmosphere to hold in or keep out the sun's heat. The side of Mercury facing the sun reaches 427°C. The side away from the sun drops to −183°C.

This image is actually many small photos put together. The smooth band and patches are areas that Mariner 10 *did not photograph.*

Venus

The planet that is next closest to the sun is Venus. It was named after the Roman goddess of love and beauty. Venus is the hottest planet at 460°C. It is also the brightest planet in the sky. Like the moon, you can sometimes see Venus during the day. Depending on the time of year, Venus is known as the "morning star" or the "evening star."

Venus is different from most of the other planets because it rotates in the opposite direction. Earth and the other inner planets rotate from west to east. Venus rotates from east to west. That means the sun rises in the west on Venus. Also, it takes a long time for Venus to rotate. A day on Venus is 243 Earth days.

This radar image of Venus shows surface features that are visibly hidden by clouds.

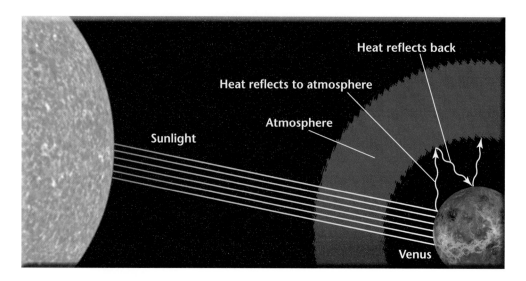

Heat reflects back

Heat reflects to atmosphere

Atmosphere

Sunlight

Venus

Unlike Mercury, Venus has an atmosphere. It contains great amounts of the gas carbon dioxide. Carbon dioxide in the atmosphere traps heat energy from the sun. As a result, the atmosphere heats up. This warming, shown above, is called the **greenhouse effect**. The clouds of Venus's atmosphere are made of tiny drops of sulfuric acid. These clouds trap heat and add to the greenhouse effect. Because of the greenhouse effect, the surface temperature of Venus is very high. The surface of the planet would be much cooler without this effect.

We cannot see through Venus's thick clouds with our eyes. However, in the 1990s, a spacecraft called *Magellan* used radar to penetrate the clouds and make images of the planet's surface. These images show areas of rolling plains, towering highlands, and craters.

Earth

Our own planet, Earth, is the third planet from the sun. It is about the same size as Venus. But Earth has several differences from the other inner planets:

◆ Earth has a mild surface temperature that changes very little.
◆ It has a dense, protective atmosphere.
◆ It is the only planet to have liquid water on its surface.

Did You Know?

People are concerned that the burning of oil and coal is adding too much carbon dioxide to the atmosphere. This activity strengthens the natural greenhouse effect and could raise temperatures on Earth. Droughts and crop losses may result.

Because of these unique features, Earth can support life. There is no evidence of life on the other planets. Earth is also the closest planet to the sun that has a moon.

The greenhouse effect occurs on Earth as well as on Venus. Without an atmosphere that traps heat, Earth would be an icy planet with temperatures no warmer than $-10°C$.

Mars

Mars, the fourth planet from the sun, is named for the Roman god of war. Its reddish color in the night sky may have reminded ancient people of blood. Mars has two small moons.

The rotation period of Mars is about the same as that of Earth. Mars rotates once every 24 hours and 38 minutes. It takes the planet 687 Earth days to complete one revolution around the sun. So, a Martian day is similar to an Earth day, but its year is almost twice as long as ours.

The atmosphere on Mars is much less dense than on Earth. The atmosphere is mostly carbon dioxide. Mars is colder than Earth because it is farther from the sun and has a thinner atmosphere. Little heat can be trapped by a thin atmosphere.

These Hubble Space Telescope photos show Mars before a global dust storm (left) and during the storm (right).

Did You Know?

Although no liquid water exists on Mars, frozen water does. The polar regions contain frozen water and frozen carbon dioxide. During spring and summer, some of the ice turns directly to water vapor—a gas.

Several space missions have landed on Mars. In 1997, the Mars Pathfinder lander visited Mars. Cameras on board sent many photographs back to Earth. One of them is shown below. The lander also brought a robotic rover to Mars. The rover rolled across the surface, testing the rocks, soil, and air. Iron in the rocks and soil makes the surface look red. Winds blow dust in the air, making the sky look pink.

Since 1960, many American and Russian spacecraft without crews have tried to orbit or land on Mars. Many did not succeed. But successful missions like Mars Pathfinder have sent back thousands of photos and other data.

In 2001, the *Odyssey* orbiter was launched. It took six months to travel the 459 million kilometers to Mars. The *Odyssey* is studying the minerals and chemicals on Mars. It will also test for hazards for future human explorers.

The two hills shown in this Martian landscape are called the Twin Peaks. They are about 30 to 35 meters tall.

Write your answers to these questions on a sheet of paper.

1. What are the names of the inner planets?

2. How would you describe Mercury?

3. Which planet has a reddish surface?

4. What does the greenhouse effect do to the temperature on a planet's surface?

5. How is Earth unique?

Achievements in Science

The Struggle to Accept the Solar System

In the early 1500s, a Polish astronomer named Nicolaus Copernicus had a new idea. Using careful observations and mathematics, he concluded that the sun must be at the center of all the planets. In such a system, Earth and the other planets revolve around the sun. Other astronomers at the time thought that Earth was at the center of everything. They believed Earth didn't move. They rejected Copernicus's idea of a sun-centered, or solar, system.

Copernicus's idea was not picked up again until almost 100 years later. In the early 1600s, an Italian astronomer named Galileo Galilei concluded that not all objects in space revolve around Earth. Galileo was one of the first astronomers to use a telescope. The more he observed the moon and the planets, the more convinced he became that Copernicus's idea was correct. Galileo published a book explaining the idea of a solar system. Still, this idea was very unpopular.

In the late 1600s, Isaac Newton, an English scientist, took a serious look at Galileo's idea. He was able to prove that Copernicus and Galileo were right. People finally accepted the fact that Earth revolves around the sun. Newton became a hero and was knighted by the queen of England.

Objectives

After reading this lesson, you should be able to

◆ identify the five outer planets.

◆ describe the five outer planets.

Except for Pluto, the outer planets have rings and are much larger than the inner planets. The outer planets are mostly frozen gas and liquid, with a small, solid core. Over the last 25 years, *Voyager* and *Galileo* spacecraft have collected much information about these planets. Look at Appendix D to learn more about space exploration.

Jupiter

Jupiter is the largest planet in the solar system. In fact, all of the other planets in the solar system could fit inside Jupiter. The diameter of Jupiter is more than 11 times larger than Earth's. It's no wonder Jupiter was named for the Roman king of the gods.

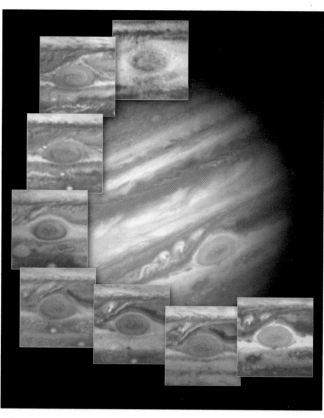

Among the most noticeable features of Jupiter are its colorful bands. These bands are clouds of gases where storms are taking place. The bands change shape every few days but generally run in the same direction. Jupiter's fast rotation might cause these bands. It takes Jupiter only 10 hours to rotate once.

A large red oval appears on the surface of Jupiter. This area is called the Great Red Spot. It is more than twice as wide as Earth. This spot is actually a spinning windstorm. It is the largest known storm in the solar system, and it has lasted at least 300 years! The Great Red Spot changes its shape and color, as shown in the photo.

The Great Red Spot rotates in a counterclockwise direction. Wind speeds inside this storm reach 400 kilometers per hour.

When two Voyager spacecraft flew by Jupiter in 1979, astronomers discovered faint rings around the planet. Astronomers also discovered more moons than they had thought existed. At least 60 moons orbit this giant planet.

Shown below is one of Jupiter's moons, Io. This moon has active volcanoes that erupt constantly. Io's volcanoes spew out sulfur, which colors the surface yellow, orange, and green.

The largest of Jupiter's moons is Ganymede. It is bigger than the planet Mercury. The smallest moon is only about 2 kilometers in diameter. A moon called Europa is an icy world with a smooth, cracked surface. It has been described as a giant, cracked cue ball.

The spacecraft Galileo *flew close to Io in 1999 and photographed its colorful surface.*

Did You Know?

One of Saturn's moons, Mimas, has a crater so huge that scientists think the object that caused the crater came close to destroying this moon.

Saturn

You are probably familiar with the rings of Saturn. Saturn, the sixth planet from the sun, was named for the Roman god of agriculture. Saturn is the second largest planet in the solar system. It revolves around the sun once every 29 years.

About 1,000 individual rings orbit Saturn's equator. They are mostly ice particles and dust. When you look at Saturn through a telescope, you can see the rings only at certain times during Saturn's orbit. That is because the rings are very thin, and Saturn rotates on a tilted axis. When the edge of the ring system is pointed toward Earth, the rings disappear from view. The images below were taken between 1996 and 2000. They show how Saturn nods as it revolves.

Like Jupiter, Saturn is a giant planet of gases with stormy bands of clouds running along its surface. Winds in these storms reach speeds of 1,800 kilometers per hour. Also like Jupiter, Saturn spins very fast. One day is about 11 hours.

Saturn has at least 31 moons, the largest of which is Titan. Titan is the only moon in the solar system that is known to have an atmosphere of its own. This atmosphere is mostly nitrogen. Titan may also have active volcanoes.

The *Cassini* spacecraft, launched in 1997, is scheduled to put a probe on Titan in 2004. Then the spacecraft will orbit Saturn for four years, studying its atmosphere, rings, and moons.

We see Saturn's rings at different angles during its revolution around the sun.

Uranus

The seventh planet from the sun is Uranus. This greenish-blue planet was named for the Greek god of the sky. One unusual thing about Uranus is the tilt of its axis. Uranus rotates on its side. During some parts of its revolution, one pole of Uranus points directly at the sun. Because of this, astronomers disagree about which of Uranus's poles is its north pole.

In 1977, astronomers discovered that Uranus has a faint, dark ring system. They were using a telescope to observe Uranus as it passed in front of a star. They noticed that the star dimmed briefly many times. Each dimming occurred as another ring passed in front of the star. In 1986, the *Voyager 2* spacecraft studied the rings and moons of Uranus up close. Since then, more rings and moons have been discovered. Uranus has at least 11 rings and 22 moons.

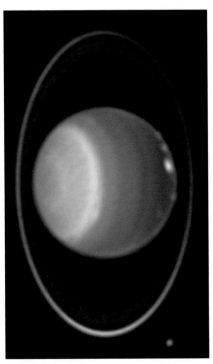

The outer planets are very cold. The cloud tops of Uranus are −200°C.

Because Uranus is so far out in the solar system, it takes 84 Earth years to complete a single orbit of the sun. Uranus rotates on its axis once every 17 hours.

Neptune

Neptune is the eighth planet from the sun. Named after the Roman god of the sea, Neptune cannot be seen without a telescope. Like Uranus, Neptune appears greenish blue because of methane gas in its atmosphere. Neptune has four rings: two thin and two thick. Like Jupiter, Neptune has a big spot in its atmosphere. The Great Dark Spot seen at the center of the photo is about as wide as Earth. The wispy, white streaks are clouds.

It takes Neptune 164 Earth years to complete a revolution around the sun. The planet rotates once on its axis every 16 hours.

The Great Dark Spot is a storm system spinning counterclockwise.

Until 1989, astronomers thought Neptune had two moons. Later, nine more moons were found. One of Neptune's 11 moons is unusual. It rotates in the opposite direction from Neptune's rotation. This moon, named Triton, also has active volcanoes.

Pluto

Pluto is the coldest, outermost planet of the solar system, but it is not always the farthest from the sun. It has a tilted, stretched-out orbit that sometimes falls inside the orbit of Neptune, as shown below. Even so, if you were to stand on Pluto, the sun would appear only as a bright star in the sky. Pluto has not yet been visited by a spacecraft.

Pluto is the smallest planet. It is the only outer planet without a ring system and a thick atmosphere. Pluto has one known moon, Charon. Even with powerful telescopes, Pluto and Charon are hard to see. At an average distance from the sun of almost 6 billion kilometers, Pluto takes 248 Earth years to make one revolution. Pluto seems to rotate about once every 6 days.

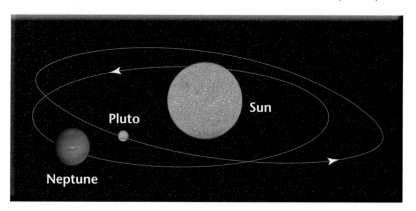

Write your answers to these questions on a sheet of paper.

1. What are the five outer planets of the solar system?

2. What are the large outer planets made of?

3. Which outer planets have rings?

4. Besides on Earth, where could you find active volcanoes?

5. How is Pluto different from the other outer planets?

▼◄▲▼◄▲▼◄▲▼◄▲▼◄▲▼◄▲▼◄▲▼◄▲▼◄▲▼◄▲▼◄▲▼◄▲▼◄▲▼◄▲▼◄▲▼◄▲▼

Science at Work

Astronomer

Astronomers study stars, planets, and other objects in space. Most astronomers do research by analyzing large amounts of data. The data are collected from satellites and powerful telescopes. Some astronomers try to solve problems with space flight or satellite communications.

The usual education needed to be an astronomer is a doctoral degree, or Ph.D. An astronomer needs to have a strong background in physics and mathematics.

Besides science skills, a successful astronomer needs to be a problem-solver. A curious mind and an active imagination are also helpful.

Many astronomers teach at colleges or universities. Other astronomers are planetarium directors. They may also be members of a research team that operates large telescopes on Earth or in space.

Materials

- ◆ one 12-meter length of adding machine paper
- ◆ meterstick
- ◆ tape

Modeling Distances in the Solar System

Purpose

What kind of model might show how far the planets are from the sun? In this investigation, you will use a scale to show distances in the solar system.

Procedure

1. Tape the strip of adding machine paper to the floor. Draw a circle at one end of the paper. The circle represents the sun.

2. The table on the next page shows the relative distances of the planets from the sun. Use this table and a meterstick to mark the location of each of the planets on the adding machine paper. Label the position of each planet with its name.

Planet	Distance from Sun in Model (centimeters)*
Mercury	12
Venus	22
Earth	30
Mars	46
Jupiter	156
Saturn	286
Uranus	574
Neptune	900
Pluto	1,180

*1 centimeter in model = 5,000,000 kilometers in space

3. Each centimeter on the strip of paper represents 5 million kilometers in space. Next to each planet on the paper, record its actual distance in kilometers from the sun.

Questions and Conclusions

1. What is the scale of this model?

2. Which four planets are closest together?

3. Which two neighboring planets have the greatest distance between their orbits?

Explore Further

Make a model that shows the diameters of all nine planets. Appendix C lists the actual diameters. What scale will you use? Use your model to compare the sizes of the planets.

Asteroids

The solar system has other objects besides the sun, the planets, and their moons. Some of these objects are **asteroids**. An asteroid is a rocky object smaller than a planet that has its own orbit around the sun. Most asteroids are smaller than a kilometer in diameter, but a few are 1,000 kilometers across.

As the diagram shows, a large number of asteroids lie between the orbits of Mars and Jupiter. This area is known as the **asteroid belt**. As many as a million asteroids make up this belt, orbiting the sun. The belt may have formed as gravity between Jupiter and much smaller matter pulled the matter into this region of space.

Asteroid

Rocky object, smaller than a planet, that orbits a star

Asteroid belt

Region between Mars and Jupiter where most asteroids orbit the sun

Meteor

Brief streak of light seen when an asteroid enters the earth's atmosphere and burns up

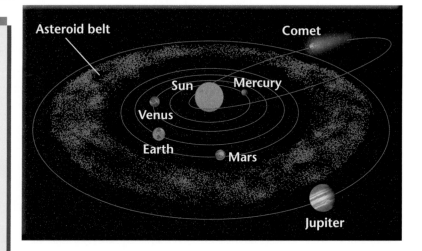

Not all of these asteroids stay in their orbits. Sometimes they are pulled out of orbit by the gravity of other planets. Asteroids may also be pulled in toward the sun.

A few asteroids come close to Earth and, at times, are captured by Earth's gravity. If an asteroid enters Earth's atmosphere, it heats up and becomes a ball of glowing gases. This brief streak of light seen in the sky is called a **meteor**. You probably know meteors as "shooting stars" or "falling stars." When many shooting stars occur, they are referred to as a "meteor shower."

Meteorite

Asteroid that hits the surface of a planet or moon after traveling through space

Comet

Ball of ice, rock, frozen gases, and dust that orbits the sun

---

One of the most well-known comets is Hale-Bopp. It was discovered in 1995 by two astronomers named Alan Hale and Thomas Bopp. The comet's closest approach to Earth was on March 22, 1997.

Did You Know?

When comets come close to Earth, they can be seen for days or weeks. They do not streak across the sky like meteors.

If an asteroid is big enough and does not completely burn up, it may hit Earth. The part that actually strikes Earth is called a **meteorite**. Large meteorites can leave craters. About 50,000 years ago, a meteorite created Meteor Crater in Arizona, shown in the photo.

Meteor Crater in Arizona is more than a kilometer across.

Comets

Other objects of the solar system include **comets.** Most of these objects follow large orbits. Most comets are not on the same orbital plane as the planets. A comet's orbit may take it far beyond the orbit of Pluto.

Scientists have found that comets are made of ice, rock, frozen gases, and dust. When a comet approaches the sun, the comet begins to warm up. Some of the ice turns to gas, and dust is also released. The gas and dust reflect sunlight, making the comet visible. A stream of particles from the sun, called the solar wind, pushes the gas and dust away from the head of the comet. This gas and dust form a tail that points away from the sun.

Comet Hale-Bopp, seen in 1997, has a very long orbit. It will not be seen again until the year 4377!

Write your answers to these questions on a sheet of paper.

1. What is an asteroid?

2. Where is the asteroid belt located?

3. What is the difference between a meteor and a meteorite?

4. What are comets made of?

5. How does the tail of a comet form?

Technology Note

A photovoltaic (PV) cell, or solar cell, uses the sun's energy to produce electricity. The biggest advantage to this kind of energy is that it's free. Since PV cells have no moving parts, they require very little maintenance and are clean and quiet.

The basic idea of a PV cell was discovered in 1839. But the details of the technology were not worked out until about 100 years later. PV cells were first used in space. In fact, PV cells are still used to power most of the satellites orbiting Earth. PV cells are especially useful in remote places where regular power lines are not available.

PV cells also have more common applications. Simple PV systems power wristwatches and solar calculators. More complicated PV systems produce electricity for water pumps and communications equipment. PV systems even provide electricity for some homes and appliances.

- Stars shine because they give off their own light. Planets and moons shine because they reflect light from the sun.

- The solar system is made of the sun, the planets and their moons, and other objects that revolve around the sun.

- The sun is a star. It is mostly hydrogen and helium gas. The sun's atmosphere has three layers: the photosphere, the chromosphere, and the corona.

- The inner planets are Mercury, Venus, Earth, and Mars. They are all solid, rocky worlds.

- Mercury has craters and almost no atmosphere.

- Venus rotates in the opposite direction from most other planets, has an atmosphere of carbon dioxide, and is very hot.

- Earth has one moon, moderate temperatures, a dense atmosphere, and much water. It is the only planet known to have life on it.

- Mars has a thin atmosphere, a reddish surface, and two moons.

- The outer planets are Jupiter, Saturn, Uranus, Neptune, and Pluto. Pluto is small and solid. The others are large and mostly gas.

- Jupiter is the largest planet and has 60 moons. A giant storm, called the Great Red Spot, can be seen in its atmosphere.

- Saturn has a big ring system and 31 moons.

- Uranus rotates on its side. It has a ring system and 22 moons.

- Neptune has a ring system and 11 moons.

- Pluto has a tilted, stretched-out orbit and one moon.

- Asteroids are small objects that orbit the sun between Mars and Jupiter. A meteor is the streak of light seen when an asteroid enters Earth's atmosphere.

- Comets are made of ice, rock, frozen gases, and dust.

Science Words

asteroid, 100	greenhouse effect, 88	moon, 78	sunspot, 82
asteroid belt, 100		planet, 78	
atmosphere, 82	meteor, 100	solar system, 79	
comet, 101	meteorite, 101	star, 78	

Chapter 4 REVIEW

Vocabulary Review

Choose the word or phrase from the Word Bank that best completes each sentence. Write the answer on your paper.

1. The planets, moons, and sun are part of the _____.

2. The sun is the _____ that the planets orbit.

3. The gases around a planet make up its _____.

4. A dark area that appears on the sun is called a(n) _____.

5. Venus has a hot surface temperature because of the _____.

6. The _____ is between Mars and Jupiter.

7. A(n) _____ is a large object that orbits a star.

8. A shooting star is a(n) _____.

9. A(n) _____ is made of ice, rock, frozen gases, and dust.

10. Another name for a natural satellite is a(n) _____.

11. A rocky object smaller than a planet is called a(n) _____.

Concept Review

Write the answer to each of the following questions.

12. Identify each member of the solar system shown in the diagram below. On your paper, write the name after each letter.

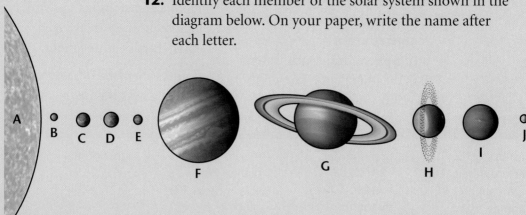

13. Name five different kinds of objects that make up the solar system.

14. What makes Earth unique compared to other planets?

15. Four of the outer planets are very similar. Give two features that they share.

Choose the word or phrase that best completes each sentence. Write the letter of the answer on your paper.

16. The sun is mostly _____.
   A helium and oxygen
   B helium and hydrogen
   C hydrogen and nitrogen
   D hydrogen and oxygen

17. The solar system is held together by _____.
   A gravity   **C** energy
   B mass   **D** gases

18. The moon shines in the sky because _____.
   A the moon is very hot
   B the moon produces its own light
   C the sun lights up part of the moon
   D the moon is a close star

Critical Thinking

Write the answer to each of the following questions.

19. What is the difference between a star and a planet?

20. One of Jupiter's moons is as big as the planet Mercury. If this moon is so big, why is it a moon and not a planet?

Test-Taking Tip When studying for a test, you will remember facts and definitions more easily if you write them down on index cards. Practice with a partner, using these as flash cards.

5 Stars and Galaxies

The sun is the closest star to Earth. It seems big, but it's an average-sized star. On a clear night, you can see many more stars in the sky. The sun is just one of at least 100 billion stars in our galaxy, the Milky Way. Beyond what you can see, there are millions of other galaxies in space. That's a lot of stars! The photo shows a star cluster found in a neighboring galaxy. This kind of star cluster isn't found in the Milky Way. In Chapter 5, you will learn about different kinds of stars and galaxies. You will discover how stars change as they grow old. You also will learn about constellations such as the Big Dipper and how far away those stars are.

Organize Your Thoughts

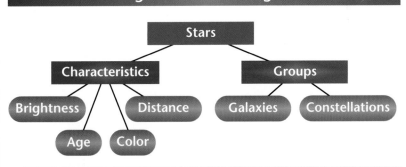

Goals for Learning

◆ To identify characteristics of stars

◆ To define a light-year

◆ To describe the life of a star

◆ To recognize constellations and explain what they are

◆ To explain what galaxies are

People have studied stars since ancient times. Ancient Egyptians, Greeks, Chinese, American Indians, and other civilizations were able to predict the movements of stars in the sky. We now know much more about stars than the first stargazers did. Scientific instruments, such as powerful telescopes, have allowed us to search farther and farther into the sky.

Why Stars Shine

A star is made mostly of hydrogen and helium gas particles. Deep inside the star, temperatures of 15,000,000°C make these particles move at incredible speeds. When moving at high speeds, the particles collide and combine, or fuse. This process is called **fusion**. The figure shows that four hydrogen particles in a star can fuse to form one helium particle plus energy. Continuous fusion produces a constant supply of energy. This energy makes its way to the star's surface. Gas particles on the surface become very hot and radiate light. We see this as a shining star.

Fusion

Process by which particles combine to form a new particle

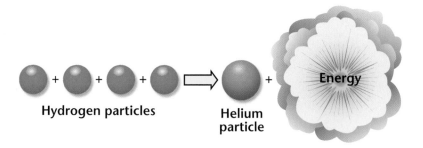

Hydrogen particles   Helium particle   Energy

Magnitude

Brightness of a star

Apparent magnitude

How bright a star looks

Absolute magnitude

How bright a star actually is

The Brightness of Stars

The first thing that you notice when you look at stars is that some of them are brighter than others. A star's brightness depends on two things:

◆ The star's distance from Earth
◆ The amount of energy that the star gives off

The closer a star is, the brighter it appears. Also, if two stars are the same distance from Earth, the star that gives off more energy will appear brighter.

To understand these ideas better, compare the brightness of stars to the flashlights in the figures below. In the first figure, both flashlights give off the same amount of light. But one looks brighter because it is closer. In the second figure, both flashlights are the same distance away. But one looks brighter because it gives off more light.

Scientists use the term **magnitude** to describe the brightness of a star. How bright a star looks is its **apparent magnitude**. The **absolute magnitude** is how bright a star really is. Absolute magnitude measures how bright the star would be if all stars were the same distance from Earth.

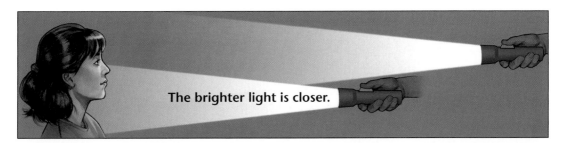

The brighter light is closer.

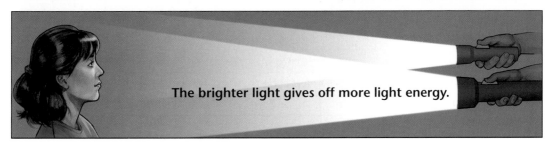

The brighter light gives off more light energy.

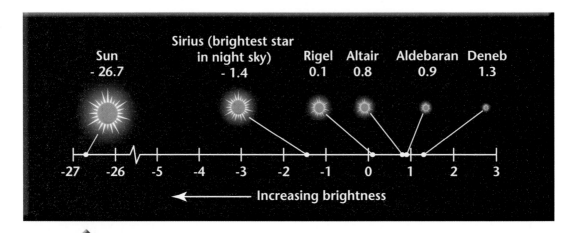

The brightness of a star is represented by a number. The apparent magnitudes of some stars are shown on the scale above. Notice that the largest negative numbers are the brightest stars.

Sirius is the brightest star in the night sky. As you can see on the scale, the apparent magnitude of Sirius is −1.4. The sun's apparent magnitude is −26.7. Of course, the sun is much brighter to us. But the absolute magnitude for Sirius is +1.4. By comparison, the sun's absolute magnitude is +4.7. This means that the sun is actually a dimmer star. If the sun and Sirius were the same distance from Earth, Sirius would shine brighter.

The Color of Stars

At first glance, you might think that all stars are white. Many of them are. But if you observe stars carefully, you will see that some are red, some are yellow, and others are blue-white. The color of a star depends on its temperature. The following table shows the temperature of stars of each color.

The sun's surface temperature is about 5,500°C. Looking at the table, you can see that the sun is a yellow star.

You may have heard the expressions "red hot" and "white hot." As a piece of metal is heated, it will first glow red. As the temperature increases, the metal will eventually turn white. In the same way, white stars are hotter than red stars.

Star Color and Temperature	
Color	**Average Surface Temperature (°C)**
blue-white	35,000
white	10,000
yellow	5,500
red	3,000

Write your answers to these questions on a sheet of paper.

1. Describe the process of fusion in stars.

2. What two factors affect a star's brightness?

3. Explain a star's apparent magnitude and absolute magnitude.

4. Which star is brighter: a star with a magnitude of 1 or a star with a magnitude of 0?

5. Which is hotter: a red star or a blue-white star?

▼◄▲▼◄▲▼◄▲▼◄▲▼◄▲▼◄▲▼◄▲▼◄▲▼◄▲▼◄▲▼◄▲▼◄▲▼◄▲▼◄▲▼◄▲▼◄▲▼

Science at Work

Telescope Technician

Telescope technicians help operate, maintain, repair, and program optical, radio, or X-ray telescopes. They often work closely with astronomers at observatories.

Technicians working at the National Radio Astronomy Observatory in New Mexico help operate a set of 27 radio telescopes. Each telescope is the size of a house and can be moved on tracks. The telescopes send and receive radio waves. Telescope technicians collect and organize this information. Astronomers use this information to map distant galaxies.

Telescope technicians need either two years of vocational training or a bachelor's degree in astronomy, mathematics, or engineering. They must have a thorough knowledge of the type of telescope they work with. Telescope technicians need to be precise and detail-oriented.

Materials

◆ masking tape
◆ marker
◆ 2 identical flashlights
◆ 2 sheets of tissue paper
◆ meterstick

Observing Brightness

Purpose

Does distance affect the brightness of a light source? In this investigation, you will demonstrate the different brightnesses of stars.

Procedure

1. Work with two partners in this investigation. Copy the data table on a sheet of paper.

Step	Observations
5	
6	
7	

2. Use masking tape and a marker to label one flashlight *A* and one flashlight *B*. **Safety Alert: Do not shine the flashlights into the eyes of others.**

3. Tape one layer of tissue paper over the front of each flashlight.

4. Darken the room.

5. Have each partner turn on a flashlight and stand together about 3 meters away from you. As they shine their flashlights toward you (but not into your eyes), compare the brightness of each light. Record your observations in the data table.

6. Have the partner holding flashlight A move about 4 meters away from you. Compare the brightness of each light. Record your observations.

7. Have the partner holding flashlight A move about 2 meters away from you. Compare the brightness of each light. Record your observations.

8. Repeat steps 5 to 7 two times, giving each partner a turn as the observer.

Questions and Conclusions

1. When did both flashlights have the same brightness?

2. Explain what you observed in steps 6 and 7.

3. In this investigation, did you change the apparent magnitude or the absolute magnitude of the flashlights?

4. How are the flashlights like stars?

Explore Further

Make one flashlight dimmer by covering it with two layers of tissue paper. Repeat the procedure. Move the flashlights until they have the same brightness. Measure the distances. Look at your results. Then, make up a system to describe the brightness of the flashlights. Consider distance and number of tissue layers. Explain your results using this system.

Light-year

Distance that light travels in one year

Did You Know?

In order to see an object, light from that object must reach your eyes. Suppose you are looking at a star that is 10 light-years away. The starlight that you see left that star 10 years ago. If that star exploded tonight, you would not see the flash for 10 years. Therefore, when you look at the stars, you are really looking back in time.

When you look at the night sky, you see some stars that seem to be closer to Earth and some that seem to be farther away. It is hard to imagine how far away stars really are.

Light-Years

Distances to stars are not expressed in kilometers or miles. Such numbers are so large that they are difficult to read and work with. Instead, scientists use a unit of length called the **light-year**. A light-year is the distance that light travels in one year.

1 light-year = 9.5 trillion kilometers

The speed of light is 300,000 kilometers per second. If a spaceship could travel at this speed, it would be going over 1 billion kilometers an hour. Moving as fast as light, this ship could travel from Earth to the moon in just over a second. The sun would be only 8 minutes and 20 seconds away. But the brightest star in the night sky, Sirius, would be almost 9 years away. That's because Sirius is 85.5 trillion kilometers, or 9 light-years, from Earth.

The distances between stars are much greater than distances between objects in our solar system. The distance between the sun and its nearest neighbor star, Proxima Centauri, is 4.2 light-years. That is more than 40 trillion kilometers.

Science Myth

Because of its name, people may assume that a light-year measures time.

Fact: A light-year is a measure of distance, not time. It is the distance light travels in one year, or about 9.5 trillion kilometers.

Sometimes, stars that look like they are near one another in space are actually very far from one another. Have you ever seen the Big Dipper? The stars in this familiar group all look like they are near one another in space. But, as the photo below shows, the stars of the Big Dipper are separated from one another by many light-years.

In this photo of a Canadian summer sky, the stars of the Big Dipper are highlighted. Each star's distance from Earth is given in light-years.

Measuring Star Distances

Astronomers determine distances to stars in different ways. One way begins by observing a star's position in the sky compared to more distant stars. Astronomers wait a few months while Earth moves in its orbit. Then they observe the star's position again. The star will appear to have shifted its position compared to the more distant stars. Closer stars appear to shift more than distant stars.

Very distant stars have shifts too small to measure. For these stars, astronomers compare their absolute and apparent magnitudes. If two stars have the same absolute magnitude, the dimmer star is farther away.

Write your answers to these questions on a sheet of paper.

1. What does a light-year measure?

2. Why do scientists use light-years instead of kilometers to describe some distances?

3. Which of the following describes a light-year?
   A trillions of kilometers
   B millions of kilometers
   C hundreds of kilometers
   D a tiny part of a kilometer

4. Compare the distance between two stars and the distance between two planets.

5. Describe two ways astronomers measure distances to stars.

Technology Note

The Hubble Space Telescope was launched in 1990. This telescope orbits Earth about every 97 minutes at 600 kilometers above its surface. The Hubble Space Telescope is a reflecting telescope with a main mirror that is 2.4 meters wide. The telescope is about as big as a bus. It is maintained regularly by NASA astronauts who travel to the telescope. NASA stands for the National Aeronautics and Space Administration, a U.S. agency.

Why did NASA launch a telescope into space? Telescopes on the ground have to "see" through Earth's dense atmosphere. This can distort and blur telescope images. Because the Hubble Space Telescope orbits above the atmosphere, it can capture sharp images that cannot be seen from the ground.

The Hubble Space Telescope has taken more than 330,000 images. It has observed at least 25,000 different objects in space.

Thanks to the Hubble Space Telescope, astronomers have learned much about the structure and evolution of our universe. This amazing telescope will continue exploring space until it retires in 2010.

Nebula

Cloud of gas and dust in space

As a star shines, fusion changes hydrogen into helium and energy. This energy is given off as light and heat. Eventually, the star's hydrogen is used up, fusion stops, and the star dies. This process takes billions of years. By studying different stars, astronomers can piece together the complete life cycle of a star.

The Birth of a Star

A star's life begins when a cloud of gas and dust is drawn together by its own gravity. This cloud is a **nebula**. The photo shows the Little Ghost Nebula. Within a nebula, gravity continues to pull gas and dust into a spinning ball. As the gas and dust pack tighter, the temperature of the ball increases. When the temperature gets high enough, fusion begins. A star is born.

Stars rotate on an axis, like planets. Stars are born rotating very fast. As stars grow old, they rotate slower and slower.

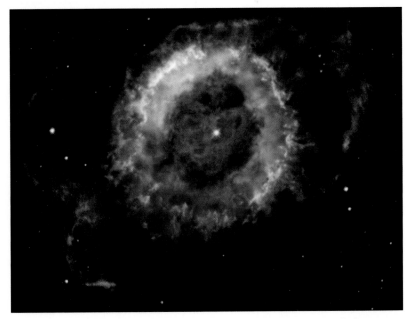

This nebula is about a light-year wide. It is more than 2,000 light-years from Earth.

The Death of a Star

The stages of a star's life depend on the balance between gravity and fusion. Gravity causes collapse, but fusion causes heat and expansion. Look at the diagram below as you read about these two forces.

Once a star uses up its hydrogen, the outer layers of the star begin to collapse toward the center. As the star collapses, particles of helium fuse. This fusion gives off energy, which expands the surface of the star. If the original star was a small- or medium-sized star, like the sun, it swells to about 100 times its size to become a **red giant**. If the star was larger and more massive than the sun, it swells even more to become a **supergiant**. These are the largest stars. Betelgeuse is the name of one supergiant. If it were placed where our sun is, Earth's orbit would be inside the star.

As the diagram shows, gravity pulls the outer parts of a red giant toward its center. It collapses. Then, its temperature increases once again, and the outer layer blows off, forming a **nova**. The center of the nova becomes a white, hot, dense star called a **white dwarf**. When the white dwarf uses up its energy, it becomes a dark, dense star that no longer shines.

Red giant

Star that has expanded after using up its hydrogen

Supergiant

One of the largest stars, formed when a star expands after using up its hydrogen; larger than a red giant

Nova

Brilliant explosion of a collapsed red giant

White dwarf

Small, white, hot, dense star that remains after a nova

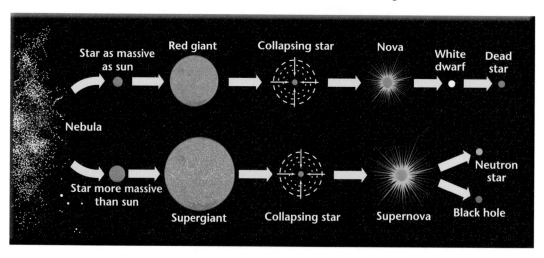

A star that becomes a supergiant has a more dramatic end. Gravity makes the supergiant collapse. Particles smashing into the center of the star make it so hot that a huge explosion occurs—a **supernova**. A supernova sends gas and dust into space and forms a nebula. After the explosion, a tiny **neutron star** may remain. A neutron star is only about 20 kilometers wide but has about as much mass as the sun. Therefore, a neutron star is very dense. One teaspoonful of a neutron star would weigh a billion tons. After a very large supernova, astronomers think the remaining star continues to collapse. The star's gravity becomes so great that light cannot escape. Thus, this region of space is called a **black hole**.

Scientists cannot visibly see black holes like they can see stars. However, black holes give off X rays, which scientists can measure. These X-ray "fingerprints" are often spotted in the centers of galaxies.

The photo on the left was taken by a camera aboard the Hubble Space Telescope. It shows a distant galaxy that formed when two smaller galaxies collided. This is what we would see if we were space observers. The image on the right was taken by an X-ray telescope in space. This X-ray image of the same galaxy shows two large black holes at the galaxy's center. The black holes appear as bright white spots, but they would not look this way to us. They are "bright" on an X-ray image because they are sending out X rays. Astronomers believe that, millions of years from now, these two black holes will combine to form one even larger black hole.

 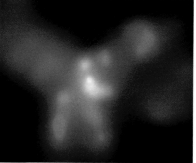

Stars can be seen on the optical image (left). Black holes and other X-ray sources can be seen on the X-ray image (right).

Write your answers to these questions on a sheet of paper.

1. How does a star's life begin?

2. Explain how gravity and fusion have opposite effects on a star.

3. Is a supergiant larger than, smaller than, or about the same size as a red giant?

4. Describe how a supergiant becomes a supernova.

5. What happens to a star when its life ends?

Achievements in Science

Black Holes

Black holes are not really holes. They are collapsed objects that are extremely heavy, yet very tiny. Because of this, they have a huge gravitational pull on objects close to them. An object on a black hole would have to go faster than the speed of light to escape this pull. Black holes are invisible because no light can escape from them.

Although black holes cannot be seen, astronomers know they exist. When gas and dust wander too close to a black hole, these particles are pulled into an orbit around it. This kind of orbit creates heat, and X rays are given off. Astronomers use powerful telescopes to measure the speed and heat of the orbiting material. From this information, they can tell that a black hole is at the center.

Stephen Hawking is a scientist who studies black holes. One of his theories is that mini black holes exist. Over time, these small black holes lose energy and mass and eventually disappear. Hawking also has shown that black holes produce their own radiant energy particles. Scientists previously thought that nothing could escape a black hole.

Hawking teaches mathematics at Cambridge University in England. He has the same teaching position as Sir Isaac Newton had 300 years ago. Hawking has amyotrophic lateral sclerosis (ALS), a disease of the nervous system. He uses a wheelchair and speaks with the aid of a computer-synthesized voice.

Objectives

After reading this lesson, you should be able to

◆ explain what a constellation is.

◆ identify some constellations.

◆ explain what a galaxy is.

◆ identify the galaxy that includes our solar system.

Constellation

Pattern of stars seen from Earth

Constellations

When ancient people looked at the sky, they imagined the stars formed the shapes of people, animals, and objects. They related these shapes to myths, or stories. Today, we still use these groups of stars, called **constellations**, to describe parts of the sky.

The ancient Greeks named 48 constellations. Today, astronomers divide the sky into 88 constellations, including the ones named by the ancient Greeks. You have probably recognized part of a constellation many times. The Big Dipper is the rump and tail of the constellation Ursa Major, also called the Great Bear.

Shown below are some constellations that can be seen from the Northern Hemisphere. Appendix E contains two sets of constellation maps: a summer set and a winter set. By comparing them, you can see that stars change position.

One star that doesn't appear to move much is Polaris. It is also called the North Star because it is located above the North Pole. During the year, the constellations appear to move in a circle around this star. To find the North Star in the sky, use the pointer stars in the Big Dipper, as shown.

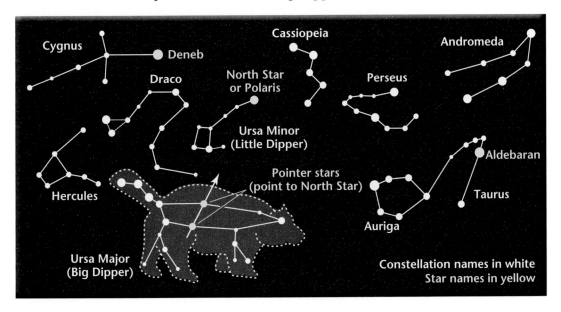

Galaxy

Group of billions of stars

Galaxies

The sun is part of a large group of stars called a **galaxy**. A galaxy may contain many billions of stars. Galaxies can be divided into three different groups, based on their shape. The three shapes are elliptical, spiral, and irregular, as shown in the photos.

An elliptical galaxy is shaped like an oval, or ellipse. Most galaxies are elliptical. An irregular galaxy has no regular shape. These galaxies look like fuzzy clouds in space.

Did You Know?

While sailing in the South Pacific in the 1500s, the crew of the explorer ship *Magellan* observed two fuzzy regions in the night sky. They were called the Large and Small Magellanic Clouds. These regions are actually irregular galaxies. They are the closest galaxies to our own—about 175,000 light-years away.

The stars in elliptical galaxies are close together. These galaxies contain very little gas or dust.

The Large Magellanic Cloud, an irregular galaxy, can be seen from the Southern Hemisphere.

A spiral galaxy might remind you of a pinwheel. Spiral galaxies are the least common, but they are very bright. Therefore, we can see many of them from Earth.

This spiral galaxy is about the same size as the Milky Way galaxy. Named M74, it is 30 million light-years away.

Most of the stars that you can see without a telescope belong to the **Milky Way galaxy**. The Milky Way galaxy is a spiral galaxy that is about 100,000 light-years wide. This galaxy contains at least 100 billion stars. The sun is one of these stars. Our solar system is a small part of one swirling arm of this galaxy.

On some nights, you can see a faint band of light across the sky. This band is called the Milky Way. It is the light from the distant stars of our galaxy. The Milky Way forms a band of light because you are looking toward the center of the galaxy. This view is like looking at a dinner plate from its side. You see only a thin portion of the plate.

There are millions of galaxies moving through space. Spiral galaxies rotate as they move. All of the galaxies together are called the **universe**. The word *universe* refers to everything that exists. The best telescopes built so far have not found an end to the universe.

Lesson 4   R E V I E W

Write the answers to these questions on a sheet of paper.

1. What is a constellation?

2. What are three kinds of galaxies?

3. To what galaxy does our solar system belong?

4. When you view the Milky Way in the night sky, what are you seeing?

5. What is the universe made of?

Science in Your Life

Light Pollution

If you step outside your front door and look up at the sky on a clear night, what do you see? If you live in or near a city, you might just see a dark sky. The farther away from city lights you live, the easier it is to see the stars. If you cannot see the stars, the problem is nighttime light, or light pollution. The sun's light blocks your view of the stars in the daytime sky. At night, other lights can block your view. Even light from cities you can't see may cause light pollution. Observatories are located in places far away from sources of light pollution. That way, telescopes get a clearer view of objects in the sky.

For hundreds of years, stargazers have tried to solve the problem of light pollution. Some ancient stargazers looked at the sky from dark holes dug in the earth. Most simply went to places away from lights to look at stars. A mountaintop is a good place because it is usually away from cities and the air is thinner. It is easier for starlight to get through.

The satellite image shows what North America looks like at night. Where does light pollution seem greatest on this map?

On the map, locate where you live. What sources of light pollution are near your home? (Don't forget street lights.) Try viewing the stars from a few different locations. How does light pollution affect your observations?

INVESTIGATION

5-2

Materials

- ◆ star guide showing constellations
- ◆ tissue paper
- ◆ black construction paper
- ◆ pin
- ◆ flashlight
- ◆ blackboard and chalk

Making a Constellation Model

Purpose

How could you model a constellation of stars? In this investigation, you will make a constellation projection.

Procedure

1. Work with a partner in this investigation. Copy the data form on a sheet of paper.

Constellation Data
Name of constellation:
Number of stars:
Reasons for choosing:
Description of pattern:

2. Choose a picture of a constellation from a star guide.

3. Trace the constellation onto a piece of tissue paper. Use a dot to mark the position of each star in the constellation.

4. Place the tracing over a sheet of black construction paper.

5. Use a pin to make a hole through both sheets of paper at each dot. Set the tissue paper aside. **Safety Alert: Use care with pins. The points are sharp.**

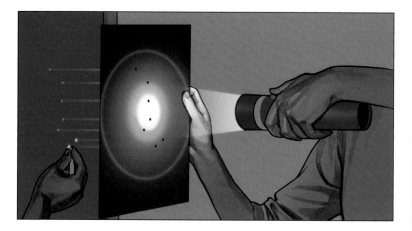

6. Darken the room. Hold the black paper in front of a blackboard. Turn on the flashlight and shine it at the paper as shown. Move the flashlight until it shines through all of the pinholes. **Safety Alert: Do not shine the flashlight into the eyes of others.**

7. Have your partner use the chalk to mark the stars in your constellation projection. Write the name of your constellation on the board.

8. Record the data about your constellation on the data form.

Questions and Conclusions

1. How is your model like an actual constellation?

2. How is your model different from a constellation?

3. How could you try to make your model better?

Explore Further

Locate the actual constellation. Use a star guide or Appendix E to find out when the constellation is in your night sky. Also, find out where to look in the sky for the constellation.

- Stars shine because of fusion. In this process, hydrogen particles combine to form helium particles plus energy. The energy makes the stars shine.

- A star's brightness depends on its distance from Earth and the amount of energy the star gives off.

- How bright a star looks is its apparent magnitude. The star's absolute magnitude is how bright it really is.

- The color of a star depends on its temperature.

- A light-year is the distance light travels in one year. Distances of stars are expressed in light-years.

- Even though stars seem to be near one another in the sky, they are far apart in space.

- Astronomers determine star distances by comparing the positions of stars and their absolute and apparent magnitudes.

- A star is created when fusion begins inside a nebula.

- A star shines until its hydrogen is used up. This process usually takes billions of years.

- The way a star dies depends on its size. A small- or medium-sized star swells to become a red giant, collapses, then explodes as a nova. A white dwarf remains.

- A massive star swells and becomes a supergiant, collapses, then explodes as a supernova. A tiny, dense neutron star may remain, or a black hole may develop.

- Constellations are groups of stars that form a pattern in the sky.

- A galaxy is a group of billions of stars. The sun is a star in the Milky Way galaxy.

- Galaxies are grouped by their shapes. The Milky Way galaxy is shaped like a spiral.

Science Words

absolute magnitude, 109	constellation, 121	Milky Way galaxy, 123	red giant, 118
apparent magnitude, 109	fusion, 108	nebula, 117	supergiant, 118
black hole, 119	galaxy, 122	neutron star, 119	supernova, 119
	light-year, 114	nova, 118	universe, 123
	magnitude, 109		white dwarf, 118

Chapter 5 R E V I E W

Word Bank

absolute magnitude

apparent magnitude

constellations

fusion

galaxy

light-years

Milky Way galaxy

nebula

supergiant

supernova

universe

white dwarf

Vocabulary Review

Choose the word or phrase from the Word Bank that best completes each sentence. Write the answer on your paper.

1. The actual brightness of a star is called its _____.

2. One of the largest stars that forms after using up its hydrogen is a(n) _____.

3. A small, hot, dense star is a(n) _____.

4. Distances to stars are measured in units called _____.

5. An explosion of a large star is a(n) _____.

6. Patterns of stars seen from Earth are called _____.

7. A group of billions of stars is called a(n) _____.

8. How bright a star looks is its _____.

9. Our solar system belongs to the _____.

10. The cloud of gas and dust in which a star is born is a(n) _____.

11. Stars shine because of a process called _____.

12. Everything that exists is called the _____.

Concept Review

Choose the word or phrase that best answers each question. Write the letter of the answer on your paper.

13. Which star magnitude is the brightest?
   A -0.1 **B** 0.5   **C** 0.1   **D** 1.5

14. Which star color is the hottest?
   A red   **B** blue-white   **C** yellow   **D** white

15. Which star color is the coolest?
   A red   **B** blue-white   **C** yellow   **D** white

16. A light-year measures _____.
   A time   **B** distance   **C** light   **D** brightness

17. A star's brightness depends on which two things?
    A distance and color
    B shape and age
    C age and energy given off
    D distance and energy given off

18. Which pair of objects is farthest apart?
    A Earth and the moon   **C** Earth and night star
    B Earth and the sun   **D** Earth and Mars

19. During fusion in stars, hydrogen particles combine to form helium and _____.
    A energy   **B** water   **C** neutron stars   **D** oxygen

20. Galaxies are divided into groups by _____.
    A temperature   **B** shape   **C** color   **D** size

21. A star that is the size of the sun will swell and become a _____ toward the end of its life.
    A supergiant   **C** nebula
    B supernova   **D** red giant

22. Light cannot escape from _____.
    A white dwarfs   **C** neutron stars
    B black holes   **D** novas

Critical Thinking

Write the answer to each of the following questions.

23. Explain what happens when a star uses up its hydrogen.

24. Order the following six objects by size, from smallest to largest: Milky Way galaxy, Earth, supergiant, white dwarf, solar system, and universe.

25. Why do Alaskans and Australians see different stars?

Test-Taking Tip When studying for a test, learn the most important points. Practice writing this material or explaining it to someone.

6

Earth Chemistry

There are many different objects in this photo of a winter scene. But they all have at least one thing in common. Everything is made of matter. Matter can take the form of a solid, liquid, or gas. The river water is in a liquid state. The snow is a solid form of water. The water that evaporates into the air is a gas. In Chapter 6, you will learn about matter and its properties. You will find out about the elements that make up matter and their atoms. You also will learn how matter combines to form mixtures and compounds.

Organize Your Thoughts

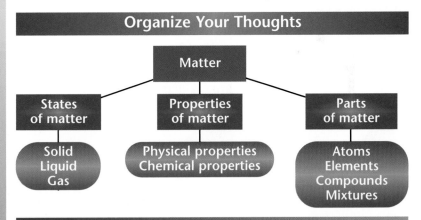

Matter

States of matter	Properties of matter	Parts of matter
Solid Liquid Gas	Physical properties Chemical properties	Atoms Elements Compounds Mixtures

Goals for Learning

◆ To define matter

◆ To identify the states of matter

◆ To identify properties of matter

◆ To locate on a diagram the parts of an atom

◆ To compare and contrast elements, compounds, and mixtures

Objectives

After reading this lesson, you should be able to

◆ define matter.

◆ recognize three states of matter.

◆ identify properties of matter.

◆ measure properties of matter.

A house is made of many parts. Not all the parts are made of the same material. For example, the lumber inside the walls is different from the shingles that cover the roof. Some parts of the house are held together with nails. The lumber, the shingles, and the nails have different characteristics. But they are all examples of **matter**.

Matter is anything that has mass and takes up space. That includes a lot of different things. Land, water, and air are matter. In fact, except for energy, everything the earth is made of is matter. Understanding some basic ideas about matter will help you understand how land, water, and air change.

States of Matter

Matter usually exists on the earth in three basic forms, or states. These **states of matter** are solid, liquid, and gas. Below are examples of these three states. What other examples can you think of?

You can describe matter by identifying it as a solid, a liquid, or a gas. The state of matter is only one way to describe something. There are many other ways.

Matter

Anything that has mass and takes up space

States of matter

Basic forms in which matter exists, including solid, liquid, and gas

Did You Know?

Matter can exist in a fourth state called plasma. This is a very hot gas made of electrically charged particles. Plasma is rare on the earth. It occurs in lightning and in stars.

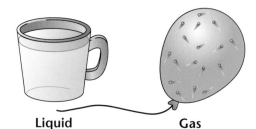

Solid   **Liquid**   **Gas**

Properties of Matter

Property

Characteristic that describes matter

Physical property

Characteristic of a substance or an object that can be observed without changing the substance into a different substance

Chemical property

Characteristic that describes how a substance changes into a different substance

How would you describe salt? It is white, solid, and made of small grains. This description is a list of three **properties** of salt. A property is a characteristic that describes matter. Properties help you identify matter.

The following table lists some properties of salt and sugar. Compare the properties to see how the two substances differ. You can use these properties to tell whether a substance is salt or sugar.

Physical Properties of Salt and Sugar		
Property	Salt	Sugar
color	white	white
state	solid	solid
size	small grains	small grains
taste	salty	sweet

The properties of salt and sugar listed above are **physical properties**. These properties can be observed without changing the substance into a different substance. Below are some common physical properties you can use to identify matter.

To identify a substance, scientists often need to know more than just its physical properties. In such cases, scientists may use chemical tests to describe **chemical properties**. A chemical property describes how a substance changes into a different substance. For example, wood burns to form ashes and gases. A chemical property of wood, then, is that it changes to ashes and gases when burned.

Reacting with air and water is another chemical property. For example, a can left in water turns into rust because iron in the can reacts with oxygen and water. So a chemical property of iron is that it reacts with oxygen and water to form rust. A complete description of matter, then, includes both chemical and physical properties.

Write your answers to these questions on a sheet of paper.

1. What is matter?

2. Give an example of a solid, a liquid, and a gas.

3. Name three physical properties of a dime.

4. How is a physical property different from a chemical property?

5. Give an example of a chemical property.

Science in Your Life

Lasting Plastic

For the past 70 years, plastic has been a useful invention. It bends. It bounces. It protects from the cold. Plastic is cheap to make and easy to mold. Because of these properties, people use a lot of plastic. But people also throw away a lot of it. Plastic has another property: it is not biodegradable. This means it does not break down in the environment. Plastic lasts and lasts, whether it is dumped in a landfill or carelessly thrown in a lake.

Recycling is one way to reduce the amount of plastic thrown away. Many cities have recycling programs for plastic and other materials. Another way to reduce plastic garbage is to use less of it. For example, when you are shopping, pick products with little plastic packaging or none at all.

You might be surprised to discover how much plastic you throw away every day. What can you do in your home to reduce plastic garbage?

6-1

INVESTIGATION

Materials

◆ assortment of objects
◆ centimeter ruler
◆ balance

Measuring Physical Properties of Objects

Purpose

What are ways of describing and identifying objects? In this investigation, you will measure the physical properties of some objects.

Procedure

1. Copy the data table on a sheet of paper.

Object	State of Matter	Color	Shape	Size	Mass	

2. List each object in the first column of your data table.

3. Describe the physical properties of each object. First, describe the properties that you can observe without making measurements (state, color, and shape). Record your observations. **Safety Alert: Use care with liquids. Wipe up any spills immediately.**

4. Use the ruler to describe the size of each object. Record these measurements.

5. Use the balance to measure the mass of each object. Record these measurements.

6. Think of another physical property that helps identify the objects. Add this property to your data table. Then, record your observations for each of the objects. **Safety Alert: Do not choose taste as a physical property. Never taste any substances used in a science investigation.**

Questions and Conclusions

1. Is it hard to describe some properties? Why?

2. Which of your descriptions are the same?

3. What property did you add to your data table? Why did you choose that property?

Explore Further

Cover the first column of your data table with a sheet of paper, or fold your data table so the first column doesn't show. Now, exchange your data table of physical properties with a classmate. Can you identify each other's objects based only on their physical properties? If not, what other properties might be helpful?

Elements

All words in the English language are made from combinations of just 26 letters. In the same way, all matter is made from combinations of 109 known **elements**.

An element is a substance that cannot be changed or separated into other kinds of substances. For example, the rock shown in the photo contains the element gold. But the gold is mixed with a mineral called quartz. You could smash the rock to separate the gold from the quartz. You could then smash the gold into tiny specks. Are the specks different elements? No, they are tiny pieces of gold, but they are still gold. What if you melted the specks? Would you have a different element? No, you would have liquid gold. You can change the physical state of an element, but it is still the same element.

Element

Substance that cannot be changed or separated into other kinds of substances

This quartz rock contains the element gold.

Atoms and Elements

Suppose you could continue to break the gold into smaller and smaller particles. Eventually you would break the gold into individual **atoms**. An atom is the smallest particle of an element that has the characteristics of that element. An element is made of only one kind of atom. For example, a chunk of pure gold is made of only gold atoms.

What makes the element gold different from any other element? The answer is in the atoms. Look at the model of a carbon atom below. An atom is made of three kinds of particles. In its center are protons and neutrons. The protons and neutrons make up the **nucleus** of an atom. Moving around the outside of the nucleus are electrons.

Did You Know?

Diamond—the hardest substance known—is made of pure carbon. Graphite, or pencil lead, is also made of pure carbon. The difference is how the carbon atoms are arranged and held together.

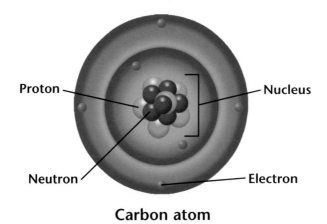

Carbon atom

Elements are different from one another because their atoms have different numbers of protons, neutrons, and electrons. However, it is the number of protons that makes each element unique. The carbon atom above has 6 protons. Each atom of gold has 79 protons. An atom of silver has 47 protons. Each copper atom has 29 protons.

The atoms in a solid are packed tightly and don't move much. The atoms in a liquid are packed tightly too, but they move freely. The atoms in a gas move very fast and spread out to fill the container they are in.

Scientists have discovered and officially named 109 elements. They have organized these elements into a chart called the Periodic Table of Elements. It is shown in Appendix E. For each element, this table gives the atomic weight and number of protons in an atom. It also lists each element's scientific symbol. Ninety-two of these elements are found in nature. For example, oxygen and nitrogen are two elements found in the air. Water contains oxygen and hydrogen.

The following table lists the 10 most common elements found in the earth's rocks. Which of these elements has the greatest number of protons? Which has the least? Notice the scientific symbol for each element. Most of these symbols are the first letter or the first two letters of the element's name. But some symbols may seem odd. For example, why is iron's symbol *Fe*? This symbol and some others are based on the element's Latin name. The Latin name for iron is *ferrum*.

Most Common Elements in Earth's Rocks		
Element	Symbol	Number of Protons
oxygen	O	8
silicon	Si	14
aluminum	Al	13
iron	Fe	26
calcium	Ca	20
sodium	Na	11
potassium	K	19
magnesium	Mg	12
titanium	Ti	22
hydrogen	H	1

Write your answers to these questions on a sheet of paper.

1. What is an atom?

2. What kind of matter is made of only one kind of atom?

3 What does an atom's nucleus contain?

4. How are elements different from one another?

5. Name five elements and give their symbols.

Achievements in Science

Creating New Elements

Several elements were discovered by creating them in a laboratory. The nine elements below were discovered by a research team led by Glenn Seaborg. This American nuclear chemist was awarded the Nobel Prize for Chemistry in 1951.

plutonium (Pu)	einsteinium (Es)
americium (Am)	fermium (Fm)
curium (Cm)	mendelevium (Md)
berkelium (Bk)	nobelium (No)
californium (Cf)	

The best known of these elements is plutonium. It is an important source of nuclear energy. Traces of plutonium are found in the earth, but this element is usually made artificially. The other elements listed have not been found in nature. Locate each one in the bottom row of the Periodic Table of Elements (Appendix E).

Seaborg made other significant discoveries. He noticed that certain heavy elements have similar properties. Because of this, the Periodic Table of Elements was reorganized. Seaborg also helped discover many isotopes. Isotopes are atoms with the same number of protons but with different numbers of neutrons. Isotopes are used to treat cancer patients.

As a tribute to Seaborg's contributions to chemistry, the element seaborgium (Sg) was named after him. Seaborg taught at the University of California at Berkeley. Look again at the list of elements he discovered. What or who are they named after?

Objectives

After reading this lesson, you should be able to

◆ explain the differences among compounds, elements, and mixtures.

◆ identify some common compounds.

◆ recognize the formula for a compound.

Compound

Substance formed when the atoms of two or more elements join chemically

Since there are only 92 natural elements, how can the earth contain so many different kinds of matter? This variety is possible because the atoms of elements combine to make different substances.

Compounds

When the atoms of two or more elements combine, a **compound** forms. Compounds have properties that are different from the elements that make them up, just as a cake is different from the eggs, flour, and milk that go into it. The example below shows this idea dramatically.

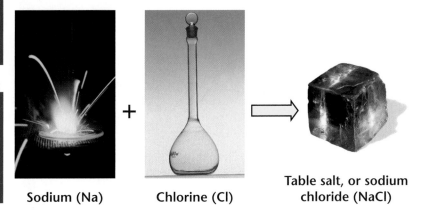

Sodium (Na)　　　Chlorine (Cl)　　　Table salt, or sodium chloride (NaCl)

Sodium is a metal. It explodes in water. Chlorine is a poisonous, greenish gas. You may have noticed the smell of this gas in a bottle of household bleach. When these two extremely dangerous elements combine, they form a compound called sodium chloride. You probably know this compound by its common name—table salt.

What does it mean to say that two or more elements combine? If a bit of sodium was placed in a container of chlorine gas, you would not suddenly have sodium chloride. To form a compound, the elements must join chemically. This means the atoms must undergo a change, such as sharing electrons. For example, the figure shows how the elements oxygen and hydrogen join chemically to form the compound water. The atoms share electrons. This sharing holds the atoms together.

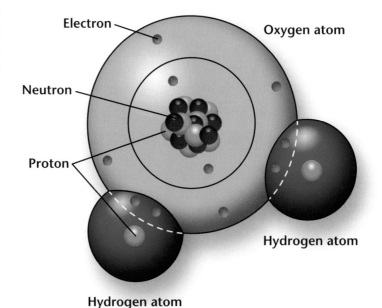

The compound water

Once elements are combined chemically, they are not easily taken apart. You cannot separate the sodium from the chlorine in salt by breaking the salt into tiny bits. You cannot separate the oxygen and the hydrogen in water by pouring it through a strainer. Usually, heat or electricity is needed to separate a compound into its elements.

Formulas for Compounds

Scientists use chemical formulas to represent compounds. Here is a list of some common compounds and their formulas. Notice how each formula includes the symbols of the elements that make up the compound.

Some Common Compounds		
Common Name	**Compound Name**	**Formula**
water	hydrogen oxide	H_2O
salt	sodium chloride	NaCl
rust	iron oxide	Fe_2O_3
baking soda	sodium bicarbonate	$NaHCO_3$
chalk	calcium carbonate	$CaCO_3$
carbon dioxide	carbon dioxide	CO_2

Besides including the symbols of the elements, a formula also tells you how many atoms of each element join to form the compound. Here's how to understand a chemical formula:

1. Identify the elements in the compound by their symbol.

   For example, water has the formula H_2O, so it contains the elements hydrogen (H) and oxygen (O).

2. Determine the number of atoms of each element. Look for a number that follows an element's symbol. This tells how many atoms of that element are in the compound. If there is no number, it means there is 1 atom of that element.

   The formula for water shows that there are 2 atoms of hydrogen and 1 atom of oxygen. In other words, the smallest unit of the compound water is formed by 2 atoms of hydrogen joined to 1 atom of oxygen.

When you think about it, a chemical formula is a lot like a recipe.

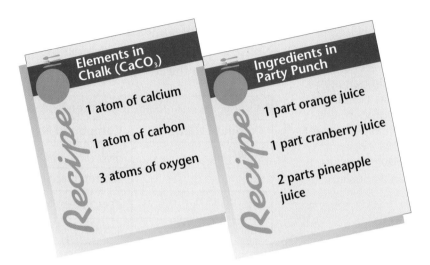

Recipe

Elements in Chalk (CaCO₃)

1 atom of calcium

1 atom of carbon

3 atoms of oxygen

Recipe

Ingredients in Party Punch

1 part orange juice

1 part cranberry juice

2 parts pineapple juice

Mixtures

The photo shows a type of matter called a **mixture**. A mixture is made of two or more elements or compounds. But a mixture is different from a compound. The substances that form a mixture do not join chemically. They are simply mixed together. The soil shown here is a mixture of dead plants, sand, clay, water and other matter. The atoms of these substances are not joined.

This garden soil is a mixture called compost.

Can you name some other mixtures? Air is a mixture of gases. Some of the gases, such as oxygen, are elements. Other gases, such as carbon dioxide, are compounds. Most rocks are mixtures of compounds. A river is a mixture of water, oxygen, soil, pebbles, and other substances that move along a riverbed. Even the taco salad you might have had for lunch is a mixture.

The parts in a mixture can vary. You can take out the dead plant material in soil and it is still a mixture of soil. You can add more oxygen atoms to air and it is still a mixture of air. Compounds, however, have a fixed recipe or formula. You cannot simply add more oxygen atoms to water. Water must have exactly one oxygen atom for every two hydrogen atoms.

Unlike a compound, you can easily separate the parts of some mixtures. For example, you can separate the dead plant material in the soil just by picking it out with your fingers. Can you think of a way to separate the salt from a mixture of salt water? You will learn how in the investigation on pages 147 and 148.

Science Myth

Some people may think that air and oxygen are the same thing.

Fact: Air is a mixture of gases. We need to breathe in oxygen, but oxygen is only about 21 percent of air. Most of the air we breathe is nitrogen gas. Air also contains small amounts of carbon dioxide, water vapor, and other gases. This mixture varies. For example, air contains more water vapor on humid days.

Write your answers to these questions on a sheet of paper.

1. What is the difference between an element and a compound?

2. Name two compounds. Describe one physical property of each.

3. The formula for water is H_2O. What kinds of atoms combine to make water?

4. The formula for silicon dioxide is SiO_2. How many atoms of silicon (Si) and oxygen (O) combine to form this compound?

5. How is a mixture different from a compound?

▼◄▲▼◄▲▼◄▲▼◄▲▼◄▲▼◄▲▼◄▲▼◄▲▼◄▲▼◄▲▼◄▲▼◄▲▼◄▲▼◄▲▼◄▲▼◄▲▼◄▲▼

Science at Work

Chemical Engineer

Engineers use science and mathematics to solve practical problems. Chemical engineers solve problems that involve chemicals.

Some chemical engineers design and test better ways to manufacture products. Others develop equipment to prevent pollution. Chemical engineers improve the ways chemicals are stored and moved. In all of these tasks, chemical engineers aim for better quality and lower cost.

Since the use of chemicals is so widespread, chemical engineers work in various fields. They develop many products, such as food, gasoline, and medical devices. They work with many materials, such as plastic cooling in a mold and liquid flowing through a pipe. They test processes to develop film and make synthetic fabric.

Chemical engineers need a bachelor's degree in chemical engineering. They also need a strong background in mathematics. Chemical engineers must be skilled problem solvers. They often work as part of a team. Good planning and communicating skills also are important.

INVESTIGATION

Materials

- ◆ clean sheet of paper
- ◆ 2 teaspoons of sand
- ◆ 2 teaspoons of salt
- ◆ spoon
- ◆ 2 beakers
- ◆ 10 tablespoons of warm water
- ◆ filter paper
- ◆ funnel

Fold once.

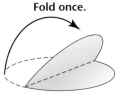

Fold twice.

Open to make a cone.

Separating a Mixture

Purpose

How would you separate a mixture of sand, salt, and water? In this investigation, you will use different methods to separate mixtures.

Procedure

1. Copy the data table on your paper.

Mixture	Description
salt and sand, dry	
salt and sand in water	
contents in beaker after filtering	
contents on filter paper after filtering	
contents in beaker after 1 day	
contents on filter paper after 1 day	

2. Use the spoon to stir the salt and sand together on a sheet of paper. Describe this dry mixture in your data table.

3. Pour the dry mixture into a beaker. Add the water. Stir the mixture well. Describe the new mixture. **Safety Alert: Never taste any substances used in a science investigation. Wipe up any spills immediately.**

4. Make a cone with the filter paper as shown. Place the cone in the funnel. Put the funnel in the empty beaker. Pour the mixture into the funnel. Describe the mixture that dripped into the beaker.

5. Describe the contents on the filter paper.

6. Remove the funnel. Place the filter paper on the paper sheet. Set the beaker containing its mixture on the paper, too. Observe both the next day. Describe what you find.

7. Clean your work space and wash the equipment.

Questions and Conclusions

1. What happened to the salt when you added water and stirred? What happened to the sand?

2. What was left on the filter paper?

3. What happened to the salt? How do you know?

Explore Further

A sand; sawdust
B sand; iron filings
C sand; pebbles

Choose one of the lettered mixtures at the left. Describe a procedure for separating it. You may use water and any equipment used earlier. You also may use a magnet, a wire screen, and a cotton square.

- Matter is anything that has mass and takes up space.

- Matter usually exists on the earth in three states: solid, liquid, and gas.

- A physical property can be observed without changing a substance into a different substance.

- A chemical property describes how a substance changes into a different substance.

- An element is made of only one kind of atom. An element cannot be changed or separated into other kinds of substances.

- An atom is the smallest particle of an element that has the characteristics of that element.

- Atoms are made of protons, neutrons, and electrons. The nucleus of an atom is made of protons and neutrons.

- Elements differ from one another because their atoms have different numbers of protons.

- Scientists have discovered and named 109 elements. Ninety-two of them are found in nature.

- The scientific symbol for each element has one or two letters.

- Compounds form when the atoms of two or more elements combine chemically.

- Scientists use formulas to represent compounds.

- Mixtures are made of two or more elements or compounds that are not combined chemically.

Science Words

atom, 138	element, 137	nucleus, 138	property, 133
chemical	matter, 132	physical	states of
property, 133	mixture, 144	property, 133	matter, 132
compound, 141			

Chapter 6   R E V I E W

Word Bank

atom

compound

element

matter

mixture

nucleus

property

state of matter

Vocabulary Review

Choose the word or phrase from the Word Bank that best matches each phrase. Write the answer on your paper.

1. solid, liquid, or gas

2. anything that takes up space and has mass

3. substance made of only one kind of atom

4. smallest particle of an element

5. center of an atom

6. NaCl, water, or calcium carbonate

7. soil, air, or salad

8. characteristic of something

Concept Review

Write the answer to each of the following questions.

9. Name three states of matter and give an example of each.

10. Describe three physical properties of an ice cube.

11. What is the difference between the atoms of two different elements?

12. Explain how a mixture is different from a compound.

Choose the word or phrase that best answers each question. Write the letter of the answer on your paper.

13. Which parts of atoms are outside the nucleus?

   A electrons   **C** neutrons

   B protons   **D** elements

14. Which of the following is a chemical property?

   A large size

   B round shape

   C salty taste

   D black compound formed when burned

15. Which compound is formed from three elements?
  A H_2O **B** CO_2 **C** $CaCO_3$ **D** NaCl

16. Which statement is true about the compound carbon dioxide (CO_2)?
  A It contains 2 carbon atoms.
  B It contains 1 carbon atom.
  C It contains 2 carbon atoms and 2 oxygen atoms.
  D It contains 2 oxygen atoms and no carbon atoms.

Critical Thinking

Write the answer to each of the following questions.

17. How could you show someone that air is matter?

18. Iron atoms combine with oxygen atoms to form rust. Is this a physical property of iron or a chemical property? Why?

19. Compare and contrast the properties of each pair below.
  A water; vinegar   **B** air; helium   **C** plastic; steel

A wood shavings; pebbles
B soil; water
C sand; iron filings

20. Choose one of the lettered mixtures at the left. Explain how you would separate it. Use any of the tools shown.

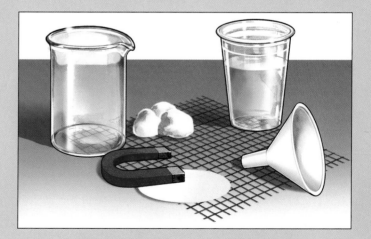

Test-Taking Tip When you review your notes to prepare for a test, use a marker to highlight key words and phrases.

Minerals

inerals are all around us. We use them every day. Can you tell what mineral is shown in the photo? The long ropes you see are really copper wires braided into cable. Copper is a mineral that can carry an electric current. It is frequently used to make electrical wires and cables. These wires are braided so that the cable will not crack when it bends. In Chapter 7, you will learn what minerals are, how you can tell them apart, and how they are used today.

Organize Your Thoughts

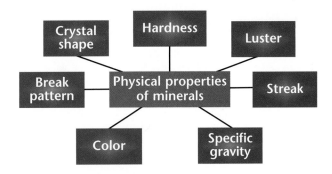

Goals for Learning

◆ To explain what a mineral is

◆ To explain how minerals are located and mined

◆ To name familiar minerals

◆ To identify basic properties of all minerals

◆ To compare minerals by their properties

◆ To describe how minerals are used

The earth around you is a mixture of useful compounds and elements. Scientists classify some of these compounds and elements as **minerals**.

Features of Minerals

What do copper, quartz, and diamond have in common? They are all minerals. Elements or compounds are called minerals if they have these five features:

◆ They are solids.
◆ They are formed naturally in the earth.
◆ They have the same chemical makeup throughout.
◆ They are not alive or made of living things.
◆ They have definite atomic patterns.

Mineral

Element or compound found in the earth

About 3,000 different minerals are found in the earth. Some are common, but most are rare. In fact, only a small number of minerals make up most of the earth's surface. The most common minerals are aluminum, quartz, feldspar, mica, calcite, dolomite, halite, and gypsum.

Copper deposits often tarnish to a brown or green color.

Some minerals, such as gold (Au) and sulfur (S), are pure elements. Graphite and diamond are different forms of pure carbon. Most minerals, however, are compounds. They are made of two or more kinds of elements. For example, quartz (SiO_2) is made of the elements silicon (Si) and oxygen (O).

Ancient miners discovered that the best places to dig for precious metals were the cracks and vents of volcanoes. They found copper, iron, silver, and gold by digging horizontal shafts near volcanoes.

Locating and Mining Minerals

Minerals can be found in rocks, sand, soil, and seashells. Many minerals are found below the earth's surface. Minerals are mined, or dug out of the earth, so they can be used. People mine for minerals on every continent except Antarctica. Some minerals are found in pure forms. But most minerals are found mixed with other minerals in rocks.

Geologists locate rocks with certain minerals by looking for clues on the earth's surface. They observe the kinds of rocks and plants in an area. Geologists might test running water for traces of minerals.

Once minerals are located, they are either skimmed off the earth's surface or dug deep out of the ground. Minerals near the surface can be strip-mined. This means that long patches of soil are stripped off. Then the exposed minerals are scooped up. Another way to reach minerals near the surface is to dig open pits.

For minerals deep underground, long shafts are dug into the earth. These shafts are often as long as 1.6 kilometers. Mining tunnels branch off the shafts. In the tunnels, explosives are used to break apart rock so the mineral deposits can be collected.

After deposits are taken out of the earth, the minerals need to be separated from the rock, or purified. One way to do this is to melt the minerals in huge smelting ovens. Another method is to use chemicals to break apart the minerals.

The mineral quartz is silicon dioxide, SiO_2.

Graphite is a soft form of pure carbon.

Lesson 1   R E V I E W

Write your answers to these questions on a sheet of paper.

1. What are the five features of a mineral?

2. Name two common minerals.

3. How do geologists know where to find minerals deep in the earth?

4. How are minerals taken out of the earth?

5. How are minerals purified?

Achievements in Science

Working with Metals

Many minerals are metals. People have been making things out of metals for thousands of years. One of the first minerals to be used was copper. Copper was mined around 9000 B.C. on the island of Cyprus in the Mediterranean Sea.

By 3000 B.C., the Sumerians had discovered bronze. They heated rocks containing copper and tin ore to produce bronze for ornaments and weapons.

Around 1900 B.C., the Hittites of Turkey began making tools and weapons out of iron. Although these ancient people were mainly farmers, they developed metal-working techniques that were more advanced than others at the time.

In the 1850s, a process for making steel was invented in America and England. This process adds carbon to melted iron by forcing air through the iron. The steel that results is stronger than iron.

More than 90 percent of all metal used in the world today is iron. Almost all of this iron is in the form of steel. Steel costs much less than other metals. It is used in thousands of products, such as cars, buildings, and paper clips.

Objectives

After reading this lesson, you should be able to

◆ identify four properties of minerals.

◆ assess color as a way to identify minerals.

◆ define luster.

◆ describe a streak test.

◆ explain how to test the hardness of a mineral.

Pyrite is sometimes called fool's gold because people can easily mistake it for gold. However, no two minerals share the same physical properties. For example, pyrite is almost the same color as gold, but it is harder than gold. In this lesson, you will learn about four properties used for identifying minerals.

Color

Some minerals have a unique color. For example, sulfur is usually bright yellow, as you can see in the photo below. However, most minerals can be found in more than one color. For example, quartz might be clear, purple, pink, black, or white. The color varies because the mineral is not usually found in a pure form. It often contains tiny amounts of different minerals called impurities.

Many minerals are similar in color, such as pyrite and gold. Color is one clue to a mineral's identity, but color alone is usually not enough of a clue.

Sulfur is easy to recognize because of its bright yellow color.

Luster

Some minerals are shiny, but others look dull. Different minerals reflect light differently. The way that a mineral reflects light is called **luster**. There are two main kinds of luster: metallic and nonmetallic. Shiny minerals, such as gold and silver, have a metallic luster.

Minerals with a nonmetallic luster can be described in several ways. For example, if a mineral looks like a pearl, its luster is described as pearly. A mineral that looks like glass is said to have a glassy luster. Compare the luster of the minerals shown here.

Talc has a pearly luster.

Calcite has a glassy luster.

Streak

When you rub a soft mineral across a tile, it leaves a mark. The color of the mark is the mineral's **streak**. A streak test helps you identify a mineral because a mineral usually has the same streak. The tile used in a streak test is called a streak plate. It is made of white, unglazed porcelain.

The streak of a mineral may be different from the mineral's color. For example, chunks of gold and pyrite are both gold colored, but you can tell them apart with a streak test. Gold has a yellow streak, but pyrite has a black streak. Some minerals are so hard, however, that they will not leave a streak.

The table below gives the luster and streak of some minerals. Notice that quartz does not leave a streak.

The Luster and Streak of Some Minerals		
Mineral	**Luster**	**Streak**
gold	metallic	yellow
silver	metallic	silver-white
pyrite	metallic	gray to black
quartz	glassy	colorless
calcite	glassy	white
talc	pearly	white
hematite	metallic or dull	red to brown

Hardness

Suppose someone offers to sell you a diamond ring. How can you tell if the diamond is real? You could do a simple test. You could see if the diamond can scratch a piece of glass. A diamond will scratch glass because it is harder than the glass. Diamond is the hardest of all minerals. It will scratch any other material. But nothing will scratch diamond.

The **hardness** of a mineral describes how well the mineral resists being scratched. Geologists measure hardness on a scale of 1 to 10, called Mohs' scale of hardness. This scale is described in a table on the next page.

Mohs' Scale of Hardness		
Mineral	Hardness	Quick Test
talc	1	scratched easily by fingernail
gypsum	2	scratched by fingernail
calcite	3	barely scratched by copper penny
fluorite	4	scratched easily by steel
apatite	5	scratched by steel
feldspar	6	scratches glass easily
quartz	7	scratches both glass and steel easily
topaz	8	scratches quartz
corundum	9	no simple test
diamond	10	no simple test

The higher the number on Mohs' scale, the harder the mineral. A mineral will scratch any other mineral that has a lower number. In the table, the mineral fluorite has a hardness of 4. It scratches calcite but does not scratch apatite. Feldspar will scratch calcite, fluorite, and apatite.

You can use Mohs' scale to find the hardness of an unknown sample. Scratch the sample against each mineral on the scale, starting with the softest mineral. If the unknown sample scratches one mineral, test it with the next. Keep moving up the hardness scale, testing until the sample itself is scratched by one of the minerals. Its hardness is between that of the last two minerals tested. For example, a mineral that scratches feldspar but is scratched by quartz has a hardness of about 6.5.

If you do not have a set of minerals, you can use the "quick test" instead. The quick test shows how to use common materials to test hardness. For example, suppose you cannot scratch a mineral with your fingernail but you can easily scratch it with a penny. The mineral probably has a hardness between 2 and 3. Geologists working in the field usually use the quick test.

Write your answers to these questions on a sheet of paper.

1. Why might the same mineral be found in different colors?

2. Describe both the color and the luster of silver.

3. How do you determine a mineral's streak?

4. The hardness of quartz is 7. The hardness of topaz is 8. Will quartz scratch topaz? Explain.

5. What is the hardness of a mineral that is scratched by steel but does not scratch glass?

Technology Note

Gold isn't just for rings and earrings. This mineral has many useful properties besides being a popular metal for jewelry.

Gold doesn't tarnish or rust when exposed to air and water. It easily conducts, or carries, an electric current. These properties make it a good choice for use in electronic products. Examples of such products include computers, telephones, and home appliances.

Gold can reflect heat without becoming hot. In the industrial and medical fields, gold-coated reflectors are used to focus light energy. Some face shields for firefighters are coated with gold.

Gold is easily hammered into tiny wires or thin sheets without breaking. For example, 28 grams of gold can be drawn into a wire 8 kilometers long. Similarly, 28 grams of gold can be flattened into a single sheet that is 30 square meters. That's enough to cover the floor of a small bedroom.

Gold is also an excellent conductor of heat energy. The main engine nozzle on a space shuttle contains gold. Temperatures around a space shuttle can reach 3,300°C. The purpose of the gold is to draw this heat away from sensitive instruments.

Observing Color, Streak, and Hardness

Materials

◆ labeled samples of minerals

◆ streak plate

◆ copper penny

◆ steel spoon

Purpose

How could you show that minerals have unique physical properties? In this investigation, you will describe the color, streak, and hardness of known mineral samples.

Procedure

1. Copy the data table on a sheet of paper.

Mineral Name	Color Observations	Streak Observations	Quick Test Observations	Hardness Estimate

2. Write the name of each mineral sample in the first column of the data table.

3. Observe the color of each sample. Record your observations in the data table.

4. Rub each sample across the streak plate, as shown here. Record your observations in the data table.

5. Refer to the Quick Test column of Mohs' scale on page 160. Try to scratch each sample with your fingernail, the penny, and the spoon. Record your observations. Wash your hands and fingernails.

6. Using Mohs' scale and your observations from step 5, estimate the hardness number of each sample.

7. Return the samples and equipment.

Questions and Conclusions

1. Which property was the easiest to observe?

2. Which property was the hardest to observe?

3. How did the color of each mineral compare to its streak?

Explore Further

Ask your teacher for an unknown mineral sample. Identify it by finding its hardness. Use the materials and minerals you already have. Explain how you tested the sample.

Crystal

Basic shape that a mineral tends to take

Did You Know?

Scientists have grown crystals on several space shuttle missions. Nearly perfect crystals can be grown in weightlessness.

Lesson 2 explored some of the properties that can help you identify minerals: color, luster, streak, and hardness. In this lesson, you will learn about some other properties you can use.

Crystal Shape

The atoms of most minerals are arranged in an orderly, repetitive pattern. The arrangement of a mineral's atoms causes it to form in solid chunks with a characteristic shape, called **crystals**. The shape of a crystal depends on the arrangement of its atoms. For example, if you look at a few grains of salt through a magnifying glass, you will see that all the grains have the same shape. Each salt grain is a tiny cube. The cubes are salt crystals.

Crystal shapes can help you identify a mineral. For example, salt and quartz have the same color and luster. However, salt crystals always form cubes, but quartz crystals have six long sides. As you can see in the photos below, the shape of a quartz crystal is very different from the shape of a salt crystal.

Salt crystals are shaped like cubes.   *Quartz crystals have six sides.*

Most minerals form crystals. The crystals of some minerals are easily visible. Some crystals, however, are so small that they cannot be seen without a microscope.

Break Pattern

The arrangement of atoms in a mineral also makes it break in a specific way. Some minerals tend to break along flat surfaces. That kind of break is called **cleavage**.

Other minerals do not leave flat surfaces when they break. Instead, they break unevenly, leaving jagged edges. A jagged break pattern is called **fracture**.

Cleavage

Ability to split along flat surfaces

Fracture

Tendency to break with jagged edges

Specific gravity

Mineral's weight compared to the weight of water

Cleavage break

Fracture break

Specific Gravity

You can compare the density of many materials just by picking them up. If you pick up a hammer, you can tell that the steel head is denser than the wooden handle. The steel feels heavier, as if more matter is packed into it.

Density can help you identify minerals. To measure the density of a mineral, you compare the weight of a sample to the weight of the same volume of water. This comparison is called **specific gravity**. It can be calculated using this formula:

$$\text{specific gravity} = \frac{\text{weight of sample}}{\text{weight of same volume of water}}$$

Water has a specific gravity of 1. A mineral that is twice as heavy as water has a specific gravity of 2. If a mineral has a specific gravity of 3.5, it is 3.5 times heavier than water.

The table lists the crystal shape, break pattern, and specific gravity of several minerals. Compare the properties of the metals copper, gold, and silver. What do you notice? Check the specific gravity of diamond and corundum. Do minerals with a high hardness have to be very dense?

Crystal Shape, Break Pattern, and Specific Gravity of Some Minerals			
Mineral	Crystal Shape	Break Pattern	Specific Gravity
calcite	6-sided	cleavage	2.7
copper	rarely forms crystals	fracture	8.8 to 8.9
corundum	6-sided	fracture	3.9 to 4.1
diamond	8-sided	cleavage	3.1 to 3.5
fluorite	cubed or 8-sided	cleavage	3 to 3.2
garnet	12-sided	fracture	3.5 to 4.3
gold	rarely forms crystals	fracture	15.5 to 19.3
graphite	rarely forms crystals	cleavage	1.9 to 2.3
gypsum	sword-shaped	cleavage	2.3 to 2.4
halite	cubed	cleavage	2.1 to 2.6
magnetite	8-sided	fracture	4.9 to 5.2
mica	6-sided	cleavage	2.7 to 3.1
pyrite	cubed	fracture	4.9 to 5.2
quartz	6-sided	fracture	1.9 to 2.8
silver	rarely forms crystals	fracture	9.6 to 12
sulfur	cubed	fracture	2 to 2.1
talc	not visible	cleavage	2.7 to 2.8

Write your answers to these questions on a sheet of paper.

1. What determines a crystal's shape?

2. What is the difference between cleavage and fracture?

3. What does specific gravity measure?

4. If a mineral is 10 times heavier than water, what is its specific gravity?

5. What is the specific gravity of water?

▼◄ ▲ ▼◄ ▲ ▼◄ ▲ ▼◄ ▲ ▼◄ ▲ ▼◄ ▲ ▼◄ ▲ ▼◄ ▲ ▼◄ ▲ ▼◄ ▲ ▼◄ ▲ ▼◄ ▲ ▼◄ ▲ ▼

Science at Work

Jeweler

Jewelers design and manufacture, or make, pieces of jewelry. They cut, polish, and set stones and gems used in jewelry. Jewelers also repair jewelry. Some jewelers own or work in a small retail shop. Others own or work for a large manufacturing company.

To design a piece of jewelry, jewelers may use a computer. Then they shape a solid model or create a wax mold for pouring liquid metal. To finish a metal piece, jewelers may need to solder pieces together, polish it, mount a gem, or engrave a design. Lasers are often used in the process.

Most jewelers learn their trade in vocational or technical schools, or on the job. Some schools offer a bachelor's or master's degree in jewelry design.

Jewelers need to know the properties of the metals, stones, and gems they use. They must be precise in their work and give attention to detail. Hand and finger control is important, as well as creativity, patience, and concentration. Knowing how to use computer-aided design software is helpful.

Finding Specific Gravity

Materials

◆ spring scale

◆ string

◆ 3 mineral samples in envelopes marked A, B, and C

◆ beaker of water

Purpose

How could you determine the specific gravity of a mineral? In this investigation, you will find the specific gravity of unknown mineral samples.

Procedure

Part A: Collect Your Data

1. Copy the data table on a sheet of paper.

Property	Sample A	Sample B	Sample C
weight in air			
weight in water			
difference			
specific gravity			

2. Tie one end of the string to the scale. Tie the other end around a dry mineral sample.

3. Read the weight of the mineral. This is the mineral's weight in air. Record the weight in the data table, including the measurement unit.

4. Lower the sample into the beaker of water, as shown on the next page. Make sure the sample is completely underwater and is not touching the sides or bottom of the beaker. **Safety Alert: Wipe up any spills immediately.**

5. With the sample suspended in water, read its weight again. Record the weight of the sample in water. Then untie the sample and return it to its envelope.

6. Repeat steps 2 to 5 for the other two samples. Return the equipment and clean your work space.

Part B: Calculate Your Results

To find the specific gravity of your samples, use this formula and the data table.

$$\text{specific gravity} = \frac{\text{weight in air}}{\text{weight in air} - \text{weight in water}}$$

1. Begin with sample A. Subtract its weight in water from its weight in air. The difference equals the weight of the water that the sample replaced. Record this difference in the data table.

2. Divide the weight of the mineral in air by the difference you just recorded. This number is the specific gravity of the sample. Record it in the data table. (Specific gravity has no measurement unit.)

3. Repeat your arithmetic for samples B and C.

Questions and Conclusions

1. The specific gravity of water is 1. Compare the specific gravity of water to the specific gravity of your samples.

2. Which sample has the lowest specific gravity?

3. Which sample has the highest specific gravity?

Explore Further

Gather all of the class samples. Use your classmates' results to group the samples by their specific gravities. What characteristics do minerals with the same specific gravity have in common?

Objectives

After reading this lesson, you should be able to

◆ relate the usefulness of minerals to their properties.

◆ identify minerals that are precious metals or gems.

Most diamonds are not gem quality. Instead of being used for jewelry, these diamonds are used in industry. Their hardness makes them ideal for tools used for drilling or cutting.

Minerals are all around you. Look at the objects shown below. All of them are made from minerals.

Minerals are important to people for many different reasons. Most minerals have been cut, crushed, melted, or chemically changed to do a specific job. Each mineral has a property that makes it valuable for the job it does. For example, diamond is so hard that it makes excellent drill tips.

Gold conducts electricity well and is often used in computer circuits and communications equipment. Copper also conducts electricity well and is cheaper than gold. Copper wire is used inside power cords for many household appliances. Some copper wire is braided into cable, as shown in the photo on page 152.

The lead in your pencil is not the mineral lead. It is the soft mineral graphite. When crushed, graphite can be used as a lubricant for metal locks. Talc is another soft mineral. It is crushed to make talcum powder, which some people use after a shower or bath.

Quartz is found in sand, which is melted to make glass for windows, bottles, and drinking glasses. Quartz vibrates at a precise, constant speed when electricity is passed through it. Clocks and watches contain tiny quartz crystals to keep time. The circuits in computers and televisions also contain quartz.

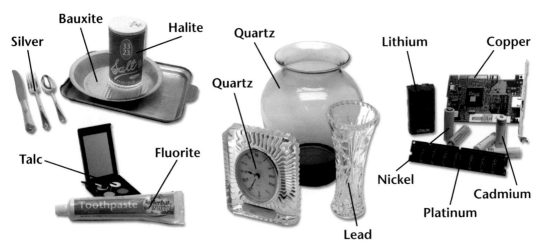

Silver Bauxite Halite Quartz Lithium Copper
Quartz
Talc Fluorite Nickel Cadmium Platinum
Lead

The mineral bauxite contains aluminum, which is used to make soft-drink cans and cookware. Aluminum is a popular packaging material. It is light, does not rust, cools and heats fast, and is easy to shape.

The table below lists a few of the minerals used to build a house.

Minerals Used in Building Products		
Mineral	How It Is Changed	Product
talc	crushed	paint
iron	melted	nails
bauxite	melted	ladder
gypsum	crushed	wallboard
corundum	crushed	sandpaper
quartz	melted	glass

Besides practical uses, minerals are valued because they are rare or beautiful. Rare, gleaming metals, such as gold and silver, are called precious metals. People use them in jewelry, coins, and objects for ceremonies. People cut and polish certain minerals to make gems for jewelry and other decorations. Precious gems are made from minerals such as diamond, topaz, garnet, quartz, and tourmaline.

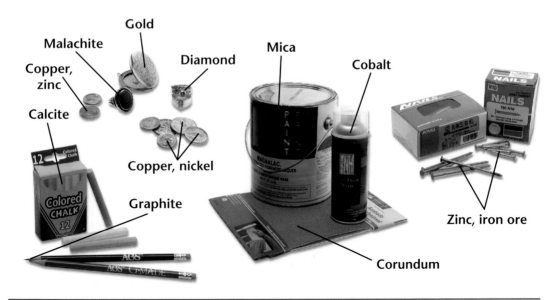

Write your answers to these questions on a sheet of paper.

1. Why is diamond used to make drill tips?

2. What property of gold and copper makes them useful in computer parts?

3. What mineral is used to make glass?

4. Name two minerals used to make gems.

5. List five minerals that you use. Name the products or objects in which they are found.

Science in Your Life

Recycling Aluminum

Aluminum comes from bauxite, a common mineral in the earth. Aluminum has a variety of uses in manufacturing, transportation, electronics, construction, and the food industry. Aluminum has been recycled for as long as it has been produced, well over 100 years.

Most people are familiar with recycling aluminum cans. In some cities, curbside recycling programs bring used aluminum cans to a recycling center. The center sorts, packages, and ships the cans to a smelting plant. Here the cans are shredded and have the paint removed from them. Then they are melted in hot furnaces and blended with other molten, or melted, metal. The molten metal is poured into large molds, where it cools and hardens. Steel rollers flatten the metal into sheets that can be used to make new aluminum cans.

Curbside recycling isn't the only way to recycle aluminum cans. Some grocery stores have recycling machines that pay people for depositing aluminum cans. Are there any recycling machines near you? Does your community have curbside recycling? Do you know where your local recycling center is?

- A mineral is an element or a compound that occurs naturally, is a solid, is not alive or made of living things, has the same chemical makeup throughout, and has a definite arrangement of atoms.

- Common minerals include quartz, feldspar, mica, calcite, halite, and gypsum.

- Many minerals are found in rocks below the earth's surface. Some of these minerals are mined and purified for different uses.

- A mineral can be identified by its properties. These include color, luster, streak, hardness, crystal shape, break pattern, and specific gravity.

- The color of a mineral may vary because of impurities.

- Minerals have either a metallic or nonmetallic luster.

- A mineral's streak is tested by rubbing the mineral across a streak plate.

- Mohs' scale of hardness ranks minerals according to how well they resist being scratched.

- Most minerals form crystals. A crystal is the basic shape that a mineral tends to take.

- The shape of a crystal depends on the arrangement of its atoms.

- Cleavage is the ability of a mineral to easily split along flat surfaces.

- The tendency of some minerals to break unevenly is called fracture.

- Specific gravity is a measure of density. It compares the weight of a mineral to the weight of the same volume of water.

- Minerals are used to make many products. Some examples are jewelry, coins, electrical wire, glass, pencils, cake pans, and nails.

Science Words			
cleavage, 165	fracture, 165	luster, 158	specific gravity, 165
crystal, 164	hardness, 159	mineral, 154	streak, 158

Chapter 7   R E V I E W

Word Bank

cleavage
crystal
fracture
hardness
luster
mineral
specific gravity
streak

Vocabulary Review

Choose the word or phrase from the Word Bank that best matches each phrase. Write the answer on your paper.

1. breaks with jagged edges

2. shape caused by a mineral's atomic arrangement

3. can be tested by scratching

4. breaks along flat surfaces

5. solid element or compound that is found in the earth

6. color of the mark left on a tile

7. glassy, pearly, or metallic

8. density compared to water

Concept Review

Choose the word or phrase that best completes each sentence. Write the letter of the answer on your paper.

9. Not all minerals are _____.
   A solids   C shiny
   B found in the earth   D formed naturally

10. Mineral A is harder than mineral B if _____.
    A A weighs more than B
    B A scratches B
    C A leaves a bigger streak than B
    D A is more dense than B

11. Gold and pyrite are different in _____.
    A color   C feel
    B luster   D streak

12. Two kinds of luster are _____.
    A shiny and dull
    B metallic and nonmetallic
    C yellow and cube-shaped
    D silver and gold

13. You test for streak by _____.
   A rubbing a mineral sample on a white tile
   B breaking a mineral sample
   C weighing a mineral sample in water
   D scratching a mineral with your fingernail

14. On Mohs' scale of hardness, diamond has the _____.
   A lowest hardness
   B brightest luster
   C darkest streak
   D highest number

Cinnabar

Use the photos to answer questions 15 and 16.

15. Which mineral has fracture?

16. Which mineral has a cube-shaped crystal form?

Critical Thinking

Write the answer to each of the following questions.

17. Describe two ways minerals are mined.

18. Explain how you would find the specific gravity of an unknown mineral sample.

19. Two unknown mineral samples are different colors. Their other properties are the same. What does this tell you?

Galena

20. Two mineral samples are colorless and have a colorless streak. One sample is quartz. How would you identify which one it is?

Test-Taking Tip When you have vocabulary words to learn, make flash cards. Write each word on the front of a card. Write its definition on the back. Use the flash cards in a game to test your vocabulary skills.

8

Rocks

A large part of the earth is made of rock. The cliffs in the photo are made of a rock type called sedimentary rock. Rocks also form mountains, islands, valleys, and even the ocean floor. The rocks you see around you are thousands of years old. They haven't always looked the same. They haven't always stayed in the same place. Rocks change. In Chapter 8, you will learn how to classify, compare, and describe different types of rocks. You will also find out how one type of rock can change over time into another rock type.

Organize Your Thoughts

Igneous

Rock types and the rock cycle

Metamorphic

Intrusive   Extrusive

Foliated   Nonfoliated

Sedimentary

Clastic   Chemical   Organic

Goals for Learning

◆ To explain what a rock is

◆ To describe igneous, sedimentary, and metamorphic rocks

◆ To explain how each rock type is formed

◆ To compare and contrast different rocks within each rock type

◆ To describe the rock cycle and the forces involved in it

Objectives

After reading this lesson, you should be able to

◆ explain what rocks are.

◆ explain why scientists study rocks.

◆ name three types of rocks.

Rock

Natural, solid material made of one or more minerals

Igneous rock

Rock formed from melted minerals that have cooled and hardened

About 3,000 minerals occur in the earth. Most of them are not found in a pure form. They are mixed together in **rocks**. A rock is a solid, natural material made of one or more minerals. Only about 20 minerals make up 95 percent of the earth's rocks.

Geologists are interested in how rocks are formed and what minerals they contain. This information helps scientists and engineers locate valuable resources, such as oil and metals. Knowledge of rocks is necessary for undertaking construction projects and understanding the environment. Rocks also provide clues about the history of the earth and how the earth changes.

Geologists classify, or group, rocks into three main types, depending on how they form. Some rock forms when hot, melted minerals cool and harden. This rock is **igneous rock**. Igneous rock can form above or below the earth's surface.

Basalt is an example of igneous rock.

Another type of rock forms when bits of other rocks and the remains of living things are pressed and cemented together. The result is **sedimentary rock**. Sedimentary rock can form under a body of water or on the earth's surface.

Sandstone is an example of sedimentary rock.

Heat, pressure, and chemical reactions can change sedimentary or igneous rock into another type—**metamorphic rock**. Metamorphic rock always forms below the earth's surface.

The photos show examples of the three rock types. What features do you notice about each one? In this chapter, you will learn more about how each type of rock forms.

This metamorphic rock shows the squeezing effect of heat and pressure deep in the earth.

Lesson 1   R E V I E W

Write your answers to these questions on a sheet of paper.

1. What is a rock?

2. What information about the earth can rocks provide?

3. What are the three main types of rocks?

4. Which type of rock is formed from melted minerals?

5. Which type of rock is formed by intense heat, pressure, and chemical reactions?

▼◄▲▼◄▲▼◄▲▼◄▲▼◄▲▼◄▲▼◄▲▼◄▲▼◄▲▼◄▲▼◄▲▼◄▲▼◄▲▼◄▲▼

Science at Work

Stonemason

Stonemasons build things out of stone. They build stone walls along shorelines and in landscapes. They lay tiles and paving stones for floors and patios. They cut and polish stone slabs for kitchen countertops and fireplaces. They fix old buildings and carve cemetery statues. They work with either natural stone, such as marble, granite, and limestone, or artificial stone, such as concrete.

A stonemason begins a project by looking at or creating a plan drawing. In these drawings, stones may be numbered so they are correctly cut and placed. The stonemason then selects, splits, cuts, and shapes the stones. Stones can be set in different ways. For a wall, stones are first set in a shallow bed of mortar, then aligned and leveled. The wall is built by alternately placing stones and mortar.

Most stonemasons start out as apprentices. Apprentices observe and help experienced workers until the apprentices learn how to do the job alone. Vocational and technical schools also offer stonemason training.

Stonemasons need to be highly skilled at handwork. They need to be precise and creative in solving visual problems. Strength and physical fitness are important because of the tools, machines, and heavy materials involved. Stonemasons should be comfortable working at heights and in noisy environments.

How Igneous Rocks Form

Deep below the earth's surface, between 50 and 200 kilometers down, temperatures are about 1,400°C. These temperatures are high enough to melt minerals, forming hot, liquid rock called **magma**.

Magma sometimes rises toward the surface of the earth through openings in the rock. As the magma rises, it cools and hardens, becoming igneous rock. Geologists classify igneous rocks into two types, based on where they form. Under the ground, magma hardens into rock slowly. On the earth's surface, magma hardens into rock quickly.

Intrusive Rocks

Magma

Hot, liquid rock inside the earth

Intrusive rock

Igneous rock that forms underground from cooled magma

Igneous rock that forms underground is called **intrusive rock**. Look at the diagram. Find the pockets of magma that have cooled and hardened below the earth's surface.

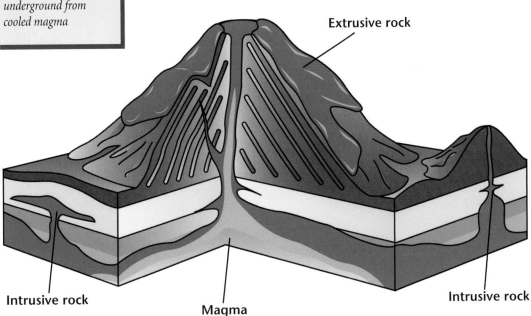

Extrusive rock

Intrusive rock

Magma

Intrusive rock

Long ago, scientists did not think granite was an igneous rock. They thought all igneous rocks were like the fine-grained surface rocks formed from cooling lava. In the late 1700s, scientists correctly identified granite as igneous rock.

Many intrusive rocks have large crystals because magma below the surface cools slowly. The size of the mineral crystals in an igneous rock is called the rock's **texture**. Rocks with large crystals are said to have a coarse-grained texture. Therefore, most intrusive rocks have a coarse-grained texture.

One of the most common intrusive rocks is granite. The minerals in this coarse-grained rock are large enough for you to see. Find the feldspar, quartz, and mica that make up the granite in the photo. Most of the rock that forms the foundations of the continents is granite. Granite might be gray, pink, or red, depending on the kind of feldspar in it. Because granite is strong and can be highly polished, it is used for buildings and monuments.

Feldspar—

Mica—

Quartz—

You can see the individual minerals that make up granite.

Lava

Magma that comes out onto the earth's surface

Extrusive rock

Igneous rock that forms from cooled lava on the earth's surface

Did You Know?

Gases sometimes escape from the top layer of lava so quickly that the lava swells into a foam. The foam hardens into a rock that looks like a sponge. This rock is called pumice. It has so many holes that it floats in water. Powdered pumice is used in making abrasive soaps. Many toothpastes contain pumice.

Extrusive Rocks

Magma that reaches the earth's surface is called **lava**. When lava cools, it forms igneous rock called **extrusive rock**. Find the extrusive rock in the diagram on page 181.

Extrusive rocks have small crystals because lava cools too quickly for larger crystals to form. Most extrusive rocks, therefore, have a fine-grained texture. Andesite, pumice, and rhyolite are examples of fine-grained extrusive rock.

The most common extrusive rock is basalt. Most of the ocean floor is made of basalt. The Hawaiian Islands are made of basalt, resulting from volcanic eruptions. Much of the exposed rock of eastern Washington and Oregon is also basalt. It was formed during lava flows that spread away from large cracks in the ground.

Sometimes lava cools so quickly that no crystals have time to form. Such is the case with the extrusive rock obsidian. The lack of any crystals gives obsidian a glassy texture, as the photo shows. Obsidian forms in lava flows or from clots of lava thrown from a volcano. Like glass, obsidian can be chipped to make a very sharp edge. People have used obsidian to make knives, arrowheads, and ornaments.

Compare obsidian, above, with basalt, shown on page 178.

Write your answers to these questions on a sheet of paper.

1. How do igneous rocks form?

2. What is the difference between an intrusive igneous rock and an extrusive igneous rock?

3. What is the difference between magma and lava?

4. Name one region where basalt is common.

5. Compare the texture of granite, basalt, and obsidian.

Achievements in Science

Field Guides for Rocks and Minerals

A field guide is a book used to identify natural objects. You may have seen a field guide for identifying things such as birds or trees. Geologists and rock collectors use field guides to identify rocks and minerals.

In 1546, German doctor Georgius Agricola wrote the first field guide for rocks and minerals. Agricola was a rock collector. He wrote the field guide as a way to organize all of the information he had gathered about rocks. Agricola classified rocks and minerals by their physical properties. These included color, crystal shape, hardness, and luster.

Since Agricola's time, thousands of mineral species have been discovered. More detailed systems for classifying rocks and minerals have been designed. Some systems still organize rocks and minerals by their physical properties. Other systems are based on chemical, genetic, or structural properties.

Modern field guides identify rocks and minerals using one or more of these classification systems.

Objectives

After reading this lesson, you should be able to

◆ explain how sedimentary rocks form.

◆ compare clastic, chemical, and organic sedimentary rocks.

◆ identify samples of sedimentary rocks.

Sediment

Solid material, such as sand, soil, pebbles, and organic matter, that is carried in air, water, or ice and settles out

How Sedimentary Rocks Form

What happens if you fill a jar with river water and let the jar sit for a while? Solid particles settle out on the bottom of the jar. These particles are **sediment**. They may include sand, soil, pebbles, and the remains of dead plants and animals. Sediment is the main ingredient of sedimentary rock.

How do bits of sand and soil get turned into rock? The diagram shows the most common way. Rivers carry sediment to a lake or ocean. The sediment settles to the bottom. As layers of sediment accumulate, the weight of the overlying sediment presses the bottom sediment together. In addition, the bottom sediment is cemented together by minerals, such as calcite, dissolved in the water. The result is sedimentary rock.

The formation of sedimentary rock does not require high temperatures or pressures. Although it commonly forms under a lake or ocean, sedimentary rock can also form on land.

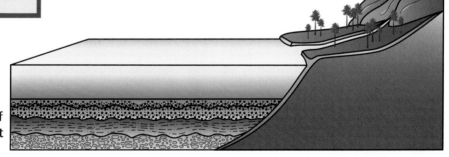

Layers of sediment

Seventy-five percent of the rocks exposed at the earth's surface are sedimentary. These rocks are classified into three main types, based on the kinds of sediment that form them.

Clastic Rocks

Clastic rock is the most common type of sedimentary rock. Clastic rock forms from fragments of other rocks. Shale, for example, is made from fine particles of clay, mica, and other tiny grains that form as rocks break down on the earth's surface. These tiny particles form a muddy mixture of sediment on the bottom of a lake or ocean. Overlying layers squeeze out the water and air, forming shale. This process is similar to squeezing a handful of mud. As you force out the water and air, the mud becomes more compact and solid.

Compare the two clastic rocks in the photos below. Notice the size of the sediment in each sample. Sediment particles are clues to the environment in which the rock formed. For example, notice the rounded pebbles of the **conglomerate**. Rounded pebbles often form in rivers, where particles in the moving water break off sharp edges of rocks, making them round. The pebbles fall to the river bottom when the water slows down. So conglomerate might indicate the location of an ancient river.

The tiny particles that make up shale, however, tend to settle out of ocean water far from where a river would empty into an ocean. So shale suggests the location of an ancient ocean.

Conglomerate contains large, rounded pebbles.

Shale is made of fine grains of clay, mica, and other minerals.

Another kind of clastic rock is sandstone. As the name suggests, it is made of sand-sized grains that are mostly quartz. What do these rocks tell you about the environment in which they formed? You might have correctly guessed that sandstone formed from ancient beaches and sand dunes. This rock may also indicate an ancient delta—the land that builds up where a river empties into a body of water. A lot of sand from river water settles out to form a delta.

Chemical Rocks

A second type of sedimentary rock is **chemical rock**. It forms from chemicals dissolved in water. Some limestones are chemical rocks. Chemical and temperature changes in ocean water can cause particles of calcium carbonate to form. These particles accumulate on the ocean floor and become limestone. Other chemical rocks include rock salt and gypsum. These rocks form when seawater evaporates, leaving minerals behind.

The photo shows Mono Lake in California. This lake is unusual because it has no water outlet. As a result, the water has become very salty. As the lake water evaporates, fantastic shapes of rock salt remain.

Rock salt is a chemical sedimentary rock that is left behind when salt water evaporates.

Organic Rocks

A third type of sedimentary rock is **organic rock**. It forms from the remains of living things. Some limestones form from the shells of sea animals. When shellfish, such as clams and mussels, die, their shells accumulate on the ocean floor. Layers of shells, which are made of calcite, are pressed and cemented together to form organic limestone. One type of organic limestone is chalk. This soft rock is made of the shells of microscopic organisms. The White Cliffs of Dover in England are made of chalk.

Coal is an organic rock that forms very slowly from layers of dead animals and plants. Coal is high in carbon and is mined and burned as a fuel source.

Technology Note

More than half of the electricity produced in the United States comes from burning coal. But how does a lump of coal turn on your lights and run your stove?

Once it is mined from the earth, coal is transported by trains and barges. Approximately 2.5 million metric tons of coal are delivered to power plants and factories in the United States every day.

When coal reaches a power plant, it is first washed. Then it is pulverized into a heavy powder. The coal powder is blown into a furnace, where it burns in the air. Water runs through tubes in the furnace. As the water boils, it produces steam. The steam passes through a turbine, which turns a generator. The generator produces electricity. This electricity is sent to your home.

Lesson 3 R E V I E W

Write your answers to these questions on a sheet of paper.

1. How do sedimentary rocks form?

2. What are the three main types of sedimentary rocks?

3. How do the sizes of grains in shale, conglomerate, and sandstone compare to one another?

4. Give an example of a chemical rock.

5. What are organic rocks made of?

Science in Your Life

The Good and Bad of Coal

Coal is an organic sedimentary rock that forms from decaying plants and animals. Coal forms very slowly. In fact, it takes millions of years of heat and pressure to turn plant and animal remains into coal. The diagram below shows the stages of coal formation.

Coal is a source of energy. People mine and burn coal to create electricity and to run plants such as steel mills. The energy content of anthracite and bituminous coal is the highest. Some countries, such as Poland, use lignite for energy. In the United States, only Texas and North Dakota use lignite.

Sixty-four percent of the world's coal is used by China, the United States, India, Russia, and Germany. Most of the coal reserves in the world are found in Europe, Asia, Australia, and North America.

Using coal has some disadvantages. First, there is a limited amount of coal in the earth. It won't last forever. Second, coal must be mined by digging deep in the earth or by stripping off a shallow layer of earth. This harms the earth's surface and can be dangerous for miners. Third, burning coal increases air pollution. Find out about other sources of energy that are less harmful in Appendix B.

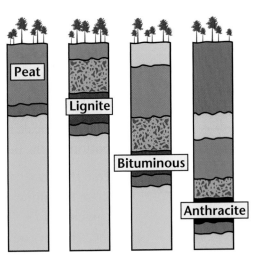

Making Calcite

Purpose

What happens when you mix washing soda and calcium chloride? In this investigation, you will observe the formation of calcite.

Materials

- safety glasses
- apron
- 2 test tubes in a stand
- teaspoon
- washing soda
- plastic stirrers
- calcium chloride
- 2 beakers
- filter paper
- funnel

Procedure

1. Copy the data table on a sheet of paper.

Material	Action	Observations
washing soda	mixed with water	
calcium chloride	mixed with water	
both mixtures	mixed together in beaker	
new substance	collected on filter paper	

2. Safety Alert: Put on the safety glasses and apron.

Fold once.

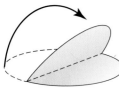

3. Fill one test tube with water. Slowly add 1 teaspoon of washing soda to the water. Stir to dissolve the washing soda. Use your data table to record what you see. **Safety Alert: Never taste any substance used in a science investigation. Wipe up any spills immediately.**

Fold twice.

4. Fill the other test tube with water. Dissolve 1 teaspoon of calcium chloride in the water. Record your observations.

5. Pour the contents of both test tubes into one beaker.

Open to make a cone

6. Allow the beaker to stand for a few minutes. Observe the bottom of the beaker. Record your observations.

7. Fold the filter paper to fit inside the funnel as shown. Place the funnel over the empty beaker. Gently pour the contents of the first beaker through the filter and into the other beaker.

8. Look closely at the substance on the filter paper. Record your observations.

9. Clean your work space and wash the equipment.

Questions and Conclusions

1. Describe the substance on the filter paper.

2. The solid that formed is calcite, or calcium carbonate ($CaCO_3$). Suggest where this solid came from in your investigation. (Washing soda is sodium carbonate, Na_2CO_3. Calcium chloride is $CaCl_2$.)

3. What type of sedimentary rock is formed in this investigation?

4. How is this investigation different from the formation of real rock?

Explore Further

Design and perform an investigation in which you model the formation of a clastic rock, a chemical rock, or an organic rock. Explain to classmates how your model is similar to and different from the formation of real rock.

Objectives

After reading this lesson, you should be able to

◆ explain how metamorphic rocks form.

◆ identify samples of foliated and nonfoliated metamorphic rocks.

Foliated rock

Metamorphic rock in which minerals have been rearranged into visible bands

Nonfoliated rock

Metamorphic rock that does not show bands

How Metamorphic Rocks Form

Deep in the earth, heat and pressure from all sides can squeeze, bend, and twist rock. Hot fluids move through the rock. The heat, pressure, and liquids change the appearance and texture of the rock. The result is metamorphic rock. Metamorphic rocks can also form when liquids and gases escape from magma. The liquids and gases add new minerals to the surrounding rock. Geologists classify metamorphic rocks into two types.

Foliated Rocks

Foliated rocks form when heat and pressure have flattened the minerals into bands. Slate, schist, and gneiss are examples of foliated rocks. Slate forms from shale and has very thin bands. Slate contains a lot of mica, which has good cleavage. Therefore, slate splits easily along its bands into sheets of rock. This property makes slate a good

Slate splits into flat sheets.

material for tiles. Gneiss forms from granite and other rocks as mica and other minerals rearrange into bands. But gneiss does not have as much mica as slate and therefore does not split as well.

Marble has no bands.

Nonfoliated Rocks

Rocks that are made largely of only one material, such as limestone and sandstone, result in metamorphic rocks without bands, called **nonfoliated rocks**. The crystals combine and interlock to form a harder rock. For example, marble is a nonfoliated rock formed from limestone. Pure marble is white. Small amounts of various minerals produce the colorful streaks and swirls in some marbles.

Lesson 4 **REVIEW**

Write your answers to these questions on a sheet of paper.

1. How do metamorphic rocks form?

2. What is the difference between foliated and nonfoliated rocks?

3. From which rock type does slate form?

4. From which rock type does marble form?

5. Why is slate used to make tiles and gneiss is not?

Technology Note

Huge blocks or slabs of marble are often needed as building materials. Because of this, explosives are not used to mine marble. Explosives would shatter marble into pieces that are much too small.

Instead, special machines, called channeling machines, are used to mine marble. These machines cut holes in a "dotted line" across a marble rock. More "dotted lines" are cut until a large block shape is outlined. Then wedges are driven into the holes. The marble block is pried away from the surrounding marble and hauled to the surface.

Some marble blocks weigh as much as 2,000 tons. These blocks are later sawed into the desired sizes.

Rocks are always changing. Some melt deep in the earth, then harden. Some are built by layers of sediment. Others twist and bend because of underground heat and pressure. Each type of rock—igneous, sedimentary, and metamorphic—can also change into another type. The series of changes that cause one type of rock to become another type of rock is called the **rock cycle**. This cycle occurs over a long period of time.

Study the rock cycle diagram below. Each arrow is one possible pathway in the cycle. The label by each arrow tells you what force is causing the rock to change. There is no special starting place in the rock cycle. You can start with any type of rock and follow any pathway leading from it.

Rock cycle

Series of natural changes that cause one type of rock to become another type of rock

Follow the arrows as we travel along the cycle, starting with magma. As magma rises from deep in the earth, it cools and hardens into igneous rock. Volcanoes quickly deposit lava on the earth's surface as extrusive rock. Pressure eventually lifts intrusive rock to the surface as well.

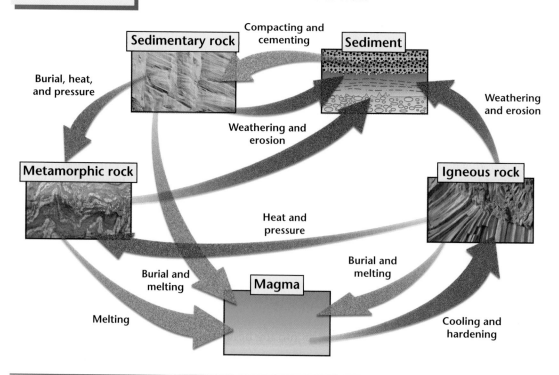

Once on the earth's surface, all rock types begin to slowly break apart and move. When rocks break down into pebbles and then into fine grains like sand, they are easily carried away. This sediment often ends up in a large body of water. Many factors cause this breaking down and carrying away: wind, water, air, living things, ice, and gravity. You will learn more about this process when you study weathering and erosion in Chapter 12.

At the bottom of a lake or an ocean, sediment forms layers. Over time and under pressure, the layers compact and cement into sedimentary rock. Sometimes sedimentary rock is later brought to the earth's surface, where it begins to break down again.

Other times, sedimentary rock becomes buried deeper in the earth. There the rock is exposed to heat and pressure. These underground forces can bend and twist it into metamorphic rock. In the same way, intrusive rock can become metamorphic rock. Sometimes metamorphic rock is brought to the surface, where it begins to break down again.

In extreme underground heat, all three types of rock can melt. Most rocks melt at temperatures of 800°C or higher. Then they become magma deep in the earth, and the rock cycle continues.

Rocks do not always cycle from igneous to sedimentary to metamorphic. Each type of rock can change into the two other types. For example, how does igneous rock change into metamorphic? Follow the pathways on the diagram to find out. To become igneous rock, the other two types must first become magma.

Rocks change by forces inside the earth and by forces on the earth's surface. Look again at the diagram. Below the earth's surface, forces of heat and pressure cause rocks to bend or melt. Above ground, forces such as wind and water cause rocks to break down, move, and settle.

Write your answers to these questions on a sheet of paper.

1. Name two ways that rocks on the earth's surface are changed.

2. Name two underground forces that change rocks.

3. What is required for a rock to become magma?

4. How might sedimentary rock become metamorphic rock?

5. How might metamorphic rock become igneous rock?

Achievements in Science

The Rock Cycle Theory

The idea of a rock cycle was first proposed in the 1700s. At that time, geology as a formal science did not exist. Most people believed the earth was only about 6,000 years old. Many thought that only major disasters such as earthquakes could change the earth's surface.

James Hutton was a Scottish physician and farmer. He loved to study science and ask questions. In particular, he wanted to find the origin of rocks and minerals.

By studying rocks in Scotland, Hutton noticed streaks of granite among sedimentary rock. He thought this showed that there was heat, even fire, deep in the earth. He also found vertical layers of rock topped with horizontal layers. He concluded that the lower layers had to be very old. They must have been tipped on their side before the new layers were added.

In 1785, Hutton published his theory of rocks in a book. He proposed that one rock type changes into another over time. These changes are caused by pressure and heat deep in the earth. He also stated that erosion, weathering, moving of sediment, and the uprising of rocks from beneath the earth's surface are all part of a cycle. Hutton believed that this cycle has been repeating for millions of years, not for thousands of years. Because of his contributions, James Hutton is called the father of geology.

Materials

- ◆ numbered rock samples
- ◆ hand lens

Identifying Rocks

Purpose

How can you identify unknown rocks? In this investigation, you will observe properties of rocks and identify rock samples.

Procedure

1. Copy the data table on a sheet of paper.

Rock Number	Observations	Rock Name	Rock Type

2. Write the number of the first sample in the first column of your data table.

3. Use the hand lens to observe the sample. Is the sample foliated or nonfoliated? Is it fine-grained or coarse-grained? What is its color? Do you see any remains of past life? Do you see crystals? Pebbles? Layers? Write your observations in the second column of your data table. Be as detailed as you can.

4. Repeat steps 2 and 3 for each of the samples.

5. Use the table on page 198 to identify each rock sample. Record your findings in your data table.

6. Review the chapter to determine each sample's rock type: igneous, sedimentary, or metamorphic. Record your findings in the last column of your data table.

7. Clean your work space.

Name of Rock	Description
basalt	dark gray to black; crystals not visible; many small holes
coal	black; smudges fingers; no crystals
conglomerate	cemented pebbles
gneiss	bands of color that may or may not be bent; often visible crystals
granite	interlocking white, pink, gray, and dark crystals
limestone	may contain tiny shells or interlocking crystals; usually light colored
marble	often has swirling colors; large interlocking crystals
obsidian	dark; glassy; fractures with curved surface
pumice	lightweight and filled with holes; looks like a hardened sponge; light colored
rhyolite	pinkish tan; often contains larger visible crystals against a mass containing crystals too small to see
sandstone	cemented sand grains; color varies but often yellow-brown
schist	flaky, parallel layers; may sparkle
shale	color varies but usually dark; smells musty when moistened; fine grained; thin layers
slate	gray or gray-blue; harder than shale

Questions and Conclusions

1. Which samples were easiest to identify?

2. Which samples were hardest to identify?

Explore Further

Collect rock samples in a nearby park or along a shoreline. Repeat step 3 for each sample. What conclusions can you make from your observations?

- A rock is a solid, natural material made of minerals. The three types of rocks are igneous, sedimentary, and metamorphic.

- Information about rocks helps us understand the environment.

- Igneous rocks form from magma or lava that hardens.

- Intrusive igneous rocks form from magma underground and have a course-grained texture. Granite is an intrusive rock.

- Extrusive igneous rocks form from lava at the earth's surface and have a fine-grained or glassy texture. Basalt is an extrusive rock.

- Sedimentary rocks form from particles called sediment. The layered sediment gets pressed and cemented into rock.

- Clastic sedimentary rocks are made from fragments of other rocks. Shale and sandstone are clastic rocks.

- Chemical sedimentary rocks form from dissolved minerals. Gypsum and some limestones are chemical rocks.

- Organic sedimentary rocks form from the remains of plants and animals. Chalk, coal, and some limestones are organic rocks.

- Metamorphic rocks form from other rocks that are twisted and bent by heat and pressure.

- In foliated metamorphic rocks, minerals in the rocks have been rearranged into bands that can be seen. Slate is a foliated rock.

- Nonfoliated metamorphic rocks do not show banding. Marble is a nonfoliated rock.

- Rocks change from one type to another in the rock cycle. This cycle is driven by forces above and below the earth's surface.

Science Words

chemical rock, 187	intrusive rock, 181	nonfoliated rock, 192	sediment, 185
clastic rock, 186	lava, 183	organic rock, 188	sedimentary rock, 179
conglomerate, 186	magma, 181	rock, 178	texture, 182
extrusive rock, 183	metamorphic rock, 179	rock cycle, 194	
foliated rock, 192			
igneous rock, 178			

Chapter 8 R E V I E W

Vocabulary Review

Word Bank

conglomerate

extrusive rock

igneous rock

lava

magma

metamorphic rock

rock cycle

sediment

sedimentary rock

texture

Choose the word or phrase from the Word Bank that best completes each sentence. Write the answer on your paper.

1. Hot, liquid rock on the earth's surface is called _____.

2. Fragments of rocks, minerals, and remains of living things are _____.

3. Rocks change from one type to another in the _____.

4. Hot, liquid rock beneath the earth's surface is _____.

5. _____ forms from rocks that have been changed by heat, pressure, and hot fluids.

6. Layers of sediment that are pressed together and cemented can form _____.

7. Liquid rock that cools on or below the surface forms _____.

8. Some igneous rocks have a coarse-grained _____.

9. _____ forms when lava cools on the earth's surface.

10. Rock made of pebbles cemented together is _____.

Concept Review

Choose the word or phrase that best completes each sentence. Write the letter of the answer on your paper.

11. A rock is a mixture of _____.
    A animals **B** minerals **C** plants **D** bands

12. The two kinds of igneous rocks can be identified by _____.
    A texture **B** color **C** bands **D** weight

13. An igneous rock that formed from magma cooling slowly would have _____.
    A a fine grain **C** no crystals
    B large crystals **D** no grain

14. The three main types of rocks are _____.

    A clastic, extrusive, and intrusive

    B sedimentary, organic, and foliated

    C quartz, feldspar, and mica

    D metamorphic, igneous, and sedimentary

15. Limestone is mostly the mineral _____.

    A mica   **B** talc   **C** quartz   **D** calcite

Copy the list below on your paper. Decide whether each rock or kind of rock is igneous, sedimentary, or metamorphic. Write the answer next to each item.

16. clastic   **19.** organic   **22.** basalt

17. chemical   **20.** nonfoliated   **23.** coal

18. granite   **21.** sandstone

Critical Thinking

Write the answer to each of the following questions.

24. A handful of sand contains bits of igneous rock. How did the igneous rock get there? How might the sand become sedimentary rock? To answer these questions, make a rock cycle diagram using the following words: magma, igneous rock, breaking into fragments, cooling, sediment, and pressing and cementing.

25. The wall of a canyon is layered and seems to be made of sand cemented together. In one part of the wall, you see a pattern like the one shown. What rock type is it? How was the rock formed? Where did it form and why?

Test-Taking Tip When studying for a test, write your own test questions with a partner. Then answer each other's questions. Check your answers.

9 The Earth's Atmosphere

The earth's atmosphere is around us all the time. The air we breathe is part of the atmosphere. The clouds in the sky are part of the atmosphere. Rainbows remind us that the atmosphere contains moisture. When sunlight passes through water droplets in the air, the different colors that make up the light separate. We see this separation of light as a rainbow. In Chapter 9, you will learn about the gases and layers that make up our atmosphere. You will also learn about clouds, precipitation, and wind patterns.

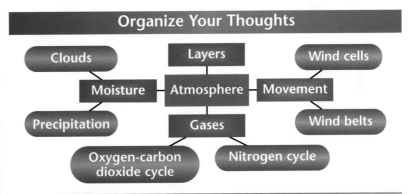

Organize Your Thoughts

Clouds — Moisture — Atmosphere — Movement — Wind cells

Precipitation

Layers

Gases — Oxygen-carbon dioxide cycle — Nitrogen cycle

Wind belts

Goals for Learning

◆ To explain what the earth's atmosphere is

◆ To explain how gases in the air cycle through the environment

◆ To describe the structure of the atmosphere

◆ To classify clouds

◆ To explain how precipitation forms

◆ To describe the earth's wind patterns

Objectives

After reading this lesson, you should be able to

◆ identify the gases in the atmosphere.

◆ describe the oxygen-carbon dioxide cycle.

◆ describe the nitrogen cycle.

Atmosphere

Layer of gases that surrounds the earth

Did You Know?

The composition of the atmosphere has changed over time and will continue to change. Scientists can study actual samples of ancient air. The samples come from air bubbles trapped for millions of years in ice and hardened tree sap.

What basic things do you need in order to live? At the top of the list is the air you breathe. When you breathe in (inhale), you take in gases that your body needs to work. When you breathe out (exhale), you release gases that are needed by other living things.

The layer of gases that surrounds the earth is called the **atmosphere**. Most people simply refer to the atmosphere as the air. Although some other planets have atmospheres, ours is the only one known to support life.

The earth's atmosphere contains many different gases. Some of these gases are elements. Others are compounds. From the circle graph, you can see that oxygen and nitrogen make up most of the earth's atmosphere. What other gases are in the air you breathe?

Oxygen and nitrogen are needed by all living things. Plants and animals take these gases from the atmosphere, use them, and then return them to the atmosphere. Oxygen and nitrogen go through these natural cycles over and over.

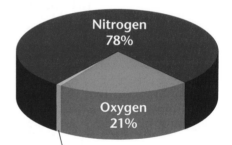

Nitrogen 78%

Oxygen 21%

Argon, carbon dioxide, water vapor, neon, helium, krypton, xenon, methane, hydrogen, ozone 1%

The Oxygen-Carbon Dioxide Cycle

Plants make their own food: sugar. They use sunlight to change carbon dioxide and water into sugar and oxygen. This process is called photosynthesis.

The diagram below shows how oxygen and carbon dioxide circulate between living things and the atmosphere. When animals and people breathe in air, their bodies use the oxygen to change the food they eat into energy. When they breathe out, they release carbon dioxide into the air. Plants take in this carbon dioxide. They use carbon dioxide, water, and the sun's energy to make sugar and oxygen. Plants use or store the sugar, but release the oxygen into the air. Animals and people take in this oxygen, and the cycle continues.

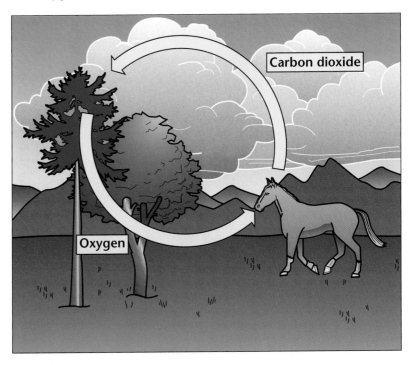

The Nitrogen Cycle

Nitrogen also cycles through the environment, as shown below. All living things need nitrogen. Most living things cannot use nitrogen gas directly from the air. However, bacteria in the soil can use this form of nitrogen. These organisms change nitrogen gas into chemical compounds that plants use. Animals take in nitrogen when they feed on plants or on plant-eating animals. Nitrogen is returned to the soil in animal waste. Nitrogen is also returned to the soil when plants and animals die. Bacteria in the soil break down these wastes, releasing nitrogen into the air and into the soil. The return of nitrogen gas to the atmosphere allows the cycle to continue.

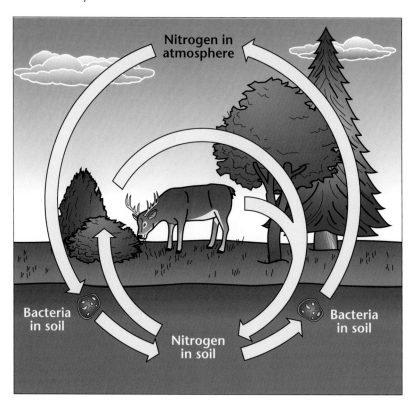

Lesson 1   R E V I E W

Write your answers to these questions on a sheet of paper.

1. What are the two main gases in the atmosphere?

2. Describe the path oxygen and carbon dioxide take through the environment.

3. What is the source of oxygen in the oxygen-carbon dioxide cycle?

4. What living things in soil are needed to change nitrogen into a form plants can use?

5. How is nitrogen released back into the atmosphere?

Science in Your Life

Ozone: Protector and Pollutant

Ozone makes up a tiny but important part of the atmosphere. Ozone is a form of oxygen. A thin layer of ozone high in the atmosphere absorbs ultraviolet radiation from the sun. This prevents most of the radiation from reaching the earth. This radiation can cause sunburn and skin cancer.

People have damaged this protective ozone layer. For example, certain gases from spray cans and refrigeration equipment drift high into the atmosphere and break down ozone. Laws now limit the use of such gases.

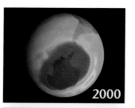

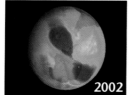

Scientists have been monitoring a hole that has appeared in the ozone layer over Antarctica. In 2000, this hole reached a size of 17.6 million square kilometers. But in 2002, the Antarctic ozone hole decreased to 9.6 million square kilometers. It also split into two separate holes.

Ozone holes in the atmosphere are harmful. But too much ozone at the earth's surface is also harmful. Ozone is one of the ingredients of smog. This hazy mixture of gases damages people's lungs and worsens heart disease. How does ozone collect at ground level? It is made by people. Factories make and use ozone for cleaning flour, oil, fabrics, and water. Car exhaust also releases ozone.

Objectives

After reading this lesson, you should be able to

◆ identify the four layers of the atmosphere.

◆ name one characteristic of each layer.

Troposphere

Bottom layer of the atmosphere, extending from ground level up to about 16 kilometers above the earth

Imagine four glass balls, one inside the other. Now picture the earth at the very center of the glass balls. You've just imagined a model of the earth and its atmosphere. The atmosphere consists of four layers. Refer to the diagram below as you read about each one.

You live in the **troposphere**, the bottom layer of the atmosphere. The troposphere extends from the earth's surface upward to about 16 kilometers. Air particles are packed more tightly in this layer than in other layers because of the weight of the air above. Therefore, even though the troposphere is the smallest of the four layers, it contains 75 percent of the air particles in the entire atmosphere.

Air gets colder and thinner, or less dense, as you go higher in the troposphere. That's why mountain climbers often need extra clothing and oxygen tanks when they climb. The troposphere is characterized by up-and-down as well as side-to-side air movements, or air currents. Most of the clouds you see in the sky are in the troposphere.

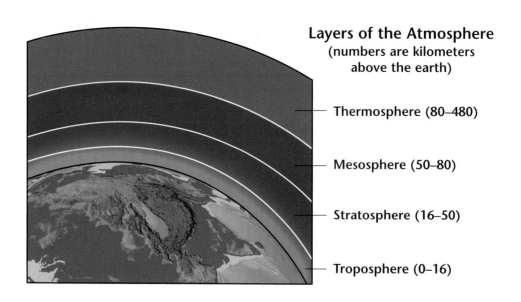

Layers of the Atmosphere
(numbers are kilometers above the earth)

Thermosphere (80–480)

Mesosphere (50–80)

Stratosphere (16–50)

Troposphere (0–16)

The **stratosphere** is above the troposphere. It extends from about 16 to 50 kilometers above the earth's surface. The stratosphere is clear and dry. Temperature increases with increasing height in the stratosphere. The ozone layer is in the lower half of the stratosphere. The ozone layer is important because it absorbs harmful radiation from the sun.

Above the stratosphere is the **mesosphere**. Here, temperature decreases with increasing height. The mesosphere is the coldest layer of the atmosphere. It is located from about 50 to 80 kilometers above the earth's surface.

The outermost layer is called the **thermosphere**. The air is the thinnest here. Temperature increases with height. It can reach 2,000°C because nitrogen and oxygen atoms absorb the sun's energy. This energy strips electrons from these atoms, making them electrically charged particles, or ions. Most of these ions are found between 60 and 300 kilometers above the earth. Therefore, this section of the atmosphere is called the **ionosphere**.

If you have ever wondered how you are able to pick up a radio station hundreds of kilometers away, the answer is the ionosphere. AM radio waves bounce off the ions in the ionosphere and travel back to the earth. As the diagram shows, this reflection of waves can carry radio messages great distances. This is especially true at night, when the sun's energy does not cause interference.

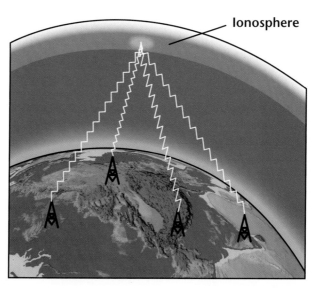

Ionosphere

Write your answers to these questions on a sheet of paper.

1. Describe the four layers of the atmosphere.

2. Which layer of the atmosphere do you breathe?

3. Where is the ozone layer?

4. Why is part of the atmosphere called the ionosphere?

5. Explain how the ionosphere is used to transmit radio waves.

Achievements in Science

Balloon Pilots

Aeronauts, or balloon pilots, have been challenging the atmosphere for hundreds of years. In 1783, the first hot-air balloon to fly with passengers was built by the Montgolfier brothers in France. The passengers included a duck, a rooster, and a sheep. Following the historic 8-minute flight, all three landed safely.

To launch their cloth-and-paper balloon, the brothers placed it over a fire. They thought the balloon flew because it was filled with smoke. They didn't understand that the key to flight was hot air. Hot air is less dense than cool air. Because hot air in a balloon is lighter than the air outside it, the balloon rises.

Since then, aeronauts have also piloted gas balloons. These are balloons filled with a light gas such as hydrogen. The record holders for the highest gas-balloon flight are two United States Navy officers. In 1961, they reached the middle of the stratosphere, more than 34 kilometers above the earth.

Evaporate

Change from a liquid to a gas

Water vapor

Water in the form of a gas

Condense

Change from a gas to a liquid

Have you ever seen your breath on a cold day? You are seeing a cloud. It forms the same way as a cloud in the sky.

How Clouds Form

Much of the earth's surface is covered with water. The sun's heat causes some of this liquid water to **evaporate**, or change into a gas. This gas, called **water vapor**, becomes part of the air. When this air is heated, it becomes less dense than the surrounding air. Therefore, the heated air rises, taking the water vapor with it. As the air continues to rise, it cools. Then the water vapor **condenses**, or changes back to liquid water. The droplets of water are so tiny that they stay afloat in the air. Billions of tiny droplets form a cloud, as shown in the left diagram.

The diagram at the right shows that clouds also form when air containing water vapor is forced up a mountainside. As the air rises, it cools. The water vapor condenses into tiny droplets of water to form clouds. The tops of some mountains are often hidden in clouds.

So how is a cloud like the breath you can see? Air in your lungs contains water vapor. When you breathe out, the vapor meets the cold air outside and condenses into tiny droplets—a cloud.

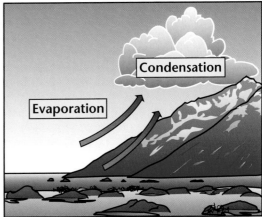

Types of Clouds

Altitude

Height above the earth's surface

Stratus cloud

Low, flat cloud that forms in layers

Fog

Stratus cloud that forms near the ground

Clouds are grouped according to their shape and **altitude**, or height above the earth's surface. There are three basic types of clouds.

Stratus clouds are low, flat clouds that form in layers. Their altitude is less than 2,000 meters. These clouds are wider than they are high, often covering the entire sky like a blanket. Often, you can see only their gray bottoms because they block out much of the sunlight. Stratus clouds often bring rain.

A stratus cloud near the ground is **fog**. How does this kind of cloud form? Without sunlight, the ground cools quickly at night. The cold ground cools the air directly above it. If the water vapor in this air condenses, a cloud forms. Fog usually develops in the early morning after a clear, calm, cold night. Fog settles in low areas. Sometimes fog forms over warm bodies of water.

Stratus clouds are flat and low in the sky.

Cumulus cloud

Puffy, white cloud occurring at medium altitudes

Cirrus cloud

High, wispy cloud made of ice crystals

Cumulus clouds are puffy, white clouds at altitudes from 2,000 to 7,000 meters. They look like piles of cotton balls. You can usually see their sides and tops shining brilliant white in sunlight. Their shaded bottoms are flat and may look gray. Cumulus clouds are often seen in fair weather.

When you think of clouds, you probably picture white, puffy cumulus clouds like these.

Cirrus clouds look like thin, wispy streaks high in the sky. Their altitude ranges from 7,000 to 13,000 meters. They are made of ice crystals instead of water droplets because the air at that altitude is below freezing. Cirrus clouds often accompany fair weather, but they may mean rain or snow is on the way.

Thin, wispy cirrus clouds are made of ice crystals.

Write your answers to these questions on a sheet of paper.

1. What is a cloud?

2. Describe two ways that clouds form.

3. Explain how fog forms.

4. Compare cumulus and cirrus clouds.

5. Name and describe the type of cloud that may indicate rain.

▼◄▲▼◄▲▼◄▲▼◄▲▼◄▲▼◄▲▼◄▲▼◄▲▼◄▲▼◄▲▼

Science at Work

Environmental Science Technician

Environmental science technicians perform tests to identify and measure pollution in air, water, or soil. They collect samples to test. They look for ways to reduce or prevent pollution. Environmental science technicians also manage and control hazardous wastes. They make sure pollution laws are carefully followed.

Environmental science technicians use science and mathematics to solve problems. They use laboratory equipment to perform tests or analyze samples. They often use computers. They keep detailed reports and interpret data.

Some environmental science technicians have a bachelor's degree in chemistry, biology, or environmental science. Others have two years of specialized training or an associate degree in a field of applied science. Successful environmental science technicians are organized, enjoy detailed tasks, and can interpret and communicate scientific results. They are often very concerned about protecting the environment.

Observing Clouds

Purpose

Can you identify cloud types? In this investigation, you will observe and classify clouds over several days.

Procedure

1. Copy the data table on your paper.

Date	Time	Weather Conditions	Cloud Observations

2. Find a location where you can observe a large portion of the sky. You should use this place for all of your observations.

3. In your data table, record the date, the time, and your observations about the weather conditions.

4. In the last column of your table, record your observations about the clouds. Include a sketch of the clouds you observe. Label the sketch with its cloud type.

5. Make observations on four or more days. Follow steps 3 and 4 each day.

Questions and Conclusions

1. Which types of clouds were most common?

2. What relationship did you find between cloud type and weather?

Explore Further

Make cloud observations in the morning and evening for several days. Is there a relationship between cloud type and time of day?

Precipitation

Moisture that falls to the earth from the atmosphere

The movement of water between the atmosphere and the earth's surface is known as the water cycle. This is described fully in Chapter 11.

The droplets of most clouds are small enough to stay in the air, suspended by air currents. But if the droplets grow large enough, they fall to the earth. Any moisture that falls from the atmosphere to the earth's surface is called **precipitation**. There are several kinds of precipitation.

Near the equator, between 30°N and 30°S latitudes, the sunlight is most direct. Here, temperatures within most stratus clouds are above freezing. These clouds are made entirely of water droplets. The droplets collide and combine to form larger drops. When the drops become large enough, they fall as rain.

Clouds in the middle and high latitudes usually form in air that is below freezing. Then water vapor turns directly to ice crystals. In a cloud, ice crystals combine until they are heavy enough to fall. If the air temperature beneath the cloud is above freezing, the ice crystals melt and fall as rain. If the air temperature is below freezing, the crystals fall as snow. If rain falls through a layer of cold air and freezes into ice particles, sleet, or freezing rain, results. If the temperature near the ground is between 3°C and 0°C, rain will not freeze until it hits an object. The result is an ice storm. You can see the effects of an ice storm in the photo.

The weight of sleet can break tree branches.

Hailstones form in tall cumulus clouds that produce storms. The temperature is below freezing at the top of the clouds. Strong winds toss the ice crystals up and down many times through the clouds. Each time, a layer of water freezes around the crystal, forming a hailstone. Hailstones are usually the size of a pea, but can be bigger than a baseball.

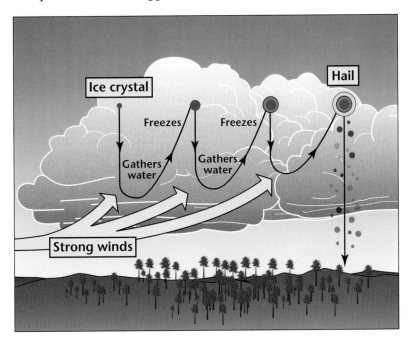

Science Myth

Some people may think that raindrops are shaped like teardrops.

Fact: Small raindrops (less than 2 millimeters in diameter) are spherical, or round. Larger raindrops are shaped more like hamburger buns. The largest raindrops (about 4.5 millimeters in diameter) are shaped like hot-air balloons.

Write your answers to these questions on a sheet of paper.

1. How does precipitation form?

2. What are four kinds of precipitation?

3. Why doesn't it snow near the equator?

4. What is the difference between sleet and snow?

5. How does hail form?

Achievements in Science

Cloud Seeding

Cloud seeding is the science of forcing clouds to release precipitation. Cloud seeding began in the 1940s. It is often used to increase the amount of rain or snow. It helps farmers grow crops. Cloud seeding also can help scatter fog and prevent or decrease hail.

There are two types of cloud seeding: cold cloud seeding and warm cloud seeding. In cold cloud seeding, an ice-forming material, such as silver iodide, is dropped from airplanes into clouds. This increases the production of snowflakes within the clouds. It can also make clouds larger and longer lasting. Warm cloud seeding is used when clouds have temperatures above freezing. A material, such as salt, is dropped into these clouds. This increases the condensation of water droplets within clouds.

During cold months, cloud seeding works less than 30 percent of the time. However, during warm months, the success rate for cloud seeding is nearly 100 percent.

INVESTIGATION

9-2

Materials

- ◆ newspaper
- ◆ books
- ◆ plastic binder (or other flat, plastic surface)
- ◆ spray mister containing water
- ◆ magnifying glass
- ◆ paper towels

Making a Model of Rain

Purpose

How does a raindrop form? In this investigation, you will make a model of water droplets and observe how they combine.

Procedure

1. Copy the data table on your paper.

Spray Number	Description of Mist on Surface	Number of Running Droplets
1		
2		
3		
4		
5		

2. Cover your work surface with newspaper. Use the books to prop open the binder cover as shown in the figure on page 220. The plastic surface should make a slope.

3. Adjust the mister nozzle to produce a fine mist. Hold the mister about 30 centimeters from the plastic surface. Then gently spray the surface just once with the mister. **Safety Alert: Wipe up any spills immediately.**

4. Using a magnifying glass, look closely at the mist on the surface. Notice the different sizes of water droplets. In your data table, describe the mist. Count any water droplets running down the slope. Record this in your data table.

5. Repeat steps 3 and 4 at least four more times.

6. Use the paper towels to dry all wet surfaces. Clean your work area and return the equipment.

Questions and Conclusions

1. How many times did you spray before one droplet ran down the surface?

2. How did the size of the mist droplets on the plastic surface change?

3. How does this activity model raindrops forming?

Explore Further

Use a mister to repeat this investigation on an inside wall of a freezer. Compare your observations with the observations made at room temperature.

Objectives

After reading this lesson, you should be able to

◆ explain what causes air to move.

◆ recognize how air moves in wind cells.

◆ identify three wind belts.

Wind cell

Continuous cycle of rising warm air and falling cold air

When you see a flag waving or leaves blowing, you know that moving air is moving these objects. But what do you think starts the air moving?

Wind Cells

The earth's atmosphere is constantly in motion. Moving air is known as wind. The motion of air is caused by unequal heating of the earth's surface by the sun. When the sun's energy heats air, the air expands because the air particles are moving farther apart. This makes the warmed air lighter, or less dense, than the cold air around it. The lighter air begins to rise. Then cold air moves in to take the place of the rising air. The new air is then warmed. This cycle of air flow is called a **wind cell**. As the diagram shows, a wind cell is a continuous cycle of rising warm air and falling cold air.

On the earth, some of the warmest air is near the equator. Warm air near the equator rises. It moves toward the North Pole and the South Pole. As the air gets closer to the poles, it becomes colder. The cold air falls back to the earth and moves back toward the equator. As this air warms up, the cycle repeats.

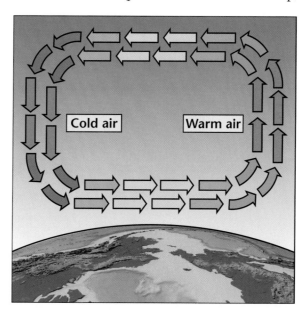

Cold air   Warm air

Global Winds

The rotation of the earth breaks large wind cells into smaller cells. These smaller wind cells are shown by black circular arrows in the diagram below. These wind cells make up the wind patterns of the earth. For example, at about 30°N and 30°S latitudes, some of the air headed for the poles falls back to the earth. As this mass of air hits the surface, it divides into two masses. One half of the air returns to the equator. The other half moves toward the North or South Pole. Look at the diagram to see where other wind cells occur.

Winds move around the earth in patterns called **wind belts**. On different parts of the earth, the belts move in different directions. Wind belts are shown by the wide arrows in the diagram.

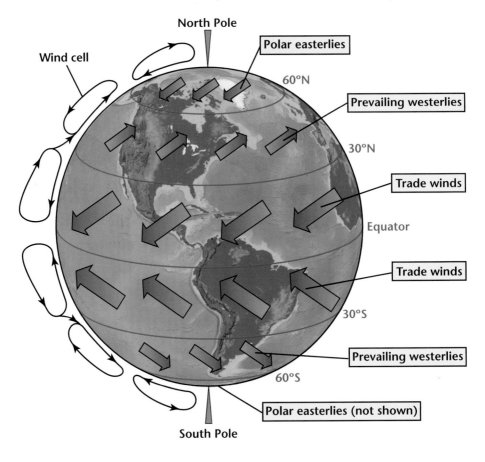

North Pole

Wind cell

Polar easterlies

60°N

Prevailing westerlies

30°N

Trade winds

Equator

Trade winds

30°S

Prevailing westerlies

60°S

Polar easterlies (not shown)

South Pole

Trade wind

Strong, reliable wind just north or south of the equator; blows from the east

Prevailing westerly

Wind generally between 30°N and 60°N latitudes (or 30°S and 60°S); blows from the west

Polar easterly

Wind near a pole; blows from the east

The equator is an area of rising air. Winds blowing along the surface are very light. Without enough wind, ships sailing in this area can become stranded.

The two wind belts just north and south of the equator are known as **trade winds**. Find these wind belts on the diagram. These winds blow from the northeast in the Northern Hemisphere and from the southeast in the Southern Hemisphere. Trade winds are strong and reliable. They have been called trade winds since the days when trading ships were powered by wind alone. The captains of those sailing ships sought out the steady trade winds to help them on their way. Hawaii lies within this wind belt.

Most of the United States and southern Canada are affected by the northern belt of the **prevailing westerlies**. Find the two prevailing westerly belts on the diagram. These winds generally occur between 30°N and 60°N latitudes and between 30°S and 60°S latitudes. They usually blow from west to east, the opposite direction of trade winds. Prevailing westerlies are not as predictable as the winds in other belts. The next time you watch a weather forecast, notice that weather moves across these wind belts from west to east. The weather comes from the west because it is carried by prevailing westerlies.

Wind belts also blow from the poles toward warmer latitudes. Winds in these belts are called **polar easterlies**. They move from east to west, like trade winds. Polar easterlies bring cold, stormy weather. Most of Alaska lies within this wind belt.

Lesson 5 REVIEW

Write your answers to these questions on a sheet of paper.

1. What causes air to move?

2. What is a wind cell?

3. Where is the earth's warmest air?

4. Where are trade winds found? From what direction do they blow?

5. Does the weather in the United States and southern Canada usually move to the east or to the west? Why?

Technology Note

Wind has been a source of power for centuries. As early as the 1100s, people in Europe used windmills to pump water and grind grain. Many windmills used broad sails to catch the wind.

The first windmill that powered an electric generator was built in 1890 in Denmark. These electricity-making windmills were improved and became popular. However, by the 1940s, coal-burning steam plants could produce electricity faster and cheaper.

In 1931, the first large-scale wind turbine was built in what is now Russia. A wind turbine is usually driven by two or three blades, much like an airplane propeller. The blades are mounted on a tall structure. Today, wind turbines are used to generate electricity for cities and farms. Often, many turbines operate together on a wind farm.

A wind farm may have several hundred wind turbines. The location of the wind farm is important. There must be a steady and strong wind. For this reason, most wind farms are near mountain passes and coastal hills. In 1984, the electricity produced by U.S. wind farms was more than 150 million kilowatt-hours. This seems like a lot. But it is much less than 1 percent of the total U.S. electricity produced. To learn more about sources of energy, see Appendix B.

Chapter 9 SUMMARY

- The atmosphere is the layer of gases that surrounds the earth.

- The earth's atmosphere consists mostly of the elements nitrogen and oxygen.

- Oxygen and nitrogen move between the atmosphere and living things through the oxygen-carbon dioxide cycle and the nitrogen cycle.

- The four layers of the atmosphere are the troposphere, stratosphere, mesosphere, and thermosphere.

- The ozone layer is in the stratosphere.

- The ionosphere is located in the upper mesosphere and lower thermosphere. It contains ions, which are positively charged particles.

- Clouds are masses of water droplets or ice crystals in the atmosphere.

- Clouds form in the atmosphere when water evaporates into the air and then cools and condenses.

- Three main types of clouds are stratus, cumulus, and cirrus. Fog is a stratus cloud near the ground.

- Precipitation is moisture that falls to the earth from the atmosphere. It may fall as rain, snow, sleet, or hail.

- The sun's unequal heating of the earth's surface causes wind.

- Continuous cycles of rising warm air and falling cold air occur in the atmosphere and are known as wind cells.

- Trade winds, prevailing westerlies, and polar easterlies make up the earth's major wind belts.

- Prevailing westerlies carry weather from west to east.

Science Words

altitude, 212	fog, 212	prevailing westerly, 223	troposphere, 208
atmosphere, 204	ionosphere, 209		water vapor, 211
cirrus cloud, 213	mesosphere, 209	stratosphere, 209	wind belt, 222
condense, 211	polar easterly, 223	stratus cloud, 212	wind cell, 221
cumulus cloud, 213	precipitation, 216	thermosphere, 209	
evaporate, 211		trade wind, 223	

Chapter 9   R E V I E W

Word Bank

altitude

cirrus clouds

condenses

evaporates

polar easterlies

precipitation

stratus clouds

trade winds

water vapor

wind belt

Vocabulary Review

Choose the word or phrase from the Word Bank that best matches each phrase. Write the answer on your paper.

1. steady winds north and south of the equator

2. height above the earth's surface

3. water that falls from the atmosphere

4. what water vapor does to become cloud droplets

5. what liquid water does to become water vapor

6. gas form of water

7. winds near the poles that blow from the east

8. pattern of wind movement around the earth

9. low, flat, gray clouds

10. high, wispy clouds

Concept Review

11. Refer to the diagram. Name each lettered layer of the atmosphere. Write your answers on your paper.

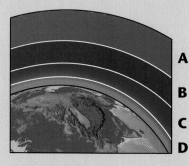

Choose the word or phrase that best completes each sentence. Write the letter of the answer of your paper.

12. The gases of the atmosphere that move in cycles as living things use them are _____.
   A oxygen, carbon dioxide, and nitrogen
   B methane, hydrogen, and helium
   C argon, neon, and ozone
   D nitrogen, xenon, and oxygen

13. The _____ reflects radio signals.
   A troposphere   **C** mesosphere
   B stratosphere   **D** ionosphere

14. The _____ is important because it absorbs most of the harmful ultraviolet radiation from the sun.

  A troposphere   **C** mesosphere

  B ozone layer   **D** ionosphere

15. Fluffy, white clouds are called _____.

  A cirrus clouds   **C** cumulus clouds

  B stratus clouds   **D** rain clouds

16. Rain forms when _____.

  A cumulus clouds are present

  B radio waves reflect from a layer of the atmosphere

  C water collects as heavy droplets in clouds

  D sunlight hits the earth at an indirect angle

17. A continuous cycle of rising warm air and falling cold air is called _____.

  A water vapor   **C** the nitrogen cycle

  B a thunderstorm   **D** a wind cell

18. The prevailing westerlies are _____.

  A winds coming from the west

  B the wind belts nearest the equator

  C trade winds

  D winds blowing to the west

Critical Thinking

Write the answer to each of the following questions.

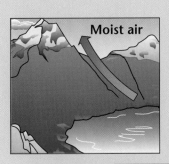

Moist air

19. When a rain forest is destroyed, how does this affect the composition of the atmosphere?

20. Moist air is pushed up a mountainside, as shown. How might the weather on the right side of the mountain be different from that on the left side?

Test-Taking Tip Do not wait until the night before a test to study. Plan your study time so that you can get a good night's sleep before a test.

10 Weather and Climate

Weather takes many different forms. One form of severe weather begins as a tropical storm over an ocean. As the storm gains energy, it becomes a spinning hurricane. This satellite photo shows what a hurricane looks like from space. Can you see the eye of the hurricane at its center? The swirling white masses around the eye are clouds. In Chapter 10, you will learn about different weather conditions and how they are measured. You also will explore weather patterns and climate zones.

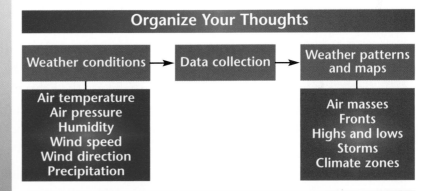

Organize Your Thoughts

Weather conditions → Data collection → Weather patterns and maps

Weather conditions:
Air temperature
Air pressure
Humidity
Wind speed
Wind direction
Precipitation

Weather patterns and maps:
Air masses
Fronts
Highs and lows
Storms
Climate zones

Goals for Learning

◆ To describe weather conditions

◆ To identify instruments that measure weather conditions

◆ To explain how fronts, highs, and lows affect weather

◆ To read a weather map

◆ To describe various kinds of storms

◆ To describe the earth's major climates

Weather

State of the atmosphere at a given time and place

Look out the window. Is it a cloudy day? Is it windy? *Cloudy* and *windy* refer to conditions of the atmosphere. **Weather** is the state of the atmosphere at a given time and place.

The weather is always changing because conditions in the atmosphere are always changing. A meteorologist measures these conditions, looks for patterns, and uses this information to predict the weather.

Air Temperature

One of the first weather conditions you hear on a weather report is the temperature of the air. Air temperature is measured with a thermometer. Most thermometers are made of a thin tube filled with colored alcohol. Heat causes a liquid to expand, or take up more space. So when the air gets warmer, the liquid in the thermometer expands and moves up the tube. If the air gets cooler, the liquid contracts, or takes up less space. Then the liquid moves down the tube.

The unit of measure for temperature is the degree (°). Two scales for measuring temperature are shown in the diagram. People in the United States usually use the Fahrenheit scale. People in most other countries use the Celsius scale. All scientists use the Celsius scale. Compare the common temperatures shown on both scales.

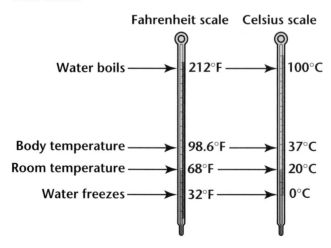

Fahrenheit scale   Celsius scale

Water boils ⟶ 212°F ⟶ 100°C

Body temperature ⟶ 98.6°F ⟶ 37°C
Room temperature ⟶ 68°F ⟶ 20°C
Water freezes ⟶ 32°F ⟶ 0°C

Air Pressure

Air pressure

Force of air against a unit of area

Barometer

Instrument used to measure air pressure

Think about what happens when you blow air into a balloon. The balloon gets bigger because the air particles push against the inside wall of the balloon. The push, or force, of air against an area is called **air pressure**.

Air in the atmosphere exerts pressure, too. The air above you and around you constantly pushes against your body. You don't feel this pressure because air in your body pushes out with the same amount of force. But what happens if air pressure suddenly changes? For example, while riding upward in an elevator, you may have felt your ears "pop." Your ears pop because they are adjusting to a drop in air pressure. As you move higher in the atmosphere, there is less air present to push on you, so air pressure drops.

Air pressure is measured with an instrument called a **barometer**. Two kinds of barometers are shown here. In a mercury barometer, air pushes down on a dish of mercury, forcing the mercury to rise in a tube. In an aneroid barometer, air pushes on a short metal can. A pointer connected to the can shows the amount of air pressure. Aneroid barometers are lightweight and portable.

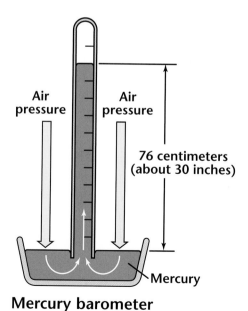

Air pressure   Air pressure

76 centimeters (about 30 inches)

Mercury

Mercury barometer

Aneroid barometer

Different scales are used to measure air pressure. Most weather reports give the air pressure in inches. Air pressure usually ranges from 29 to 31 inches (74 to 79 centimeters), which is the height of mercury in a mercury barometer.

A change in air pressure indicates a change in weather. A rise in air pressure usually means drier weather is on the way. A drop in air pressure often means precipitation is coming.

Humidity

Have you ever described a hot day as sticky or muggy? Such days are uncomfortable because of high **humidity**. Humidity is the amount of water vapor in the air. When the air contains a lot of water vapor, the humidity is high. The maximum amount of water vapor that the air can hold, or its capacity, depends on the air temperature. Warmer air can hold more water vapor than colder air can.

The amount of water vapor in the air compared to its capacity is called **relative humidity**. It is calculated as a percent. A relative humidity of 50 percent means that the air contains half, or 50 percent, of its water vapor capacity. When the air is completely filled with water vapor and cannot hold more, the relative humidity is 100 percent.

A **psychrometer** is an instrument used to measure relative humidity. It is actually made up of two thermometers. The bulb of one thermometer is covered with a damp cloth. As water evaporates from the cloth, it cools. The temperature of this thermometer is lower than the temperature of the dry thermometer. The lower the humidity, the faster the water evaporates and the lower the temperature drops. The relative humidity is then found by comparing the temperatures of the two thermometers to a special chart.

Wind Speed and Direction

The speed of the wind is an important weather condition. It helps meteorologists predict how fast an approaching storm will arrive. Wind speed is measured with an **anemometer**. An anemometer has three or four arms, with a cup attached to the end of each arm. These cups catch the wind and cause the arms to rotate. When the wind speed increases, the arms rotate faster. This spinning rate may be indicated on a dial or digital display.

The photo shows a simple anemometer with three arms. It also shows another important weather instrument: a **wind vane**.

A wind vane shows the direction from which the wind is blowing. It is often shaped like an arrow. Wind hits the larger back section of the vane. The vane turns so that it points into the wind.

Wind is named by the direction from which it comes. A wind that moves from north to south is called a north wind. A north wind causes a wind vane to point north.

A quick glance at this anemometer and wind vane will tell you both wind speed and direction.

Precipitation

Rain gauge

Instrument used to measure the amount of rainfall

Chapter 9 described four kinds of precipitation: rain, snow, sleet, and hail. If any precipitation falls, a weather report usually tells you how much. A **rain gauge** measures the amount of rainfall. As you can see, a rain gauge is a container that collects rain. A scale along the side shows the amount in centimeters or inches. Snow depth is usually measured simply by inserting a meterstick in a flat area of snow. Hail can be measured in two ways: by its depth on the ground and by the diameter of the hailstones.

Did You Know?

The wettest place on the earth is Mount Waialeale. This soggy mountain is on the island of Kauai in Hawaii. It receives about 12 meters of rain a year. This rain comes from trade winds carrying rain clouds up the side of the mountain.

Rain gauges come in different shapes and sizes. To accurately measure rainfall, rain gauges should be placed in open areas.

Write your answers to these questions on a sheet of paper.

1. What is weather?

2. How does a thermometer work?

3. What does a change in air pressure tell you about the weather?

4. Why does air pressure drop as you go higher in the atmosphere?

5. What weather condition does each of these instruments measure: barometer, thermometer, rain gauge, anemometer, psychrometer?

Science at Work

Atmospheric Scientist

A scientist who studies the atmosphere is called an atmospheric scientist. These specialists study the atmosphere's properties and patterns. They also study how weather affects the environment and how people affect the atmosphere.

Atmospheric scientists collect air samples and gather data from weather satellites, Doppler radar, and weather balloons. They use this information to create computer models of the atmosphere and to design experiments.

Atmospheric scientists predict long-term weather changes. They research the effect of pollution on clouds. They study how processes in the ocean and on the sun change weather. They design better instruments and give advice to government and industry leaders.

Atmospheric scientists must have at least a bachelor's degree in meteorology, atmospheric science, or a related science field. A graduate degree is often helpful.

People who want to work in this field should have strong computer and mathematics skills. A good atmospheric scientist is creative, patient, organized, and stays up-to-date on research methods.

Measuring Air Pressure

Materials

◆ large, round balloon
◆ scissors
◆ glass baby-food jar
◆ rubber band
◆ drinking straw
◆ glue
◆ marking pen
◆ index card
◆ centimeter ruler
◆ masking tape

Purpose

Does the air pressure change in your classroom? In this investigation, you will construct a barometer and collect weather data.

Procedure

1. Copy the data table on your paper.

Date and Time	Barometer Reading	Weather Observations

2. Cut off the neck of a balloon. Stretch the balloon tightly over the top of a jar. Hold the balloon in place with a rubber band. **Safety Alert: Use care when stretching the balloon. It can snap and cause injury.**

3. Cut one end of a drinking straw so that it forms a point. Glue the other end of the straw to the center of the balloon cover, as shown in the figure.

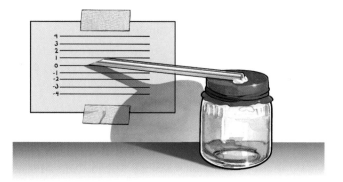

4. With a pen, mark a scale on the unlined side of an index card, as shown. Make the lines 0.5 centimeter apart. Number them from −4 to 4.

5. Place your barometer near a wall. Tape the index card to the wall so that the straw on the barometer points to the zero line. Make sure the barometer is not in direct sunlight.

6. When the glue has dried, observe the position of the straw. In your data table, record the number indicated by the straw. Also record the date, time, and outside weather conditions.

7. Repeat step 6 at least once each day for the next four days.

Questions and Conclusions

1. What does an upward movement of the straw indicate about air pressure?

2. What does a downward movement of the straw indicate about air pressure?

3. How did air pressure change during the five days of observations?

4. Use your readings to make a prediction about upcoming weather. Explain your prediction.

Explore Further

Find out how accurate your predictions were. Use a local newspaper to compare your data with weather reports for the same days.

After reading this lesson, you should be able to

◆ describe ways that weather data are collected.

◆ explain how fronts, highs, and lows affect weather.

◆ read the information on a weather map.

Did You Know?

In 1869, more than 1,900 ships sank in the Great Lakes during storms. The U.S. government reacted to this huge loss by setting up a weather service for the nation. The service was called the Army Signal Service. Its job was to predict the weather and post weather warnings.

Collecting Weather Data

To predict the weather, meteorologists need data from many places. At about 10,000 weather stations worldwide, measurements are taken at the exact same time several times a day. In the United States, the National Weather Service (NWS) collects these data for meteorologists to use.

Weather information is collected in many ways. Weather stations are collections of instruments that measure temperature, air pressure, humidity, cloud cover and type, precipitation, and wind speed and direction. Measurements are recorded automatically or taken by weather observers and transmitted to NWS centers.

Weather balloons more than a meter in diameter carry instruments high into the atmosphere. Weather satellites in orbit around the earth provide views of cloud patterns. Radar sends out radio waves that bounce off rain or snow. The returning waves make an image that shows where precipitation is occurring, as shown in the photo.

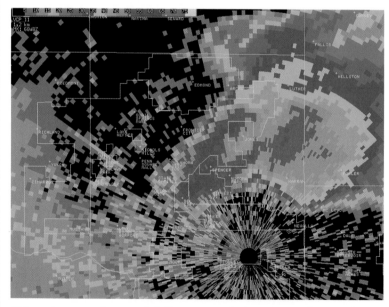

This radar map shows rainfall amounts during a tornado system. Notice the colored legend: red is heavy rain, lavender and gray are light rain, and black is no rain.

Air Masses and Fronts

Air mass

Large section of the atmosphere with the same temperature and humidity throughout

Front

Moving boundary line between two air masses

Warm front

Boundary ahead of a warm air mass that is pushing out and riding over a cold air mass

Cold front

Boundary ahead of a cold air mass that is pushing out and wedging under a warm air mass

Weather data from a large area of the earth show meteorologists where **air masses** are located. An air mass is a huge body of the lower atmosphere that has similar temperature and humidity throughout. An air mass can be warm or cold. It can have a lot of water vapor or very little. Air masses are so large that two or three of them can cover the United States. As air masses move, they bring their weather to new places.

A **front** is a moving boundary line between two air masses. Look at the diagrams below as you read about two types of fronts.

A **warm front** occurs where a warm air mass glides up and over a cooler air mass. As the warm air rises, it cools and water vapor condenses. Typically, high cirrus clouds appear. Low stratus clouds follow. The barometer falls continuously, and a period of steady precipitation begins. When the front passes, skies clear and the barometer rises. The temperature rises as warm air replaces the cooler air.

A **cold front** occurs where a cold air mass pushes out and wedges under a warmer air mass. The warm air mass rises quickly. If the warm air mass has a lot of water vapor, towering storm clouds form quickly. Heavy precipitation follows, but only for a short period of time. Several hours after the front passes, the weather becomes clear and cool.

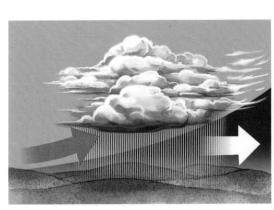

Warm front

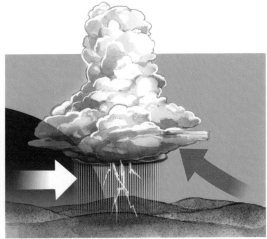

Cold front

Highs and Lows

High

Cold area of high air pressure

Low

Warm area of low air pressure

Isobar

Line on a weather map connecting areas of equal air pressure

Cold air is more dense than warm air. Therefore, cold air exerts more pressure on the earth's surface than does warm air. A cold air mass, then, is usually an area of high pressure, or a **high**. Highs often have fair weather. Look at the map below. You can see that air moves outward from a high in a clockwise rotation. However, air moves into an area of low pressure, or a **low**. The air coming into a low is warm and rotates counterclockwise. Lows often have clouds and precipitation. On a map, lines called **isobars** connect areas of equal pressure. Isobars form a circular pattern around highs and lows.

In most of the United States and Canada, weather moves from west to east. Therefore, a high passing through Oklahoma may soon pass through Arkansas. The high will likely bring similar weather to both places.

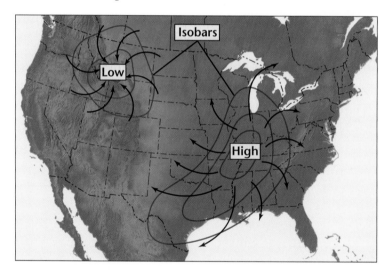

Weather Maps

As you can see, meteorologists must consider a lot of data to develop a weather forecast. They organize these data on weather maps, like the one above and the one on page 243. Weather maps generally include information about precipitation, cloud cover, air masses, highs, lows, and fronts. Weather maps may also include isobars, temperatures, wind speeds, and wind directions. As you learned in Chapter 1, to read these maps, you first need to understand their symbols.

Lesson 2 REVIEW

Write your answers to these questions on a sheet of paper.

1. Describe four ways weather data are collected.

2. How is a cold front different from a warm front?

3. What is the difference between a high and a low?

4. What are isobars?

5. Name three kinds of information found on a weather map.

Achievements in Science

Doppler Radar

The ability to predict weather events has improved greatly in the last century. Even as recently as 15 years ago, meteorologists could provide only a 2-day forecast. Today, improved technology helps them provide a mostly accurate 4-day forecast.

One of the tools that meteorologists use is a Doppler radar system. This type of radar uses a high-powered antenna that rotates and sends out radio waves. Some of these waves bounce off raindrops or snowflakes in the air and return to the antenna. A computer detects and measures how these waves have changed. It also measures the time it took for the waves to return. From this information, the computer calculates the distance and direction of the precipitation. Wind speed and direction also can be calculated.

This information is used to create a Doppler map. The map shows the locations and amounts of precipitation. You have probably seen a Doppler map on television weather reports. Meteorologists are trained to use these maps and other resources to understand and predict weather.

Using a Weather Map

Purpose

How can you show weather conditions on a map? In this investigation, you will make and interpret a weather map.

Materials

◆ map without weather symbols

Procedure

1. On your map, copy the weather information from the weather map on page 243. Copy the legend of symbols, too.

2. Show that it is raining across southern Florida.

3. Show that snow is falling in Minnesota and Ontario behind the cold front.

4. Show that a warm front is occurring across Alabama, Georgia, and South Carolina and heading toward Florida.

5. Show that it is now cloudy in Honolulu, Hawaii, and partly cloudy in Juneau, Alaska.

Questions and Conclusions

1. Which cities have clear skies?

2. Which kind of front is heading toward Dallas and Chicago? What kind of weather will these cities have after the front passes them?

3. From your map, predict what will happen to temperatures in Florida tomorrow. Explain your answer.

4. Suggest two more symbols that could be added to your map. Explain the symbols. How do they make the map more useful?

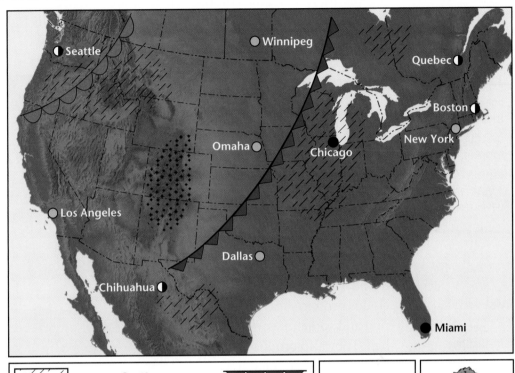

/// Rain	◐ Clear	Cold front	Honolulu
✦✦ Snow	◑ Partly cloudy	Warm front	Juneau
	● Cloudy		

Explore Further

Compare local weather maps for two days in a row. How accurate was the first day's forecast? Did the fronts move as expected? Are there any new fronts? From which direction did they arrive?

Storms are violent kinds of weather. They are caused by rapid changes in the movement of air masses. Storms usually include precipitation and high winds.

Thunderstorms

Perhaps the most familiar kind of storm is the thunderstorm. This kind of storm occurs when warm air is forced upward by a cold front. Large, dark, cumulus clouds form. Such clouds are also called thunderheads. These clouds produce heavy rain and sometimes hail. They also produce lightning and thunder.

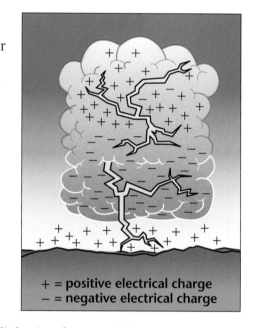

+ = positive electrical charge
− = negative electrical charge

The diagram shows how lightning forms. Within a thunderhead, air moves up and down. This motion causes electrical charges to build. An electric current passes between the negative and positive charges. This current is lightning. A streak of lightning may be only a few centimeters wide, but it heats that part of the air intensely. The heated air expands so quickly that it produces a sound wave we call thunder. You see the lightning before you hear the thunder because light travels faster than sound.

Tornadoes

A **tornado** is a small but powerful wind storm with a whirling, funnel-shaped cloud. Tornadoes sometimes form in thunderstorms when warm, humid air rushes up to meet cool, dry air. Tornadoes have very low air pressure and can rotate at speeds up to 450 kilometers per hour. When they touch the ground, they can uproot trees, toss cars, and destroy houses. Tornadoes last for a very short time.

Tornadoes usually form in open, level areas like the prairies of the central and southern United States. In these areas, there are few mountains or forests to break the high winds.

Tornadoes usually occur in April, May, and June.

Hurricanes

A **hurricane** is a large tropical storm that often covers thousands of square kilometers. Winds spiral toward the center of the storm, with speeds up to 320 kilometers per hour. At the center of a hurricane is an area of calm air called the eye. In the satellite photo on page 228, notice how the clouds spiral around the eye of a hurricane.

All hurricanes form over the ocean near the equator. They collect warm, moist air and begin to spin. They grow stronger over the warm tropical water. As hurricanes approach land, their wind pushes the water of the ocean against the shore, and flooding occurs. Hurricanes may drop tremendous amounts of rain as they move inland, causing further damage. Hurricanes lose their force as they continue to move over land because they are no longer fed by the heat and moisture of tropical seas. Friction with the land also slows the winds of the storm.

Lesson 3 R E V I E W

Write your answers to these questions on a sheet of paper.

1. How does a thunderstorm form?

2. What is lightning?

3. What is a tornado?

4. Under what conditions does a hurricane form?

5. What causes a hurricane to lose its force?

Technology Note

Weather satellites allow meteorologists to see weather patterns that can't be observed from the ground. There are two basic types of weather satellites. One type, the polar-orbiting satellite, circles the earth. The first weather satellite sent into space was a polar-orbiting satellite. It was launched in 1960. It circled the earth every 2 hours at about 1,000 kilometers above the earth's surface. It has since been replaced by more complex polar-orbiting satellites.

The other type of weather satellite is the geostationary satellite. It stays in a fixed position about 36,000 kilometers above the equator. The most well-known satellites of this type are the geosynchronous operational environmental satellites (GOES). The first one was launched in 1975. Several more have been launched since. These satellites take pictures of the earth's atmosphere and measure weather conditions in space. They even help with search and rescue operations.

The National Weather Service uses GOES images to monitor severe storms and hurricanes. GOES technology also allows local meteorologists to take pictures of small areas of weather.

What kind of weather do people have on the other side of the world? It may be similar to yours. Scientists have identified global patterns in weather.

Climate Zones

Like weather, **climate** describes conditions of the atmosphere. Weather is the state of the atmosphere at a given time and place. Climate is the average weather of a region over a long period of time. A region's climate depends on two kinds of measurements:

◆ The average temperature pattern during a year
◆ The average amount of precipitation in a year

The climates of the world are divided into three major groups, called climate zones. Find each zone on the map. Refer to this map as you learn more about these zones.

Objectives

After reading this lesson, you should be able to

◆ compare and contrast the three world climate zones.
◆ identify factors that affect climate.

Climate

Average weather of a region over a long period of time

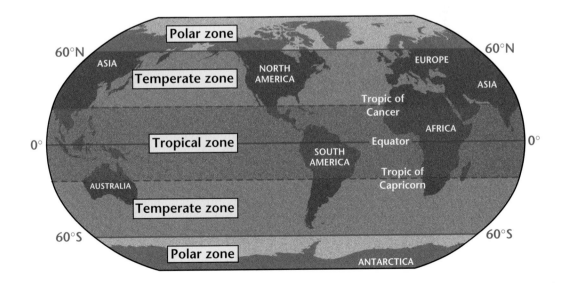

The mild climates in areas near large bodies of water are called marine climates. The more extreme climates in areas far from water are called continental climates.

Polar climates are marked by generally cold temperatures. There is little precipitation in these climates, and it is usually in the form of snow. The temperatures are so low that very little snow melts. Polar climates generally extend from the poles to about 60° latitude. They also exist at very high elevations on mountains.

Temperate climates generally extend from 60°N latitude to the tropic of Cancer and from 60°S latitude to the tropic of Capricorn. These climates feature the greatest changes in weather. There are four different weather seasons in these climates, where winters are cold and summers are warm.

Tropical climates occur near the equator between the tropic of Capricorn and the tropic of Cancer. These climates are marked by the highest average temperatures on the earth. Tropical climates are also the most humid regions. There is little variation in the kind of weather from one month to the next.

Each of the three major climate zones is further divided into climate regions. The table on page 249 provides some information about these regions.

Factors That Affect Climate

Why is one climate different from another? The main factor is the angle at which sunlight hits the earth. Because the earth is a sphere, sunlight hits the tropics more directly than areas toward the poles. The more direct sunlight provides warmer temperatures.

Climate is also affected by how high a place is above sea level. The temperatures in a mountain region are cooler than the temperatures in a nearby valley. In general, higher places tend to be cooler. This is why you can find snow-capped mountains near the equator.

The nearness of large bodies of water also affects climate. In general, areas that are close to an ocean or a large lake get more precipitation than areas farther from water. Water heats up and cools off more slowly than land. As a result, areas near large bodies of water have more mild temperatures than areas far from water.

Polar Climates

Ice cap climate

Temperatures below freezing | Precipitation less than 25 centimeters per year | No visible plant life

Tundra climate

Temperatures slightly higher than ice cap | Precipitation less than 25 centimeters per year | Mosses and small shrubs

Subarctic climate

Short summer, cold winter | Precipitation 25–30 centimeters per year | Small pines, spruce, and fir

Temperate Climates

Marine west coast climate

Temperatures generally above freezing | Precipitation 50–76 centimeters per year | Thick evergreen forests

Deserts and steppes

Warm to hot summer, cold winter | Precipitation less than 25 centimeters per year | Cactus in deserts, grasses in steppes

Mediterranean climate

Warm summer, mild and wet winter | Precipitation 25 centimeters per year | Scattered trees, low shrubs

Humid subtropical climate

Warm and humid summer, mild winter | Precipitation 76–165 centimeters per year | Heavy plant growth and forests

Humid continental climate

Warm and humid summer, cold winter | Precipitation 76 centimeters per year | Hardwood and softwood forests, grass prairies

Tropical Climates

Tropical rain forest

Always hot and humid | Precipitation 254 centimeters per year | Very thick forests and plant growth

Tropical desert

Dry and relatively hot | Precipitation less than 25 centimeters per year | Almost no plant life

Savannah

Humid and warm summer, dry and cool winter | Precipitation 76–152 centimeters per year | Scattered trees and shrubs, tall grasses

Lesson 4   R E V I E W

Write your answers to these questions on a sheet of paper.

1. Where do polar climates occur?

2. Where do tropical climates occur?

3. Which climate zone has warm summers and cold winters?

4. How does height above sea level affect climate?

5. What effect does a large body of water have on climate?

Science in Your Life

Your Climate Zone

Now that you have learned about climate zones, identify the zone you live in. How would you describe the climate in your zone? If you have friends or family who live in other climate zones, compare your zone with theirs. Do you think you'd rather live in their climate zone?

What kinds of severe weather occur in your climate zone? How would you know if severe weather was predicted for your area? Local newspapers provide important weather information. They may also show radar and satellite images of weather patterns that could affect your area. Radio stations regularly broadcast weather reports.

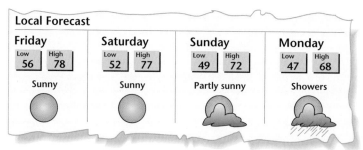

Local Forecast

Friday	Saturday	Sunday	Monday
Low 56 High 78	Low 52 High 77	Low 49 High 72	Low 47 High 68
Sunny	Sunny	Partly sunny	Showers

Are you prepared for severe weather? In your class or at home, discuss what you should do in a weather emergency. How can you prepare now for severe weather?

The Federal Emergency Management Agency recommends that you have a disaster supply kit ready in case of a weather emergency. The kit should include water, a first-aid kit, a flashlight, a radio, a few basic tools, extra clothes, canned food, and a can opener.

■ Weather is the state of the atmosphere at a given time and place.

■ To study weather, meteorologists gather information about air temperature, air pressure, humidity, wind speed, wind direction, type of precipitation, and amount of precipitation.

■ A barometer measures air pressure. A psychrometer measures relative humidity. An anemometer measures wind speed. A wind vane shows wind direction.

■ Weather data are collected by using weather balloons, weather satellites, and radar.

■ An air mass is a large body of air near the earth's surface. It has the same temperature and humidity throughout.

■ Fronts are the moving boundaries of air masses.

■ At a warm front, warm air glides up and over cooler air. Steady precipitation often results.

■ At a cold front, cold air pushes under warmer air. A short storm often results.

■ Data about fronts, air masses, highs, and lows are recorded on weather maps and used to predict weather.

■ Storms are severe weather conditions and include thunderstorms, tornadoes, and hurricanes.

■ Climate is the average weather of a region over a long period of time.

■ The major world climates are divided into three zones: polar, temperate, and tropical.

■ Climate is affected by the angle of sunlight, height above sea level, and nearness of large bodies of water.

Science Words

air mass, 239	front, 239	psychrometer, 232	weather, 230
air pressure, 231	high, 240	rain gauge, 234	wind vane, 233
anemometer, 233	humidity, 232	relative	
barometer, 231	hurricane, 245	humidity, 232	
climate, 247	isobar, 240	tornado, 245	
cold front, 239	low, 240	warm front, 239	

Chapter 10 REVIEW

Vocabulary Review

Choose the word or phrase from the Word Bank that best matches each phrase. Write the answer on your paper.

1. tropical storm that forms over an ocean

2. instrument for measuring air pressure

3. state of the atmosphere at a given time and place

4. large section of the atmosphere having the same humidity and temperature throughout

5. storm with a dangerous funnel cloud

6. instrument for measuring wind speed

7. instrument for measuring relative humidity

8. average weather over a long period of time

9. line on a weather map connecting areas of equal air pressure

10. amount of water vapor in the air

Concept Review

Choose the word or phrase that best completes each sentence. Write the letter of the answer on your paper.

11. In an area of low pressure, the _____.

    A air is moving out   **C** air rotates clockwise

    B temperature is warm   **D** skies are sunny

12. The force of the atmosphere against the earth's surface is _____.

    A air pressure   **C** wind

    B air temperature   **D** precipitation

13. A wind vane shows _____.

    A altitude   **C** air pressure

    B wind speed   **D** wind direction

14. Lightning is best described as _____.
   A positive electrical charges
   B a moving thunderhead
   C electric current
   D high pressure

15. A moving boundary between two air masses is called a(n) _____.
   A eye   **B** front   **C** isobar   **D** storm

16. A hurricane forms over a(n) _____.
   A ocean   **C** forest
   B prairie   **D** mountain

17. The _____ climate zone has warm summers and cold winters.
   A polar   **B** tropical   **C** temperate   **D** tundra

18. A warm front often brings _____.
   A storm clouds   **C** heavy rain
   B cool weather   **D** steady rain

Critical Thinking

Write the answer to each of the following questions.

19. Two cities are located in the temperate climate zone. One city is located on the coast at sea level. The other city is located in the mountains, high above sea level. How would you expect the climates of the two cities to be the same and different? Explain your answer.

20. If a high pushes out a low in your area today, what weather changes would you expect?

Test-Taking Tip To prepare for a test, study in short sessions rather than in one long session. During the week before the test, spend time each evening reviewing your notes.

The Earth's Water

Earth is called the water planet for a good reason. More than 70 percent of the earth's surface is covered with water. Water is also in the atmosphere and under the ground. All of this water is continuously moving. For example, ocean water evaporates into the air. Clouds gather and carry this moisture. Eventually, water droplets in clouds fall back to the earth. In Chapter 11, you will learn how water moves and changes. You will also learn about different bodies of water, such as rivers, lakes, and oceans.

Organize Your Thoughts

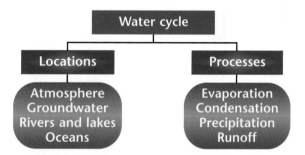

Water cycle

Locations
Atmosphere
Groundwater
Rivers and lakes
Oceans

Processes
Evaporation
Condensation
Precipitation
Runoff

Goals for Learning

◆ To explain the water cycle

◆ To compare fresh water and salt water

◆ To explain the water table

◆ To describe the sources and movement of fresh water

◆ To describe ocean water, waves, currents, and the ocean floor

Water is everywhere. Almost all of the earth's water is in the oceans. But it is also in rivers and lakes, under the ground, in the air, and even in your own body.

Earth's water is in continuous motion. It moves from the atmosphere to the earth's surface and back to the atmosphere. This movement of water is called the **water cycle**. Study the diagram below and notice the different forms that water takes as it goes through a complete cycle.

The water cycle is powered by the sun. Heat from the sun evaporates surface water, and the water vapor rises into the atmosphere. The rising water vapor cools and condenses into clouds. Water droplets or ice crystals in the clouds grow larger, then fall to the earth as precipitation.

Water cycle

Movement of water between the atmosphere and the earth's surface

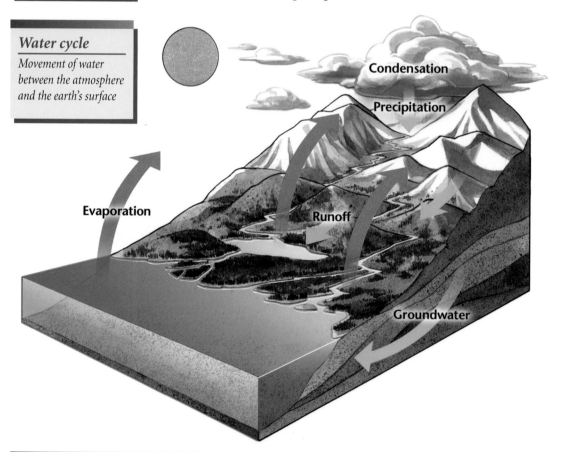

Groundwater

Water that sinks into the ground

Runoff

Water that runs over the earth's surface and flows into streams

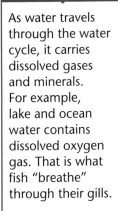

As water travels through the water cycle, it carries dissolved gases and minerals. For example, lake and ocean water contains dissolved oxygen gas. That is what fish "breathe" through their gills.

Did You Know?

The Dead Sea is a saltwater lake in the Middle East. It is almost nine times saltier than any ocean. Nothing lives in the Dead Sea except bacteria.

What happens after precipitation falls? Some of it sinks into the ground and becomes **groundwater**. This water collects in the spaces between rocks and moves slowly underground. Precipitation that does not sink into the ground is called surface water. Some surface water evaporates. But most of it becomes **runoff**—surface water that flows over the land and into streams and rivers.

Why doesn't all precipitation sink into the ground? There are three main reasons.

1. The ground may be saturated, or completely soaked, and unable to hold any more water. It is like pouring water on a sponge. Eventually, the sponge fills and water runs off it.

2. On a slope, the water may run off too quickly to sink in.

3. The ground may not have enough vegetation to stop the water from flowing elsewhere. Plants and their roots soak up water.

Eventually, surface water evaporates or rivers carry it to the oceans. If you have ever tasted ocean water, you know it is much too salty to drink. Salt water also cannot be used for farms and industry. Salt water kills most land plants and ruins machinery. In Lesson 3, you will learn more about the properties of salt water.

Like the water on land, ocean water evaporates and moves back into the atmosphere. Dissolved salts are left behind, however. So the water that condenses in the atmosphere and falls onto the land contains no salt. It is fresh water.

Write your answers to these questions on a sheet of paper.

1. How does water move between the atmosphere, the land, and bodies of water?

2. What is the difference between groundwater and surface water?

3. What is runoff?

4. Why doesn't all precipitation soak into the ground?

5. How are salt water and fresh water different?

Science in Your Life

Your Water Budget

How much water do you use? Probably more than you think. The table lists the average amount of water used for different tasks. Estimate how much water you have used so far today. Think about ways to cut down on the water you use. Then make a water budget by planning the amount of water you will "spend" each week.

Water Uses	
Task	**Average Amount Used**
drinking water	2 liters per person per day
flushing a toilet	11 to 19 liters per flush
taking a shower	19 liters per minute
taking a bath	133 to 152 liters per bath
running a dishwasher	38 to 57 liters per load
doing laundry	72 to 171 liters per load
washing hands	1 liter
brushing teeth	4 liters
washing a car	76 to 114 liters
watering a lawn	912 liters per half hour

Where does used water go? If your home is connected to a sewer system, the water you use drains into a sewer. Sewer pipes carry this water to a treatment plant, where it is cleaned and filtered.

Objectives

After reading this lesson, you should be able to

◆ explain how groundwater moves and forms the water table.

◆ describe springs, geysers, and caves.

◆ describe how runoff creates rivers, drainage basins, and lakes.

◆ identify three purposes of reservoirs.

Porous

Containing many spaces through which air and water can move

Water table

Top of the groundwater layer

Fresh water is an important resource. Think of the many ways you use it every day, such as for drinking, washing, and cooking. Farms and industry, however, use 90 percent of the fresh water consumed in the United States. Fresh water can be found in many places, both above and below the ground.

Groundwater

Groundwater starts as precipitation or runoff that soaks into the earth. The water can sink into the ground because most soil is **porous**, or has spaces between its particles. Loose soil, such as sandy soil or soil with a lot of decayed plant material, is very porous. The rocks beneath the soil may also be porous. Water trickles around broken rock pieces and through cracks.

The diagram shows what happens as water continues downward. Eventually, water comes to a solid rock layer through which it cannot move. Groundwater collects on top of the rock layer, filling the spaces above it. The top of this wet earth layer is the **water table**. Find the water table in the diagram. If you drill a well down past the water table, water flows into the well and can be pumped to the surface. About half the drinking water in the United States comes from groundwater.

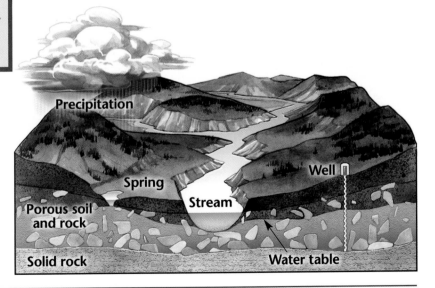

Precipitation

Spring

Stream

Well

Porous soil and rock

Solid rock

Water table

Springs, Geysers, and Caves

Spring

Place where groundwater flows naturally out of the ground

Geyser

Place where hot groundwater and steam blast into the air

Sinkhole

Funnel-shaped depression that results when the roof of a cave collapses

The water under the ground is moving. Notice in the diagram on page 259 what happens when the water table reaches the surface on a hillside. Groundwater flows out of the ground as a natural **spring**.

Certain springs, called **geysers**, shoot water and steam into the air. Geysers occur where groundwater lies close to hot rock or magma. Pockets of groundwater are heated and turned to steam. The steam rises, pushing the hot water above it. The steam and water erupt as a geyser. Geysers occur in Wyoming, New Zealand, and Iceland. The eruptions of some geysers are predictable. Castle Geyser, below left, erupts twice a day.

Moving groundwater creates some other unusual features. For example, groundwater seeping through cracks in limestone may dissolve the rock and form caves. Some caves are barely large enough to crawl through. Others are immense.

The photo below right shows what happens when the roof of a cave collapses. A funnel-shaped **sinkhole** forms. Sinkholes may fill with groundwater and rain to become ponds.

Castle Geyser in Yellowstone National Park, Wyoming, blasts water for 20 minutes, then steam for another 30 minutes.

In 1981, this sinkhole formed in one day. The city of Winter Park, Florida, made it into a lake.

Rivers and Drainage Basins

Tributary

River that joins another river of equal or greater size

Drainage basin

Land area that is drained by a river and its tributaries

Divide

Ridge that separates drainage basins

Much of the fresh water above ground flows as rivers. Rivers begin as runoff that moves over the land, carving small paths in the ground. These paths get wider and deeper as water continues to flow through them. The paths become streams. They always flow downhill because of gravity. The streams join and become rivers. These rivers then join and form even larger rivers. Rivers that join other rivers are called **tributaries**. Notice the rivers on the map below. You can see how water and sediment in the most distant tributaries end up in the main river.

The land area in which runoff drains into a river and its tributaries is a **drainage basin**. The map shows five drainage basins. The Mississippi-Missouri River basin covers about 40 percent of the United States. Notice how rain that falls in Montana can eventually reach the Gulf of Mexico. Ridges that separate drainage basins are called **divides**. One divide runs along the Rocky Mountains. Rivers east of this divide flow into the Gulf of Mexico. Rivers west of this divide flow into the Pacific Ocean. What other divide is shown?

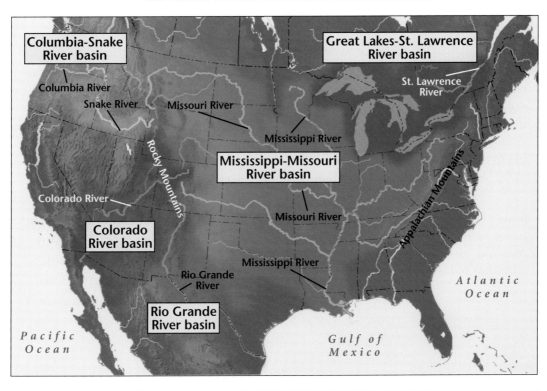

Rivers are important sources of fresh water. They provide much of the water that people use every day. Yet rivers make up a tiny percent of the earth's water. The diagram shows that only 3 percent of the earth's water is fresh water. Only 1 percent of all fresh water is not frozen or underground. Of this available fresh water, less than 1 percent is in rivers.

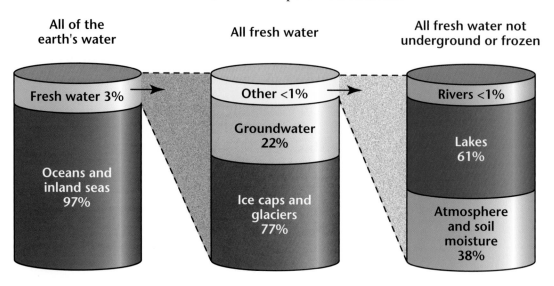

All of the earth's water

Fresh water 3%

Oceans and inland seas 97%

All fresh water

Other <1%

Groundwater 22%

Ice caps and glaciers 77%

All fresh water not underground or frozen

Rivers <1%

Lakes 61%

Atmosphere and soil moisture 38%

Lakes

Surface water does not always flow along a path. Some of it collects in depressions, or low areas. Water eventually fills the depressions, forming lakes. Even though some of the water evaporates, lakes continue to be fed by precipitation, runoff, springs, and rivers. Many lakes also lose water through outflowing streams or moving groundwater.

Lakes are many different sizes. For example, some lakes in Wisconsin are only a few meters deep. You can hear people talking from the opposite shore. The Great Lakes, on the other hand, are so wide that you cannot see across them. Lake Superior is the largest freshwater lake in the world. Its deepest point is about 400 meters. Many of the lakes in the northern United States and Canada formed when huge sheets of moving ice gouged out depressions. You will learn more about this process in Chapter 12.

Reservoir

Artificial lake created by placing a dam across a river

Reservoirs

Many cities store large supplies of fresh water in artificial lakes called **reservoirs**. Reservoirs are made by constructing dams along rivers. As you can see in the photo below, water backs up behind the dam, turning part of the river into a lake. Reservoirs serve several purposes, as described below.

Reservoirs store water for home use, farming, and industry. This water can be piped to dry areas. Much of southern California's water, for example, comes through a canal from Lake Havasu. This lake is actually a reservoir behind Parker Dam on the Colorado River between California and Arizona.

Reservoirs control flooding. During periods of heavy rain and runoff, a reservoir may fill up. This water can be released slowly and safely downstream through gates in the dam.

Reservoirs produce electricity. In a hydroelectric dam, the water moves through generators near the bottom of the dam. The rushing water turns the blades of a turbine, which spins a magnet. When the magnet spins through loops of wire, electricity is produced.

This California reservoir was built because of unreliable rains and occasional floods. Besides supplying water, it produces electricity.

Lesson 2   R E V I E W

Write your answers to these questions on a sheet of paper.

1. What is a water table?

2. How does a sinkhole form?

3. How can runoff on a mountain end up in an ocean 2,000 kilometers away?

4. How do lakes gain and lose water?

5. How are reservoirs useful?

▼◀▲▼◀▲▼◀▲▼◀▲▼◀▲▼◀▲▼◀▲▼◀▲▼◀▲▼◀▲▼◀▲▼◀▲▼◀▲▼◀▲▼

Science at Work

Hydroelectric Power Plant Operator

Hydroelectric power plant operators manage an entire plant and supervise many people. They control the water flow in the dam and the machinery that generates electricity. This includes gates, valves, turbines, and generators.

Plant operators adjust the plant's power output to meet changing electricity demands. They check water, voltage, and electricity flows. Plant operators maintain and repair equipment. They prepare reports about equipment or performance.

Hydroelectric power plant operators must have at least a high-school diploma. College-level courses in mechanical or technical fields are helpful. Computer, math, and science skills are important. A good plant operator has mechanical ability, is responsible, and understands equipment and safety procedures.

Plant operators must be willing to work under tiring conditions. Their job requires constant attention. They may spend hours sitting or standing at control stations. They also may maintain buildings, grounds, and access roads.

Exploring Evaporation

Purpose

How does heat affect evaporation? In this investigation, you will discover factors that cause evaporation.

Procedure

1. Copy the data table on your paper.

Time	Uncovered Dish	Covered Dish	Uncovered Dish with Lamp
start			
time of evaporation			

2. Place the petri dishes on a tabletop. Use the dropper to place one drop of water in the center of each dish.

3. Place a cover over one of the dishes.

4. Move one of the uncovered dishes at least 50 centimeters away from the other two. Position the lamp directly over this dish, as shown.

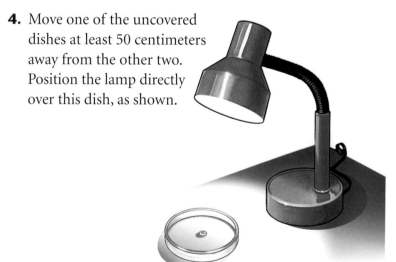

5. Turn on the lamp. If you have a clock, record the time. If you have a stopwatch, start the watch. **Safety Alert: The lamp will become very hot. Do not touch the bulb or the lamp.**

6. Observe the three dishes every 2 minutes. Record the time when each drop evaporates.

7. Clean your work area and return the equipment.

Questions and Conclusions

1. Which drop of water took the longest time to evaporate?

2. Which drop took the shortest time to evaporate?

3. What conclusions can you make about the factors that affect evaporation?

4. What predictions can you make about the evaporation rate on a hot, sunny day and on a cool, cloudy day?

Explore Further

Design an experiment to find out how wind affects evaporation. How could you model wind blowing over a petri dish? How could you vary the amount of wind modeled?

Properties of Ocean Water

The water in the oceans is salt water. The circle graph shows why. Notice that 96.5 percent of ocean water is pure water. But 3.5 percent is dissolved salt. That amount of salt makes a mouthful of ocean water saltier than a mouthful of potato chips. Most of the salt is sodium chloride—common table salt. This salt comes from rocks in the ocean floor. Salt also washes into oceans from rivers.

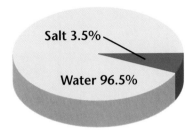

Not all parts of oceans are equally salty. The saltiness, or **salinity**, of ocean water varies. In warm, dry climates, ocean water evaporates quickly. Since salt doesn't evaporate, the salt that remains makes the salinity greater than average. In some oceans, the salinity is less than average. This happens in rainy climates or where rivers and melting ice add fresh water to oceans.

Ocean water is warmest at the surface where the sun heats it. Near the equator, the surface temperature can reach 30°C. Near the poles, the ocean surface is frozen. The diagram shows average ocean temperatures in a tropical or temperate zone. Notice how the water temperature decreases with depth.

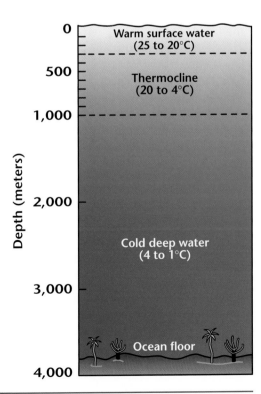

Along the edges of oceans are smaller bodies of salt water. They are called gulfs, seas, or bays. The Gulf of Alaska is part of the Pacific Ocean. The Mediterranean Sea is part of the Atlantic Ocean. The word *sea* can also be used in a general sense to mean "ocean."

The temperature is fairly constant near the surface because winds and waves keep the water well-mixed. However, in the **thermocline**, between 300 and 1,000 meters below the surface, the temperature drops sharply. Below the thermocline, the temperature decreases slowly. The bottoms of oceans are near freezing.

Ocean Waves

When you think of oceans, you probably picture **waves**. A wave is the regular up-and-down motion of water caused by energy traveling through the water. A wave gets its energy from wind. When the wind blows, it pushes up the water to start small waves. The waves become larger as the wind blows longer and harder. Most ocean waves are less than 3 meters high. However, storms can produce waves as high as 30 meters—the height of a 10-story building. No matter what the size, all waves have the parts shown below.

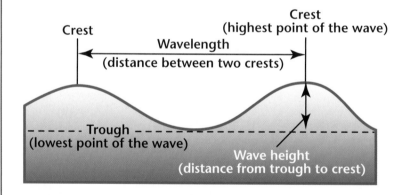

Have you ever seen a leaf bob up and down on passing waves? The waves move forward, but the leaf does not. Although it looks like waves constantly push water forward, the water generally stays in the same place. Only the waves move forward.

As a wave approaches shallow water and a shore, the wave rubs against the ocean floor. Friction slows the bottom of the wave, but the crest keeps moving at the same speed. Therefore, the crest moves ahead of the rest of the wave. The wave tilts forward and tumbles over, or breaks. After a wave breaks on a shore, the water can actually move quite a distance. It may be hurled against rocks or pushed up the slope of a beach.

Ocean Currents

Although waves do not move water, **currents** do. Ocean currents are large streams of water flowing in oceans. Winds cause currents near the ocean surface. Therefore, currents tend to follow the major wind belts. On the map below, trade winds and prevailing westerlies are shown as wide arrows. Major ocean currents are shown as thin arrows. Compare the trade winds with the currents near the equator. Both move westward.

Currents carry warm water from the equator toward the poles and bring cold water back toward the equator. In so doing, currents affect climates on land by warming or cooling the coasts of continents. Both wind and land absorb heat from warm ocean currents.

The Gulf Stream and the North Atlantic Drift are currents that have a warming effect. Find these currents on the map. The Gulf Stream carries warm water from the tropics up along the east coast of North America. The North Atlantic Drift carries this warm water across the Atlantic. It gives western Europe mild summers and winters.

Now locate the California Current on the map. This current carries cold water from high latitudes. It has an "air-conditioned" effect along the west coast of the United States and Mexico.

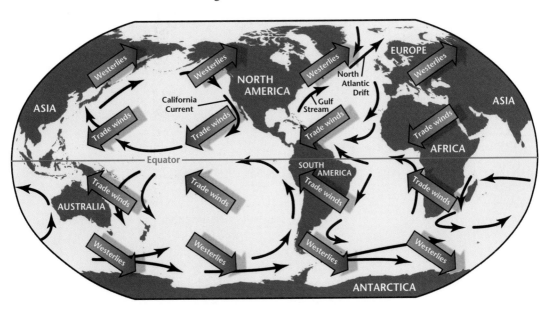

The Ocean Floor

Until the late 1800s, the ocean floor was a great mystery. Today oceanographers use complex technology to measure distances and take pictures underwater. They also travel to the ocean floor. The main features of the ocean floor are listed below and shown in the diagram.

- ◆ A **continental shelf** is the part of a continent that extends underwater. A continental shelf slopes gently. The average water depth is 130 meters. The average width is 75 kilometers.
- ◆ A **continental slope** dips sharply from a continental shelf to the deeper ocean floor.
- ◆ Plains are wide, flat areas where sediment constantly settles. About half of the ocean floor consists of plains. Their average depth is about 4,000 meters.
- ◆ A **mid-ocean ridge** is an underwater mountain chain. Such a chain may extend for thousands of kilometers along the ocean floor.
- ◆ A **seamount** is an underwater mountain. Many of these are active or extinct volcanoes. A seamount that rises above sea level forms an island.
- ◆ A **trench** is a long, deep valley. Trenches are the deepest places on the earth. Some are 10 kilometers deep.

Continental shelf

Part of a continent that extends from a shoreline out into an ocean

Continental slope

Steep slope between the continental shelf and the deep ocean floor

Mid-ocean ridge

Mountain chain on the ocean floor

Seamount

Underwater mountain that is usually a volcano

Trench

Deep valley on the ocean floor

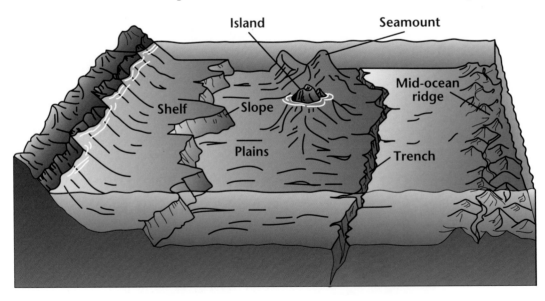

Ocean Life

Ocean environments support a rich variety of living things. Scientists divide these forms of life into three groups, based on how and where they live. Look at the cross section of ocean life below. Which group provides most of the seafood people eat?

Plankton are one form of life in oceans. This group includes tiny plants and animals that float at or near the ocean surface. Plankton are a source of food for larger animals.

Animals that swim freely are classified as **nekton**. This group includes the widest variety of sea creatures, from the tiniest fish to the largest whale.

Organisms that live on the ocean floor are called **benthos**. They do not swim. Some, such as corals, remain in one place their whole lives. Others, such as snails and crabs, crawl along the ocean floor.

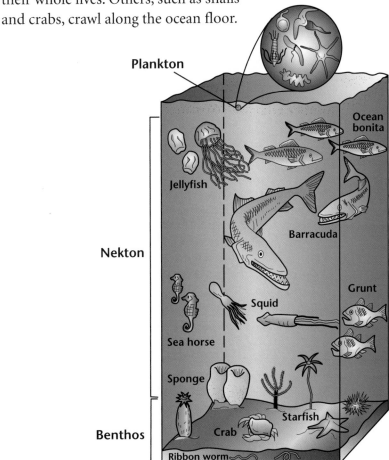

Plankton

Ocean bonita

Jellyfish

Barracuda

Nekton

Grunt

Squid

Sea horse

Sponge

Starfish

Benthos

Crab

Ribbon worm

Lesson 3   R E V I E W

Write your answers to these questions on a sheet of paper.

1. What are two sources of salt in ocean water?

2. Describe how water temperature changes with ocean depth.

3. What causes most ocean waves and currents?

4. How do currents affect climate?

5. What are several features of the ocean floor?

Achievements in Science

Protecting the Environment

Today most people know the importance of clean water, land, and air. However, protecting the environment has not always been a popular concern. Before 1960, there were few laws about what people could dump in rivers, on land, or into the air. Thousands of people died from smog, or polluted air, given off by factories in London and in U.S. cities. The Cuyahoga River in Cleveland often caught on fire because of the oil floating in it. Many fish in Lake Erie died because of pollution.

By 1960 the public began to understand how chemicals and other wastes could affect their health and the environment. Rachel Carson was a biologist who helped promote this awareness. In 1962 she wrote a book that warned about the dangers of pest-killing chemicals, or pesticides, on the environment. Her book, *Silent Spring*, had a strong impact on its readers. In fact it led to the banning of DDT and other pesticides.

In 1970 the U.S. Environmental Protection Agency was created to protect people and the environment. Now federal and state laws exist to preserve and improve the quality of our water, land, and air.

Materials

- ◆ 2 small, clear plastic soft-drink bottles
- ◆ tablespoon
- ◆ table salt
- ◆ fine-tip waterproof marker
- ◆ masking tape
- ◆ drinking straw
- ◆ centimeter ruler
- ◆ modeling clay

Measuring the Effect of Salt Water on Floating

Purpose

Will an object float higher in salt water or fresh water? In this investigation, you will observe the effect of salt water on floating.

Procedure

1. Copy the data table on your paper.

Trial	Fresh Water	Salt Water
1		
2		

2. Fill the two soft-drink bottles about three-quarters full of water. Add 6 tablespoons of salt to one bottle. Carefully swirl the contents to dissolve the salt. **Safety Alert: Never taste any substances used in a science investigation. Wipe up any spills immediately.**

3. Label the saltwater bottle *S* and the freshwater bottle *F*.

4. Make a float meter. Put a 6-centimeter strip of tape along one end of a drinking straw. Mark off 0.5-centimeter lengths along the tape. Push a pea-size ball of clay onto that end of the straw.

5. Drop the float meter into the fresh water. Count how many markings on the tape stay above water. Record your observations.

6. Drop the float meter into the salt water. Count the markings above water. Record your observations.

7. Repeat steps 5 and 6 for trial 2.

Questions and Conclusions

1. In which did the meter float higher: the salt water or the fresh water?

2. Based on your results, make a general statement about how objects float in salt water compared to how they float in fresh water.

Explore Further

Design an investigation to measure and compare the floating properties of many saltwater samples. Vary the amount of salt added to the samples from 1 to 10 (or more) tablespoons. At what amount doesn't the salt completely dissolve?

Chapter 11 S U M M A R Y

- Water moves between the land, the atmosphere, and bodies of water in the water cycle.

- The earth's water includes salt water, which is too salty to drink, and fresh water, which does not contain salt. Most of the earth's water is salt water.

- Water under the earth's surface is called groundwater.

- Springs, geysers, and caves are evidence of moving groundwater.

- Groundwater moves downward in the ground and collects to form a soaked layer, the top of which is called the water table.

- Rivers and their tributaries drain runoff from large areas of land called drainage basins.

- Lakes form when water collects in a depression on land.

- Reservoirs are lakes made when people dam a river. Reservoirs store water, control flooding, and produce electricity.

- Ocean water is salt water because it contains dissolved salt.

- The temperature of ocean water decreases with depth.

- A wave is the up-and-down motion of water caused by energy from the wind.

- Currents move ocean water. Currents are caused by winds and follow the same general pattern as global winds.

- Features of the ocean floor include continental shelves and slopes, mid-ocean ridges, trenches, seamounts, and plains.

- Ocean life includes floating plankton, free-swimming nekton, and ocean floor-dwelling benthos.

Science Words

benthos, 271	drainage basin, 261	porous, 259	thermocline, 268
continental shelf, 270	geyser, 260	reservoir, 263	trench, 270
continental slope, 270	groundwater, 257	runoff, 257	tributary, 261
current, 269	mid-ocean ridge, 270	salinity, 267	water cycle, 256
divide, 261	nekton, 271	seamount, 270	water table, 259
	plankton, 271	sinkhole, 260	wave, 268
		spring, 260	

Chapter 11 R E V I E W

Word Bank

continental shelf

drainage basin

geyser

mid-ocean ridge

salinity

trench

tributary

water table

Vocabulary Review

Choose the word or phrase from the Word Bank that best completes each sentence. Write the answer on your paper.

1. A river that flows into another river is a _____.

2. The land area in which runoff flows into a river and its tributaries is a _____.

3. Underground water forms a soaked layer, the top of which is the _____.

4. Heated groundwater blasts out of the ground at a _____.

5. A deep valley on the ocean floor is called a _____.

6. A mountain chain on the ocean floor is called a _____.

7. Water with more salt has greater _____ than water with less salt.

8. A _____ extends from a shoreline out into an ocean.

Concept Review

Choose the word or phrase that best completes each sentence. Write the letter of the answer on your paper.

9. In the water cycle, water moves from oceans to the atmosphere by _____.
  A evaporation   **C** precipitation
  B condensation   **D** runoff

10. The water cycle is powered by _____.
  A oceans and rivers   **C** the water table
  B precipitation   **D** the sun's heat

11. Precipitation that doesn't evaporate or sink into the ground _____.
  A is not part of the water cycle
  B becomes groundwater
  C flows out of the ground as a spring
  D flows into streams as runoff

12. As ocean water deepens, its temperature _____.

   A gets warmer   **C** stays the same

   B gets colder   **D** varies

13. Artificial lakes that supply fresh water, control flooding, and produce electricity are called _____.

   A water tables   **C** drainage basins

   B reservoirs   **D** tributaries

14. The top of a wave is the _____.

   A trough   **B** wave height   **C** crest   **D** seamount

15. Ocean currents are caused by _____.

   A waves   **B** tides   **C** winds   **D** runoff

16. A fish swimming in an ocean is classified as _____.

   A nekton   **B** benthos   **C** plankton   **D** salinity

17. Moisture that sinks into the ground is called _____.

   A plankton   **C** surface water

   B groundwater   **D** a reservoir

Critical Thinking

Write the answer to each of the following questions.

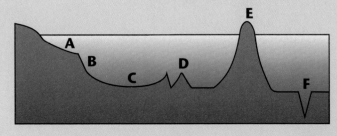

18. Refer to the diagram. Name each lettered feature of the ocean floor.

19. After a dry summer, water no longer comes up through a well. What has happened?

20. One way to make salt water fit to drink is to heat it and collect the water vapor. How is this like the water cycle?

Test-Taking Tip Before writing out an answer on a test, read the question twice to make sure you understand what it is asking.

Weathering and Erosion

Materials on the earth's surface are constantly changing. Rocks and soil break down and move. Sometimes we notice these changes. But most of the time, they happen very gradually. At one time, the tree in the photo was barely noticeable as it sprouted. What did the rock look like then? What happened to the rock as the tree grew? How did the rock crack? In Chapter 12, you will learn about the processes of weathering and erosion. You also will learn about some landforms caused by erosion.

Organize Your Thoughts

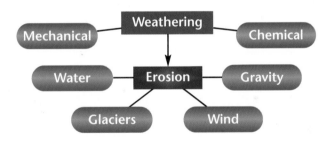

Goals for Learning

- ◆ To explain weathering and soil formation
- ◆ To describe how a river and its valley age
- ◆ To describe how water, glaciers, wind, and gravity cause erosion
- ◆ To give examples of several eroded landforms
- ◆ To describe how deposited landforms develop

The earth is constantly changing. Even a hard material like rock changes. Over the years, these carved and polished grave markers have broken down, tilted, and become discolored.

The breaking down of rocks on the earth's surface is known as **weathering**. Weathering occurs when rocks are exposed to air, water, or living things. All these factors help to break rocks apart.

How have these rocks weathered?

Weathering

Breaking down of rocks on the earth's surface

Mechanical weathering

Breaking apart of rocks without changing their mineral composition

Mechanical Weathering

In **mechanical weathering**, rocks break into smaller pieces, but their chemical makeup stays the same. The photo on page 278 shows one way that rocks break. This tree started growing in soil that collected in a small crack of the rock. As the tree grew, its roots pushed against the rock and split it. You might see this kind of mechanical weathering in a sidewalk near a tree. The growing roots often lift and crumble the sidewalk.

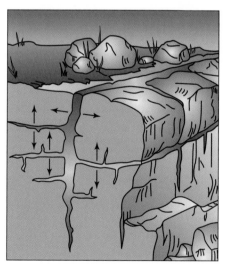

Mechanical weathering also occurs as water freezes in the cracks of rocks. When water freezes, it expands. As the freezing water expands, it pushes the rock apart, as shown in the diagram. The ice may melt, and the water may refreeze. Each time the water freezes, the cracks get bigger. Finally, the rock breaks apart.

Chemical Weathering

In **chemical weathering**, changes occur in the chemical makeup of rocks. New minerals might be added to or taken away from the rock. The minerals might be changed into new substances.

For example, in a process called **oxidation**, oxygen from the air or water combines with the iron in rocks. As a result, a new, softer substance called iron oxide, or rust, forms. Iron oxide stains rocks various shades of yellow, orange, red, or brown. How is the rocky bluff below like the rusty, old can?

A rusting can slowly crumbles.

"Rusting" rock also slowly breaks apart.

Chemical weathering also occurs when water changes minerals in the rocks. For example, the mineral feldspar is part of many rocks. Water changes feldspar to clay and washes it away. Without the feldspar to hold the other minerals together, the rock falls apart.

The limestone cave shown on the next page is the result of chemical weathering. Rain and groundwater combine with carbon dioxide in the air to form carbonic acid. This is the same acid found in carbonated soft drinks. As carbonic acid trickles through the ground, it dissolves calcite—the main mineral in limestone. As more and more limestone is dissolved, small holes become huge caves.

Soil

Mixture of tiny pieces of weathered rock and the remains of plants and animals

Topsoil

Top layer of soil, rich with oxygen and decayed organic matter

Subsoil

Layer of soil directly below the topsoil

Carlsbad Caverns are limestone caves in New Mexico.

How Soil Forms

When rock has weathered for a long time, **soil** may develop. Soil is a mixture of tiny pieces of weathered rock and the remains of plants and animals. The makeup of soil depends on the types of rock particles and remains that are found in it.

As soil develops, it forms layers. Fully developed soil has three layers. Look at the diagram as you read about soil layers.

Topsoil

Subsoil

Weathered rock

Solid rock

Most soil you see is **topsoil**. This layer has the greatest amount of oxygen and decayed organic matter. The organic matter helps the soil hold moisture.

Directly below the topsoil is the **subsoil**. It contains minerals that were washed down from the topsoil. Many of these minerals are forms of iron oxide. They give the subsoil a yellowish or reddish color. Plant roots grow into the subsoil to get minerals and water.

The next layer contains chunks of partially weathered rock. Near the bottom of this layer, rock fragments sit directly on solid rock.

Lesson 1   R E V I E W

Write your answers to these questions on a sheet of paper.

1. What factors in the environment cause weathering?

2. Name two causes of mechanical weathering.

3. Explain how a limestone cave forms.

4. What layer of soil contains the most decayed material?

5. What lies below the three layers of soil?

Technology Note

Many people study and explore caves. Maps help people find their way in unfamiliar caves without getting lost.

Early cave maps were sketched from memory and were not accurate. Today more precise cave maps are made with compasses and measuring tapes. Some maps are made with computers and electronic tools called laser range finders. Maps made with these devices accurately lay out cave features.

Computer programs allow mapmakers to gather data from cave surveys and create three-dimensional cave models. These on-screen models can be rotated to view any angle of the cave. While exploring a cave, people can use a global positioning system device to look at these computer models. These models can be used to find different cave routes and entrances.

INVESTIGATION

12-1

Materials

- hand lens
- safety glasses
- 5 limestone chips or pieces of chalk
- clear plastic, 12-ounce cup
- 1 cup of vinegar
- strainer
- water
- paper towels

Observing Chemical Weathering

Purpose

What will happen when limestone is exposed to acid? In this investigation, you will model and observe chemical weathering.

Procedure

1. Copy the data table on your paper.

Limestone	Observations
before weathering	
after weathering	

2. Use the hand lens to look at the surfaces of the limestone chips. In the data table, describe their appearance.

3. Safety Alert: Put on your safety glasses.

4. Place the chips in the cup. Pour enough vinegar into the cup to cover the chips. Let the chips sit overnight. **Safety Alert: Never taste any substances used in a science investigation. Wipe up any spills immediately.**

5. Pour the vinegar and limestone chips through a strainer over a sink. Run water over the chips to rinse off the vinegar.

6. Place the limestone chips on paper towels. Use the hand lens to look at the limestone surfaces. In the data table, describe any changes you see.

Questions and Conclusions

1. How did the surfaces of the limestone change?

2. Vinegar is an acid. What did the vinegar do to change the appearance of the limestone?

Explore Further

Design a similar experiment that varies the soaking time or uses other rocks. For example, you might soak one set of limestone chips for a day, another set for two days, another for three days, and so on. How would each set compare? What would you predict about the mass of each set before and after soaking? Another idea is to repeat the experiment using chips of sandstone, granite, and marble. Which rocks are most resistant to this kind of chemical weathering?

Erosion

Wearing away and moving of weathered rock and soil

After rock has been loosened by weathering, it is worn away and moved to another place. The wearing away and moving of weathered rock and soil is called **erosion**. The main agents, or causes, of erosion are rivers, waves, glaciers, wind, and gravity.

River Erosion

Water running downhill is a powerful force. In fact, rivers and their tributaries change more of the landscape than any other agent of erosion. After rain falls to the earth, the water flows downhill. The water pushes soil and rock fragments as it moves. These solid particles are sediment. The water and sediment flow into small gullies, which lead to rivers.

As water flows in a river, it erodes the banks and riverbed, which is the bottom of the river. Compare the eroding power of a river to a hose. The force of water from the hose can easily dig up soil and move it across a lawn. A jet of water may even chip away at a sidewalk. Similarly, river water erodes the land. Sand and stones in the river scrape against the banks and riverbed, causing more erosion. The boulders in the photo below have been worn smooth by fast-moving water and sediment.

Water and sediment act like sandpaper on these rocks in the Madison River in Wyoming.

Did You Know?

Before water-diversion projects began in the 1950s, Niagara Falls moved upriver about 1 meter per year. This was caused by eroded limestone tumbling from the top of the falls to the base of the falls.

The Life of a River Valley

As you run your finger through sand, your finger carves out a little valley. As a river erodes the land, it also carves out a valley. Some valleys are narrow with steep walls. These are called canyons. Other valleys are wide and shallow. The shape of the valley largely depends on how old it is. Rivers and their valleys go through three stages: youth, maturity, and old age. Study the diagrams below as you read about the life of a river.

A young river is narrow and fast. Its swift waters rapidly cut down through rock, carving out a V-shaped valley. The river covers all or most of the valley floor. The fast waters have a lot of energy and can push rocks along the river's path. Rapids and waterfalls are common. The Yellowstone River and Niagara River are examples of young rivers.

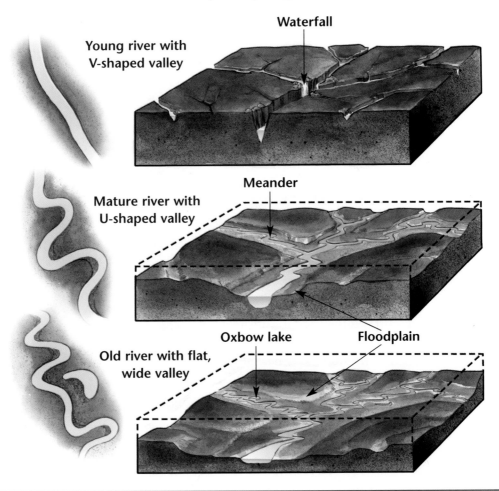

Waterfall

Young river with V-shaped valley

Meander

Mature river with U-shaped valley

Oxbow lake   Floodplain

Old river with flat, wide valley

The exact cause of meanders is not known. Objects or landforms may block the path of a river. The earth's rotation or a change in river stage may also cause a river to twist and turn.

As erosion continues, a river becomes mature. At this stage, the boulders and rocky ledges that cause rapids and waterfalls have been eroded away. The slope, or angle, of the river is less steep, so the river does not flow as fast. It can move pebbles, sand, and mud, but not large rocks. The valley of a mature river is much wider than the river itself. The Ohio River and Missouri River are mature rivers.

All rivers have curves. Mature rivers usually have more of them. Compare the rivers in the diagram on page 287. The water flows faster and pushes harder against the outside of each curve and erodes that bank faster. Water slows down on the inside of each curve, allowing sediment to settle and build up. This process creates large, looping bends called **meanders**.

As a mature river's meanders grow, its **floodplain** also grows. A floodplain is the low, flat area that a river covers when it overflows its banks. Floodwaters leave behind rich soil and nutrients on floodplains.

The valleys of old rivers are broad and flat. By this time, the river has eroded its way down to near sea level. Old rivers tend to have enlarged meanders and more of them. As a meander continues to grow, it forms almost a complete circle. During a flood, the river may break through its banks and flow straighter. The meander is cut off and becomes a C-shaped **oxbow lake**. The Mississippi River, shown in the radar image, is an old river.

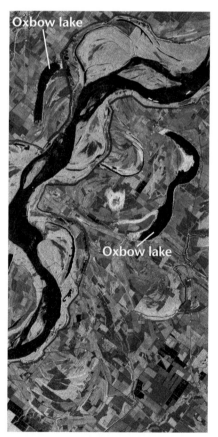

This image, taken from a space shuttle, shows oxbow lakes along the Mississippi River.

River Deposits

Deposition

Dropping of eroded sediment

Mouth

Place where a river flows into a larger body of water

Delta

Fan-shaped area of land formed when sediment is deposited where a river empties into a lake or an ocean

Alluvial fan

Fan-shaped area of land deposited where a mountain stream moves onto flat land

Sediment carried by the agents of erosion is eventually dropped in a process called **deposition**. For example, when a river slows down, it may drop, or deposit, its sediment. Heavy particles, such as stones, drop out first. As the river slows down further, lighter sediment, such as sand and clay, drops out.

A river slows down considerably as it empties into a lake or an ocean. The place where a river flows into a larger body of water is called the **mouth** of the river. Sediment settles out at the river's mouth. Eventually, the sediment builds up above the water level and forms a fan-shaped area of land called a **delta**. As the diagram below shows, a river usually branches off as it winds through the delta and empties. A delta provides rich farmland. Much of Egypt's farmland, for example, is located on the fertile Nile River delta.

An **alluvial fan** is similar to a delta. It forms at the base of a mountain where a mountain stream meets level land.

Wave Erosion

Waves in an ocean or a large lake change the shoreline through erosion and deposition. As waves pound the shoreline, they hurl not only water but also bits of rock and sand against the coast. These materials chip away at the rocky shore. Waves also force water into cracks in rocks along the shoreline. With each wave, the water presses against the sides of the cracks. The cracks get bigger, and pieces of rock split off.

This type of erosion formed the cliffs, towers, and other rocky shapes shown in the photo below. During storms, waves reach higher on cliffs and carve steep sides. Arches form when waves erode through a cliff. If the top of an arch collapses, a tower of rock called a sea stack is left standing.

How has wave erosion shaped this shoreline in Australia?

Wave Deposits

Beaches are areas where waves have deposited sand, pebbles, or shells. Some of this beach material is sediment from nearby eroded rocks. Other beach material is sediment carried to the lake or ocean by rivers. Currents near the shore carry sediment to different parts of the shoreline. As waves break on shore, the sediment is pushed onto the beach.

Currents along the shore can change the shape of a beach. One result is a spit, or curved finger of sand, sticking out into the water. Waves and currents can also carry sand away from the beach and deposit a long, underwater sandbar offshore.

Lesson 2 REVIEW

Write your answers to these questions on a sheet of paper.

1. What is erosion?

2. How does a young river differ from an old river?

3. Explain how a meander becomes an oxbow lake.

4. How does a delta differ from an alluvial fan?

5. From where does the sand on a beach come?

Science in Your Life

Erosion Caused by People

People's actions sometimes cause too much erosion. This can be harmful to the environment and to people. One way that people increase erosion is by using off-road vehicles (ORVs) such as dirt bikes, dune buggies, and all-terrain vehicles. Their overuse has damaged land and threatened the survival of plants and animals.

The photo below illustrates this problem. This hillside used to be covered with grass. The roots of grass and other plants hold soil in place and catch water runoff. Animals use the plants and the areas around them as habitats. Many of the plants are food for animals.

Within weeks, ORVs dug up the vegetation and created ruts. When it rained, the rainwater followed these ruts and formed deep gullies. The exposed soil now erodes quickly from the hill. Areas have been set aside for ORVs, but some people go into closed areas.

Are there areas around your home where people are causing erosion? Go for a walk and take your own survey. Look for evidence of erosion from human activity. Can you think of ways to prevent this erosion?

INVESTIGATION

12-2

Comparing Erosion

Purpose

Do the trees, shrubs, and plants growing on a hillside help prevent erosion? In this investigation, you will find out if vegetation affects erosion.

Procedure

1. Cover your work surface with newspaper. Spread a layer of soil in each paint tray to a depth of about 5 centimeters. Cover only the part of the tray that gently slopes downward. This will model a hillside. Wet or pack the soil a little if necessary so that it stays on the hillside.

2. Plant a handful of grass seeds evenly in the soil of one tray. Wash your hands and clean your work space. Place the trays side by side on clean newspaper.

3. Gently water the seeds every day for about a week, until the grass grows a few centimeters. **Safety Alert: Wipe up any spills immediately.**

4. Copy the data table on your paper.

Trial	Bare Soil	Soil with Grass
1		
2		
3		
4		
5		

5. Sprinkle water over each tray for 5 seconds. Sprinkle toward the top of the tray so that the water can run down the hill. In the data table, record your observations about how the water runs down each hill and how much erosion occurs.

Materials

◆ newspaper
◆ 2 paint trays
◆ soil
◆ grass seeds
◆ sprinkling can
◆ water

6. Repeat the 5-second sprinkling four more times. Record your observations after each sprinkling.

Questions and Conclusions

1. What differences in water flow did you observe between the two hillsides?

2. What differences in erosion did you observe between the two hillsides?

3. What differences did you observe about the color of the water at the bottom of the two trays?

4. How can you use the results of this experiment to prevent unwanted erosion in areas near your home?

Explore Further

Do certain kinds of vegetation reduce erosion better than others? Redesign the experiment to find out.

Objectives

After reading this lesson, you should be able to

◆ define two types of glaciers.

◆ explain how glaciers erode the land.

◆ describe features caused by glaciers.

Glacier

Thick mass of ice that covers a large area

Two conditions are needed for glaciers to form: year-round cold temperatures and heavy snowfall. Siberia in northern Russia has constant cold weather. But because it receives little snowfall, no glaciers form there.

In cold climates, water falls as snow. This snow can build up into thick layers. If the snow does not melt, increasing pressure causes the snow below to form solid ice. Year after year, more ice builds up. Eventually, a **glacier** may form. A glacier is a thick mass of ice that covers a large area. Glaciers may be as small as a football field or hundreds of kilometers long.

Glaciers form only where average temperatures stay below freezing. So they are found only in mountain regions and near the poles. Glaciers in mountain regions are called alpine glaciers. They move slowly downhill. Notice how the alpine glacier in the photo below extends down the valley. Glaciers that cover broad areas of land near the poles are called continental glaciers. Continental glaciers cover most of Antarctica and Greenland.

The Muldrow Glacier in Alaska flows down the north side of Mount McKinley. It is a popular climbing route.

Cirque

Bowl-like basin in a mountain that is carved out by an alpine glacier

Horn

Jagged, pyramid-shaped peak formed by the intersection of three or more cirques

Gravity causes glaciers to move. As glaciers move, they pick up loose sediment. Because of their great size, glaciers move huge boulders and soil. These materials freeze onto the bottom and sides of the glacier. They act like grinding and cutting tools as the glacier continues to move. The photo below shows how large rocks in the bottom of a glacier cut long grooves in the surface rock. Small rocks in a glacier act like sandpaper, smoothing and shaping the land beneath.

This limestone cliff on Kelleys Island in Lake Erie was carved by a glacier.

A horn forms where several cirques come together.

Alpine Glaciers

Alpine glaciers begin in the upper reaches of mountain valleys. As they begin to move, these glaciers carve out bowl-shaped basins called **cirques**. Several cirques around the top of the mountain may form a pyramid-shaped peak called a **horn**. The Matterhorn in Switzerland, shown in the photo on the left, is one of the most famous horns.

Before it was covered with a glacier, a mountain valley may have been shaped by a river. The valley would have had a typical V shape. As the glacier moves down the mountain, it gouges out the valley like a giant ice cream scoop. As a result, the V-shaped valley becomes a U-shaped valley.

The glacier continues to move down the mountain until it reaches temperatures warm enough to melt. As the ice melts, it deposits sediment. The sediment forms ridges called **moraines**. Moraines are the "footprints," or evidence, of a glacier, telling us it was here. In the photo, notice the U-shaped valley, glacial lake, and moraines. Trace the glacier's path with your finger.

Some glaciers move into a body of water before they melt. When a piece of a glacier breaks off in the water, it becomes an iceberg.

This Montana scene shows where a glacier slid down a mountain valley and melted. Trees now grow on the moraines around the lake.

Ice shelves are continental glaciers that extend over water. Antarctica is surrounded by many ice shelves. Ice caps are small, dome-shaped continental glaciers. Part of Iceland is covered by an ice cap.

Continental Glaciers

Continental glaciers are up to 4 kilometers thick. Because of their tremendous size and weight, these glaciers transform the surface of the land. They change the courses of rivers and create lakes great and small. Continental glaciers can even move boulders the size of houses hundreds of kilometers.

About 10 percent of the earth is currently covered by glaciers. Most of these glaciers are the continental glaciers that cover Antarctica and Greenland. These two large land areas are often shown in white on maps and globes.

Continental glaciers covered parts of North America and Europe long ago. How do we know? Like alpine glaciers, continental glaciers mark their boundaries by leaving behind moraines. The map shows the location of major moraines surrounding the Great Lakes. These moraines are left from the last ice age, when much of the Northern Hemisphere was covered by continental glaciers. This ice age started more than a million years ago and ended about 10,000 years ago.

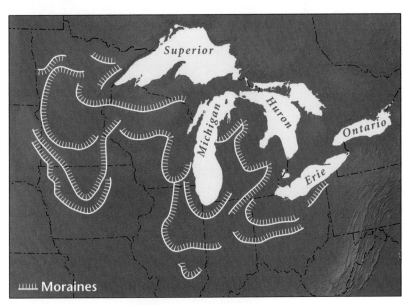

At the end of this ice age, the glaciers began to melt. Huge blocks of ice broke off from the glaciers. As shown below, these blocks became partly buried in sediment. When an ice block melted, it left a hole in the ground. The hole filled with water. Many of the small lakes in Wisconsin and Minnesota formed this way.

Large lakes formed from these continental glaciers, too. Some glaciers carved wide, deep basins. As they melted, the glaciers filled the basins with water. Moraines dammed parts of the lakes. This process created the Great Lakes, the Finger Lakes in New York, and Lake Winnipeg in Canada.

1. An ice block breaks off a glacier.

2. The ice block gets partly buried in sediment.

3. The ice block melts to form a lake.

Lesson 3 REVIEW

Write your answers to these questions on a sheet of paper.

1. Describe the two kinds of glaciers.

2. How does a glacier erode the land as the glacier moves?

3. How does a horn form?

4. How does a moraine form?

5. Describe how the Great Lakes formed.

Achievements in Science

Artificial Glaciers

A new process is being developed to capture and hold water needed for crops. This process creates artificial glaciers. Some scientists think artificial glaciers may someday help many water-starved villages around the world.

Chewang Norphel, an engineer from Ladakh, India, has experimented with artificial glaciers. Norphel wanted to solve the water shortage in Ladakh. This farming village is located high in the Himalayas. It gets very little rain.

In the 1990s, Norphel helped Ladakh build five artificial glaciers. The new glaciers increased the village's water supply and improved farming.

Creating the glaciers was simple. Before winter set in, water from an existing stream was piped to valley areas. Then this water was forced to flow downhill. Along the way, stone walls were built to stop the water flow and form pools. As temperatures fell, the pools froze. The process of flowing, pooling, and freezing was repeated for many weeks. The pools became thick sheets of ice—artificial glaciers.

It cost only $2,000 to build Ladakh's glaciers. Because of the success of Norphel's experiment, interest in artificial glaciers is growing. A major project to create glaciers in Pakistan has already begun.

Lesson 4 — Erosion Caused by Wind and Gravity

Objectives

After reading this lesson, you should be able to

◆ describe how wind erodes land.

◆ explain how sand dunes form.

◆ identify examples of erosion by gravity.

Did You Know?

Some sand dunes in the Sahara, a desert in Africa, grow to be hundreds of meters tall.

Science Myth

Many people think of deserts as hot, sandy places.

Fact: Deserts are harsh environments with little rainfall and extreme temperatures. Parts of frozen Antarctica are considered deserts.

Wind Erosion and Deposits

Wind is another cause of erosion. Like water, wind picks up and carries materials from one place to another. Wind also erodes by blowing sand against rock. This action is similar to a sandblaster used to clean buildings discolored by pollution. If you have ever been stung in the face by windblown sand, you know wind can be an effective agent of erosion. Much rock in desert areas is pitted with tiny holes from windblown sand.

You are probably familiar with wind deposits called sand dunes. These are mounds formed as the wind blows sand from one place to another. Sand dunes are most common in deserts, but they also occur around beaches.

Wind may bounce sand along the ground until it hits an obstacle, such as a small rock. A small sand pile forms behind the rock. The pile blocks other sand grains, and a larger mound forms. The mound continues to grow, forming a sand dune. The dune moves as wind blows sand up the gentle slope and deposits it on the steeper back slope, as shown below.

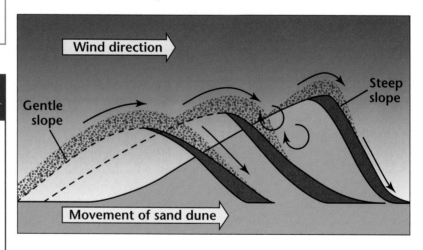

The Role of Gravity in Erosion

Gravity plays a part in all erosion. For example, rivers and alpine glaciers flow because of gravity. Gravity can move only material that has been loosened in some way. One way rock and soil are loosened is by freezing and thawing. Another way this happens is by heavy rains. A great deal of water can make soil smooth and slippery. Soil in this condition flows easily. When material on a hillside is loosened, gravity can cause rapid erosion. Mudflows and landslides are examples of this.

The photo below shows how gravity can make erosion happen rapidly. This hillside was loosened until it gave way to gravity's downward pull. In this case, the result was a landslide that damaged a Colorado road. Have you ever seen a sign that reads Caution: Falling Rock? Then you know about another result of erosion by gravity.

Gravity works slowly, too. You may have noticed old telephone poles or grave markers that tilt downhill. Loose soil and rocks move slowly downhill, tilting objects along the way.

This road in the Rocky Mountains crosses an area of landslide activity.

Write your answers to these questions on a sheet of paper.

1. What are two ways that wind erodes the land?

2. How does a sand dune form?

3. Where do sand dunes form?

4. Give examples of erosion caused by gravity.

5. How are rocks and soil loosened?

Science at Work

Floodplain Manager

Flooding can cause great loss, damage, and danger to people and the environment. Rebuilding after a flood is costly. Floodplain managers help prevent floods and reduce flood damage. They also protect water and soil resources.

Floodplain managers inspect systems that hold storm water. Floodplain managers make sure that builders follow rules for excavating, or digging, at construction sites. They also meet with government officials and city planners.

Many floodplain managers have a bachelor's degree in civil engineering. Some local governments offer floodplain management training programs. These training programs focus on storm water runoff, erosion control, and rules to prevent water pollution.

Floodplain managers should have a strong math and science background. They should be able to understand blueprints and maps. Computer and communication skills are also important. A good floodplain manager cares about the environment and safety.

Chapter 12 SUMMARY

- All rock exposed at the surface begins to break apart.

- Mechanical weathering is the process of breaking up rocks without changing their mineral makeup.

- Chemical weathering is the process of breaking up rocks by changing the minerals in them.

- Soil is a mixture of weathered rock and the remains of plants and animals.

- Fully developed soil includes a topsoil, a subsoil, and a layer of partially weathered rock.

- The process by which weathered rock bits and soil are moved is called erosion.

- Erosion is caused by water, glaciers, wind, and gravity.

- As a river erodes the land, it carves out a valley. Rivers and valleys change with time.

- A river deposits sediment where it flows into a lake or an ocean, forming a delta.

- Waves wear away the shoreline in some places and build it up in others.

- Glaciers are moving masses of ice. Alpine glaciers move down mountains. Continental glaciers cover broad areas of land.

- Glaciers form U-shaped valleys and scrape the land.

- Glaciers leave ridges of sediment called moraines. Glaciers have formed many lakes.

- Wind causes erosion by carrying sediment and by blowing it against rock.

- Sand dunes form as sand collects into a huge mound.

- Gravity moves rock and soil downhill. This process can occur quickly or slowly.

Science Words

alluvial fan, 289
chemical
 weathering, 281
cirque, 295
delta, 289
deposition, 289

erosion, 286
floodplain, 288
glacier, 294
horn, 295
meander, 288

mechanical
 weathering, 280
moraine, 296
mouth, 289
oxbow lake, 288

oxidation, 281
soil, 282
subsoil, 282
topsoil, 282
weathering, 280

Chapter 12 R E V I E W

Word Bank

alpine

cirque

delta

erosion

horn

meander

moraine

oxbow lake

soil

weathering

Vocabulary Review

Choose the word or phrase from the Word Bank that best completes each sentence. Write the answer on your paper.

1. The process of moving weathered rock and soil is _____.

2. Sediment settles out where a river empties into an ocean, forming a(n) _____.

3. The breaking down of rocks on the earth's surface is _____.

4. A large, looping curve in a river is a(n) _____.

5. Several cirques can intersect to form a jagged _____.

6. A mixture of bits of weathered rock and decayed material is _____.

7. Glaciers that form in mountain valleys are _____ glaciers.

8. Rock and sediment that drop from a glacier form a ridge called a(n) _____.

9. A C-shaped body of water formed when a meander is cut off is a(n) _____.

10. A bowl-shaped basin carved out of a mountain by an alpine glacier is a(n) _____.

Concept Review

Choose the word or phrase that best completes each sentence. Write the letter of the answer on your paper.

11. Two characteristics of a young river are a _____.
   A U-shaped valley and slow-moving water
   B V-shaped valley and fast-moving water
   C wide valley and many meanders
   D shallow valley and oxbow lakes

12. During oxidation, oxygen combines with iron to form iron oxide, or _____.

A clay   **B** carbonic acid   **C** feldspar   **D** rust

13. The land covered by an overflowing river is the river's _____.

A floodplain   **C** delta
B water table   **D** topsoil

14. Water freezing in the cracks of rocks is an example of _____.

A deposition   **C** mechanical weathering
B chemical weathering   **D** erosion

15. The main process that forms a beach is _____.

A weathering   **C** deposition
B erosion   **D** oxidation

16. An alluvial fan forms at the base of a mountain and is similar to a _____.

A sand dune   **B** cirque   **C** glacier   **D** delta

Critical Thinking

Write the answer to each of the following questions.

17. Name each lettered layer shown in the diagram.

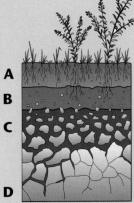

18. Why would a farmer plow across a hillside instead of plowing straight down the slope?

19. Once a rock breaks into pieces, weathering occurs faster. Explain why.

20. Sand dunes near a beach are being blown toward a neighborhood. Residents want to keep the dunes, but they don't want the blowing sand. What can they do?

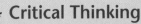

Test-Taking Tip   When studying for a test, use the titles and subtitles within a chapter to help you recall information.

13 Forces in the Earth

Red hot lava bursts forth as the Piton de la Fournaise Volcano erupts. This volcano is on an island in the Indian Ocean. What forces deep inside the earth cause such an awesome event? Why do volcanoes occur only in some locations? The answers to these questions begin with the ground on which we stand. It is moving. We usually don't notice it. But a fiery volcano or a shattering earthquake reminds us that the earth's surface and the material beneath it are moving. In Chapter 13, you will discover how parts of the earth move and what happens when they do.

Organize Your Thoughts

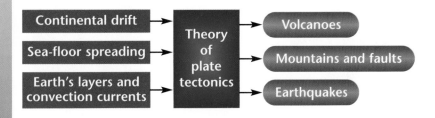

Goals for Learning

◆ To describe the structure of the earth

◆ To explain the theory of plate tectonics

◆ To relate volcanoes to plate tectonics

◆ To explain how mountains and faults form

◆ To relate earthquakes to plate tectonics

The Earth's Layers

Although we cannot directly see the interior of the earth, scientists use instruments to collect data about it. These data are used to make a model of what the inside of the earth is like.

The earth is made up of three main layers. At the center is a dense **core**. The core is solid iron and nickel, surrounded by melted iron and nickel. The core is about 3,500 kilometers thick. Outside the core is the **mantle**. The mantle is made of liquid and solid rock that moves and churns. The entire mantle is about 2,900 kilometers thick. The outermost layer of the earth is the **crust**. Compared to the other layers, the crust is very thin and cold. It is between 8 and 70 kilometers thick. The continents and ocean floor are part of the crust. The thickest part of the crust is found below large mountain ranges.

Objectives

After reading this lesson, you should be able to

◆ identify the earth's layers.

◆ explain continental drift, sea-floor spreading, and plate tectonics.

Core

Dense center of the earth made of solid and melted metals

Mantle

Layer of the earth that surrounds the core

Crust

Outer layer of the earth

The most abundant element inside the earth—including its crust, mantle, and core—is iron.

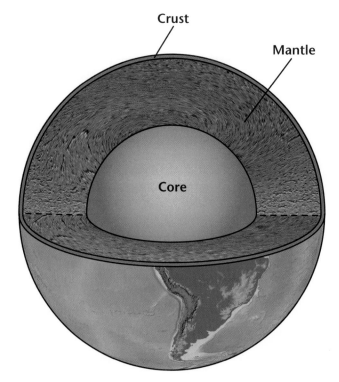

Crust

Mantle

Core

Continental Drift

Continental drift

Theory that the major landmasses of the earth move

Pangaea

Single landmass from which Alfred Wegener thought the continents separated millions of years ago

A theory, such as Wegener's theory of continental drift, is a possible explanation for many related observations.

Have you ever noticed that some continents, such as Africa and South America, look as if they might fit together? In 1912, a German scientist named Alfred Wegener proposed the theory of **continental drift** to explain why.

According to this theory, the earth's continents used to be joined as a single, large landmass called **Pangaea**. Wegener believed Pangaea started breaking up millions of years ago. The continents slowly moved to their present positions.

225 million years ago

180 million years ago

Present day

Besides the puzzle fit of the continents, Wegener had other evidence to support his theory. For example, fossils found on one continent were similar to those found on other continents. Mountain ranges and rock layers seemed to continue from one continent to another. In addition, glacial deposits were found at the equator where no glaciers could exist. Could the glacial deposits have formed when the continents were in a different place? Wegener thought so.

Sea-Floor Spreading

After World War II, new instruments allowed scientists to map the ocean floor. Here is what scientists discovered about the long, underwater mountain ranges called mid-ocean ridges:

◆ A rift valley splits these ridges in half.
◆ The amount of heat coming from a mid-ocean ridge is almost eight times greater than the heat from other parts of the ocean floor.
◆ Magma rises from beneath the ocean floor through cracks in the rift.
◆ The age of the ocean floor increases with distance from a ridge.

The theory of **sea-floor spreading** explains these observations. This theory states that hot magma from the mantle rises and pours out onto the ocean floor through cracks in a rift. The magma cools, hardens, and forms new crust. This new crust piles up around the rift, forming a mid-ocean ridge. More rising magma pushes the new crust away on both sides of the ridge. This process widens the oceans and pushes the continents apart.

Plate Tectonics

The ideas of sea-floor spreading and continental drift have led to one of the most important theories in science—**plate tectonics**. This theory states that the earth's crust is made of large sections, or **plates**. As shown on the map, most plates include ocean crust and continental crust.

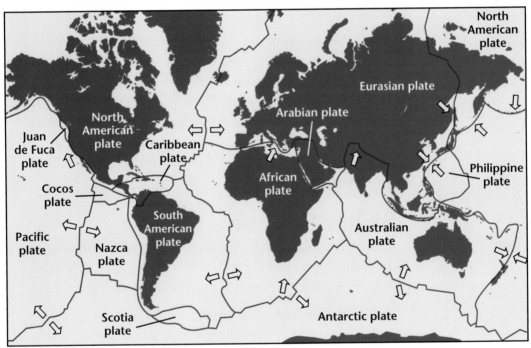

⇨ **Plate movement** — **Plate boundary**

Plates move in three different ways: they move apart, collide, or slide past each other. How they move determines what happens where they meet.

Look at the diagram below. The South American and African plates are moving apart. Where plates move apart, a rift forms. The Nazca and South American plates are moving toward each other. Here the Nazca plate is forced under the South American plate, forming a deep trench. The Nazca plate melts as it sinks into the mantle. Some plates slide past each other. The map on page 310 shows the Pacific plate sliding northwest past the North American plate.

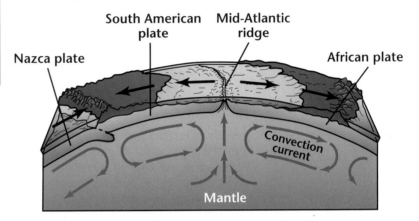

The pushing, pulling, and grinding of plates cause volcanoes and earthquakes. Magma that reaches the surface produces volcanoes where plates collide or spread apart. You will learn more about volcanoes and earthquakes later in this chapter.

Convection Currents

The last piece in the plate tectonics puzzle is what causes the plates to move. In other words, why does magma rise at mid-ocean ridges in the first place? Most scientists think the answer is **convection currents**. A convection current is the circular movement of a liquid or gas as it heats. Convection currents in the partly melted upper mantle can push the plates along as if on a conveyor belt. Look at the convection currents shown in the diagram above. Compare their movement to the movement of the plates.

Write the answers to these questions on a sheet of paper.

1. Describe the layers of the earth.

2. What is the theory of continental drift?

3. Explain how mid-ocean ridges probably formed.

4. What is the theory of plate tectonics?

5. Why do the earth's plates move?

Achievements in Science

The Theory of Sea-Floor Spreading

How did scientists discover the underwater mountain ranges known as mid-ocean ridges? They used a tool called sonar. Sonar is a device that bounces sound waves off underwater objects. The echoes of these sound waves are recorded. The time it takes for the echo to reach the sonar device tells how far away the object is. This information allowed scientists to map mid-ocean ridges.

How did scientists connect mid-ocean ridges to sea-floor spreading? They took a dive to the ocean floor in *Alvin,* a deep-sea submersible. *Alvin* can stand up to the crushing water pressure at the ocean bottom. *Alvin's* crew took pictures of rocks that looked like toothpaste squeezed from a giant tube. These strange rocks were igneous rocks. They form when liquid rock erupts from deep in the earth and quickly cools. The rocks showed evidence of many eruptions. Scientists think these eruptions from mid-ocean ridges pushed the ocean floor to the sides. This pushing is sea-floor spreading.

More evidence of sea-floor spreading came from rock samples. Scientists on a ship drilled through 6 kilometers of water. The drills took samples of the ocean floor around a ridge. The scientists determined the ages of the rock samples. They discovered that samples taken farthest from the ridge were the oldest. The youngest rocks were at the center of the ridge. This was more evidence of sea-floor spreading.

How Volcanoes Form

A **volcano** is a mountain that builds around a **vent**, or opening, where magma pushes up through the surface of the earth. The mountain is shaped like a cone. It is built up by rock particles, ash, and hardened lava that erupt from the volcano. Some of this erupted material is so tiny that it is carried by the wind for several kilometers before landing.

The vent at the top of a volcano may look like a funnel-shaped crater. A wider opening forms if the crater's walls collapse into the vent. Sometimes the top part of a volcano is completely blown off by a large eruption.

Most volcanoes form where two plates meet. For example, Mount St. Helens in Washington formed where the Juan de Fuca plate sinks beneath the North American plate. The sinking Juan de Fuca plate melts into magma, which then rises to the surface. Where plates collide beneath the oceans, the volcanoes may rise above sea level to form islands. The Aleutian Islands of Alaska and the islands of Japan formed this way.

Objectives

After reading this lesson, you should be able to

◆ explain how volcanoes form.

◆ describe three types of volcanoes.

Volcano

Mountain that develops where magma pushes up through the earth's surface

Vent

Round opening through which magma reaches the surface of the earth

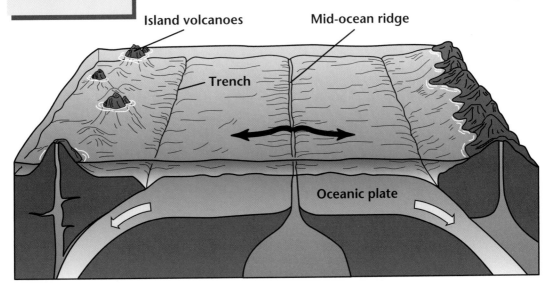

Island volcanoes

Mid-ocean ridge

Trench

Oceanic plate

Types of Volcanoes

Volcanoes are grouped into three types. This grouping is based on how the volcano erupts, the material that comes out, and the shape of the volcano. Compare the photos to the following descriptions.

Cinder cones are small volcanoes with steep sides and narrow bases. Their eruptions are explosive, shooting ash and igneous rock high into the air. Because of this, cinder cones are built up with layers of loose rock particles. Most cinder cones are less than 500 meters high. These small volcanoes are found in western North America and in other parts of the world.

Paricutín is a large, well-known cinder cone in Mexico. It began in 1943 when hot gas and lava came out of cracks in a cornfield. It erupted ash, rock, and lava almost constantly for 9 years. It grew to 410 meters high. In 1952, this cinder cone stopped erupting. Paricutín provided a rare opportunity for geologists to watch the birth, life, and death of a volcano.

Sunset Crater Volcano in Arizona is a cinder cone.

Kilauea Volcano on the island of Hawaii is a shield volcano. It has been erupting constantly since 1983. The photo on the cover of this book shows the lava from this volcano flowing over a cliff and into the ocean.

Shield volcanoes are low and broad with wide craters. They are not very explosive. Thin basalt lava flows from their quiet eruptions. Shield volcanoes are built up by layer after layer of lava that has spread out and hardened.

Mauna Loa Volcano in Hawaii is the largest volcano in the world. This shield volcano extends down to the ocean floor.

Composite volcanoes form when gentle eruptions of lava alternate with explosive eruptions of ash and rock. The gentle eruptions add thin layers of lava to the mountain. The explosive eruptions add rocky layers. Composite volcanoes grow to be very tall.

Mount Fuji in Japan is a composite volcano.

Write the answers to these questions on a sheet of paper.

1. What is a volcano?

2. How do volcanoes relate to plate tectonics?

3. What are the characteristics of a cinder cone?

4. Describe a shield volcano.

5. How do composite volcanoes form?

Science in Your Life

Living on a Tectonic Plate

Earthquakes and volcanoes usually occur where two tectonic plates come together. If you live on or near a plate boundary, you may know people who have experienced an earthquake or volcano. Perhaps you have experienced one yourself. What is the best way to prepare for these events? What should you do in such an emergency?

Many cities lie close to or on plate boundaries. Builders design structures in these cities to withstand the force of earthquakes. The worker in the photo is strengthening a freeway support in a city affected by earthquakes.

A new product may help to reduce earthquake damage to buildings. It is called magnetorheological (MR) fluid. It is a mixture of oil and metal particles. When exposed to a magnetic force, MR fluid thickens into a material like cold peanut butter. It changes back to a liquid when the magnetic force is gone.

Since earthquakes cause strong magnetic forces, scientists are testing MR fluid as a possible shock absorber for buildings. The fluid can be put in special containers controlled by a computer. Hundreds of these devices can be placed within a building's structure. When an earthquake hits, these devices can respond by cushioning and supporting the building.

Objectives

After reading this lesson, you should be able to

◆ describe two ways that mountains form (in addition to volcanoes).

◆ identify forces that cause mountains to form.

◆ name three types of movement along faults.

You may have heard the expression "as old as the hills." In fact, mountains and hills are still being built. The process is usually so slow, however, that you don't notice it. Movements of the earth's crust cause these landforms to rise above the surrounding landscape.

Folding Plates

Mountains can form when plates collide. You have already read about how volcanic mountains form when one plate sinks beneath another. This usually happens when a dense ocean plate collides with a continental plate. The Cascade Range in northwestern United States and the Andes in Peru were built this way.

When a continental plate collides with another continental plate, the plates usually crumple like a rug. The rock layers of the plates bend without breaking, as shown in the diagram. This process is called **folding**. Folding can occur either where the two plates meet or somewhere in the middle of a plate. The Himalayas in Asia were formed where two plates met and folded.

Folding

Bending of rock layers that are squeezed together

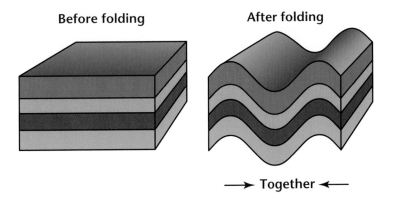

Before folding   **After folding**

⟶ **Together** ⟵

Faults

Fault

Break in the earth's crust along which movement occurs

Normal fault

Break in the crust in which the overhanging block of rock has slid down

Reverse fault

Break in the crust in which the overhanging block of rock has been raised

Strike-slip fault

Break in the crust in which the blocks of rock move horizontally past each other

When pressed together, some rocks break rather than bend. A **fault** is a break in the earth's crust along which movement occurs. Some faults are visible on the earth's surface. Most faults, however, are deep underground. Rock movement along faults can cause mountains to form.

There are three types of faults shown in the diagram below. In a **normal fault**, the two sides of the fault pull apart. The overhanging rock on one side drops down. In a **reverse fault**, the two sides push together. The overhanging rock on one side is pushed up. In a **strike-slip fault**, blocks of rock slide against each other horizontally. The San Andreas fault in California is a strike-slip fault.

Blocks of rock along a fault usually move short distances at a time. When enough pressure builds up, the rocks move and the pressure is released. When the pressure builds up again, more movement occurs.

Over time, movement along faults can raise large blocks of rock, forming mountains. Rock movement along faults built the Grand Tetons of Wyoming and the Wasatch Range of Utah.

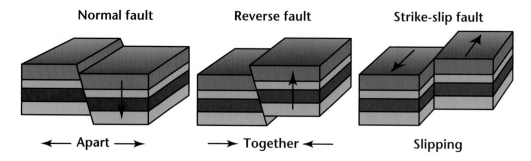

Normal fault ← Apart →

Reverse fault → Together ←

Strike-slip fault Slipping

Science Myth

Some people may think that a fault is a single crack on the earth's surface.

Fact: A fault is a deep break in the earth's crust. Most faults are very long and travel far underground. Because of this, many smaller faults actually make up a large fault.

Lesson 3 **REVIEW**

Write the answers to these questions on a sheet of paper.

1. What are three ways that mountains form?

2. Define folding.

3. What is a fault?

4. Compare the direction of movement in a reverse fault and in a strike-slip fault.

5. How do normal faults differ from reverse faults?

Technology Note

Earthquakes are best known for causing destruction. But the data collected by studying earthquakes can be useful. In the next lesson, you will learn that earthquakes cause energy waves to travel through the earth. Scientists use these waves to learn about the interior of the earth. With a technique called seismic tomography, they can even create images of the earth's flowing mantle.

To understand this technique, think of turning on a lamp in a dark room. The lamp sends out light waves. These waves light up things so you can see them. Seismic tomography uses earthquake waves to "light up" the earth's interior.

The process is not an easy one. First, a computer processes wave data from thousands of recent earthquakes. Then this information is used to make a series of images. Each image represents a slice of the earth's interior. When the slices are put together, a three-dimensional picture of the earth is produced. This picture provides information about convection currents within the earth's mantle.

INVESTIGATION

Making Models of Folding and Faults

Materials

◆ 2 thick telephone books or catalogs

Purpose

How could you model the formation of mountains? In this investigation, you will model the movement of rock layers where folding and faults occur.

Procedure

1. Copy the data table on your paper.

Type of Rock Movement	Sketch of Model

2. Work with a partner to model folding rock layers. Have your partner hold a telephone book as shown below. Your partner should grasp it firmly with both hands.

3. Have your partner slowly push both hands together, squeezing the book. In the data table, sketch the folds that appear and record the type of rock movement you modeled.

4. Switch places and repeat step 3 so your partner has a turn to sketch.

5. Use two telephone books to model rock layers along a fault. With your partner, hold the books together as shown above. Be sure to place the book spines at an angle.

6. Slowly move the books to model rock movement at a normal fault. If needed, refer to the diagram on page 318.

7. Sketch what happens to the books and record the type of movement you modeled.

8. Repeat steps 6 and 7 two more times, modeling rock movement along a reverse fault and then along a strike-slip fault.

Questions and Conclusions

1. What kind of plate motion might produce the change you saw in step 3?

2. Compare and contrast the motion of the rock layers you modeled for a normal fault and a reverse fault.

3. How did you move the books to model a strike-slip fault?

4. How do the models demonstrate mountain building?

Explore Further

Use modeling clay to create a model of a normal fault, a reverse fault, and a strike-slip fault. Use arrow labels to show the direction of movement in each model. What other ways can you model faults?

What does it feel like when you sit in the bleachers at a sporting event? When someone stands up, sits down, or walks nearby, you probably feel the bleachers shake. Shaking also occurs in the rocks of the earth's crust. This shaking is called an **earthquake**.

Causes of Earthquakes

An earthquake is a shaking of the earth's crust that occurs when energy is suddenly released. An erupting volcano releases energy and causes some earthquakes. But most earthquakes occur when rocks break or move suddenly along a fault. For example, two blocks of rock that are sliding past each other may get snagged on the jagged rocky sides. Friction holds the blocks together, but they are still being pushed. Energy builds up. When the pushing overcomes the friction, the blocks move suddenly and a lot of energy is released, causing an earthquake.

Earthquake

Shaking of the earth's crust

Like volcanoes, most earthquakes occur near plate boundaries. This is where most fault movements occur. In fact, the boundary between two plates that are sliding past each other is a large fault. Smaller faults occur near such large faults. An example of this is the San Andreas fault along the coast of California. This large fault is where the Pacific plate meets the North American plate. When these plates suddenly slip, an earthquake occurs. Many smaller faults branch off this large fault.

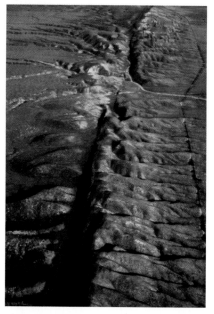

The entire San Andreas fault system is about 1,300 kilometers long. In some places, it cuts deeper than 16 kilometers into the earth.

Seismograph

Instrument that detects and records earthquake waves

Earthquake Waves

The energy from an earthquake travels through rock in waves. There are three different types of earthquake waves. Primary waves, or P-waves, cause rock particles to vibrate back and forth. Secondary waves, or S-waves, cause rocks to vibrate up and down or side to side. Both P-waves and S-waves travel inside the earth. When P-waves or S-waves reach the earth's surface, they cause long waves, or L-waves. L-waves travel along the surface of the earth. L-waves are the most destructive of earthquake waves because they cause the ground to bend and twist.

Earthquake waves are detected by an instrument called a **seismograph**, shown below. A seismograph uses a suspended pen that does not move and a roll of paper that does move. When the earth shakes, the paper chart also shakes. This makes the pen record a jagged line instead of a straight one. A seismograph records all three kinds of earthquake waves. P-waves are recorded first. They move the fastest and are the first to arrive at the recording station. P-waves also make the shortest lines on the chart. S-waves follow the P-waves. S-waves make longer lines. The L-waves arrive last. They make the longest lines. In the diagram below, you can see how the recordings of the different waves look.

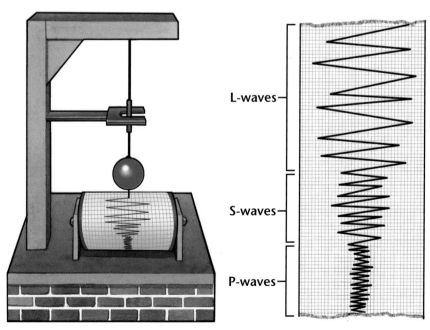

Locating the Epicenter

The point inside the earth where the earthquake starts is called the **focus**. The point on the earth's surface directly above the focus is called the **epicenter**. Scientists can pinpoint the epicenter of an earthquake. To do this, they compare the arrival times of the P-waves and the S-waves.

To locate the epicenter, scientists compare seismograph readings from at least three locations. For example, suppose Station A detects waves that show an earthquake started 100 kilometers away. On a map, a circle with a 100-kilometer radius is drawn around Station A. Readings at Station B put the earthquake at 200 kilometers away. So, a 200-kilometer-radius circle is drawn around Station B. Readings at Station C show the earthquake to be 50 kilometers away. A circle with a 50-kilometer radius is drawn around Station C. The point where the three circles meet is the earthquake's epicenter.

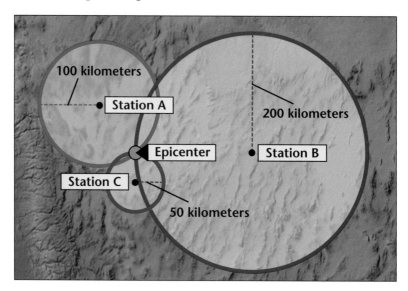

Earthquake Strength and Its Effect

The strength of an earthquake is measured on the **Richter scale**. This scale is based on seismograph wave measurements. The Richter scale assigns every earthquake a number from 1 to 9. Each number represents an earthquake that is 10 times stronger than the next lowest number. The strongest earthquake ever recorded had a measurement of 8.9 on this scale.

The effect of an earthquake on a given region depends on the strength of the earthquake and the distance from the epicenter. Earthquakes can cause great damage and loss of life. Most injuries result from the collapse of buildings, bridges, and other structures in heavily populated areas.

An earthquake damaged this Los Angeles, California, highway in 1994.

Even earthquakes on the ocean floor can cause much damage. They may trigger **tsunamis**, or large sea waves. A tsunami may reach a height of 35 meters, as tall as a 10-story building. Large tsunamis can destroy coastal towns.

Predicting Earthquakes

Scientists hope to save lives by learning to predict where and when an earthquake will occur. They watch for several signs. For example, a sudden drop in the level of well water often precedes an earthquake. Bulges in the earth's surface near a fault could indicate the buildup of stress. Near a fault, seismic activity produces an almost constant occurrence of P-waves and S-waves. A change in the speed of the P-waves may signal a coming earthquake. Scientists use these clues to predict earthquakes. If earthquakes could be accurately predicted, many lives could be saved.

Write the answers to these questions on a sheet of paper.

1. What is an earthquake?

2. What instrument is used to measure earthquake waves?

3. Compare and contrast the three kinds of earthquake waves.

4. Describe how the Richter scale is used to identify an earthquake's strength.

5. What two factors determine the effect of an earthquake?

▼◄▲▼◄▲▼◄▲▼◄▲▼◄▲▼◄▲▼◄▲▼◄▲▼◄▲▼◄▲▼◄▲▼◄▲▼◄▲▼◄▲▼◄▲▼◄▲▼◄▲▼

Science at Work

Seismologist

Seismologists study earthquakes and the seismic waves caused by earthquakes. Their job is to detect earthquakes and earthquake-related faults.

Seismologists use many instruments to collect data. Seismographs and seismometers are instruments that receive and record seismic waves. Magnetometers detect and measure magnetic fields. Seismologists interpret data from these instruments to detect the coming of an earthquake. They also determine the location and strength of earthquakes. Much of their job involves managing data on a computer.

A bachelor's degree in geology is needed for a beginning job in seismology. Research positions require a master's or doctoral degree.

Seismologists must have strong science, math, and computer skills. Good communication skills are important for writing reports and working on a team. Seismologists need to be willing to travel to faraway survey sites. Some seismologists may perform their jobs from a ship.

INVESTIGATION

13-2

Materials

◆ index card
◆ large drawing paper
◆ tape
◆ drawing compass
◆ centimeter ruler

Locating an Earthquake

Purpose

How do scientists find the epicenter of an earthquake? In this investigation, you will make a map that pinpoints the source of an earthquake.

Procedure

1. Copy the data table on your paper.

Station	Distance to Epicenter (kilometers)	Distance to Epicenter on Map (centimeters)*
1		
2		
3		

*Based on scale: ___ kilometers = ___ centimeters

2. Make a dot in the top right corner of the index card. Label the dot Station 1. Make a dot in the middle of the right edge. Label it Station 2. Make a dot in the bottom left corner. Label it Station 3.

3. Tape the index card to the middle of the drawing paper.

4. Study the report below. Record the distance information in the data table.

> National Seismographic Network
>
> To: All Member Stations
> From: A. Arliss
> Subject: Main shock at 4:42 A.M. today
>
> Based on seismograph readings, we have determined the following:
>
> | Monitoring Station | Distance to Epicenter |
> |---|---|
> | 1 | 900 kilometers |
> | 2 | 1,100 kilometers |
> | 3 | 1,150 kilometers |

5. Based on the size of your paper, determine a map scale to convert these distances from kilometers to centimeters. (Each centimeter distance will be the radius of a circle around a station on your map.) Record this scale in the data table. Record the converted distances in the third column of the table.

6. In the data table, find the epicenter's distance from Station 1 in centimeters. Use the ruler to set your compass for that distance. Place the point of the compass on Station 1. Draw a circle. **Safety Alert: Use care when drawing with a compass. The point is sharp.**

7. Repeat step 6 for the remaining stations.

Questions and Conclusions

1. Where on your map is the epicenter of the earthquake?

2. You drew your map on plain paper. What additional information would appear on an actual seismographic map?

Explore Further

Refer to the tectonic plate map on page 310. Choose an area that lies on a tectonic plate boundary. Use a map of that area to repeat this investigation. Instead of the index card, choose actual cities on the map for Stations 1, 2, and 3. Use the epicenter distances already given for these stations. Locate the epicenter of this imaginary earthquake. Is it in or near a city?

Chapter 13 SUMMARY

- The earth has three main layers: the core, the mantle, and the crust.

- The theory of continental drift states that the continents were once joined as a single landmass that slowly separated and moved apart over time.

- The theory of sea-floor spreading states that the ocean floor spreads as new crust is formed at mid-ocean ridges.

- The theory of plate tectonics states that the earth's crust is made of several large plates that move.

- Convection currents in the mantle push the crust, causing the plates to move.

- Volcanoes occur where magma pushes up through the earth's surface. This happens most often at plate boundaries.

- Volcanoes are grouped into three types: cinder cones, shield volcanoes, and composite volcanoes.

- Mountains can form from volcanic eruptions, from folding, and from movement at faults.

- An earthquake is a shaking of the earth's crust. Most earthquakes occur near plate boundaries.

- Earthquake energy travels through the earth as waves. A seismograph detects and records these waves.

- The epicenter of an earthquake can be located by using the arrival times of earthquake waves at different locations.

- The strength of an earthquake is measured on the Richter scale.

Science Words

cinder cone, 314	crust, 308	Pangaea, 309	shield volcano, 315
composite volcano, 315	earthquake, 322	plate, 310	strike-slip fault, 318
continental drift, 309	epicenter, 324	plate tectonics, 310	tsunami, 325
convection current, 311	fault, 318	reverse fault, 318	vent, 313
core, 308	focus, 324	Richter scale, 324	volcano, 313
	folding, 317	sea-floor spreading, 310	
	mantle, 308	seismograph, 323	
	normal fault, 318		

Chapter 13 R E V I E W

Vocabulary Review

Choose the word or phrase from the Word Bank that best completes each sentence. Write the answer on your paper.

1. The earth's crust shakes during a(n) _____.

2. The bending of rock layers is _____.

3. An instrument used to record earthquake waves is a(n) _____.

4. The idea that new crust forms along rifts in the ocean floor is called _____.

5. The point on the earth's surface above the focus of an earthquake is its _____.

6. The idea that the earth's landmasses move is the _____ theory.

7. The circular movement of a gas or liquid as it heats is a(n) _____.

8. The idea that the earth's crust is made of moving sections is the theory of _____.

9. The layer of the earth between the core and the crust is the _____.

10. A break in the earth's crust where the earth moves in different directions is a(n) _____.

Concept Review

Choose the word or phrase that best completes each sentence. Write the letter of the answer on your paper.

11. The earth's surface is part of the _____.

  A core

  B atmosphere

  C crust

  D mantle

12. Continental drift, sea-floor spreading, and plate tectonics all help explain _____.

   A how the earth's surface changes
   B where convection currents come from
   C why the earth has layers
   D the age of the earth

13. Where two plates meet, they usually _____.

   A explode
   B scrape or squeeze each other
   C stop moving
   D become attached

Write the answer to each of the following questions.

14. Name the three types of volcanos and one unique feature of each.

15. Describe two of the three ways that mountains form.

16. Explain what the Richter scale measures.

17. Look at the lettered diagrams. Name the type of fault each diagram represents.

A
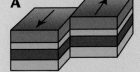

Critical Thinking

B
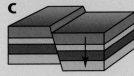

Write the answer to each of the following questions.

18. Tell how mountains, volcanoes, and earthquakes are related to the earth's plates.

19. Review the factors that determine the effect of an earthquake. What factors might determine the effect of a tsunami?

C

20. A string of active volcanoes rings the Pacific Ocean basin. In fact, the circle is called the Ring of Fire. What conclusion might you draw about the earth's crust under this ring? Why?

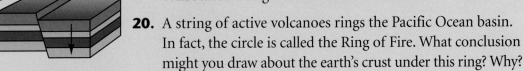

Test-Taking Tip Decide which questions you will do first and last. Limit your time on each question accordingly.

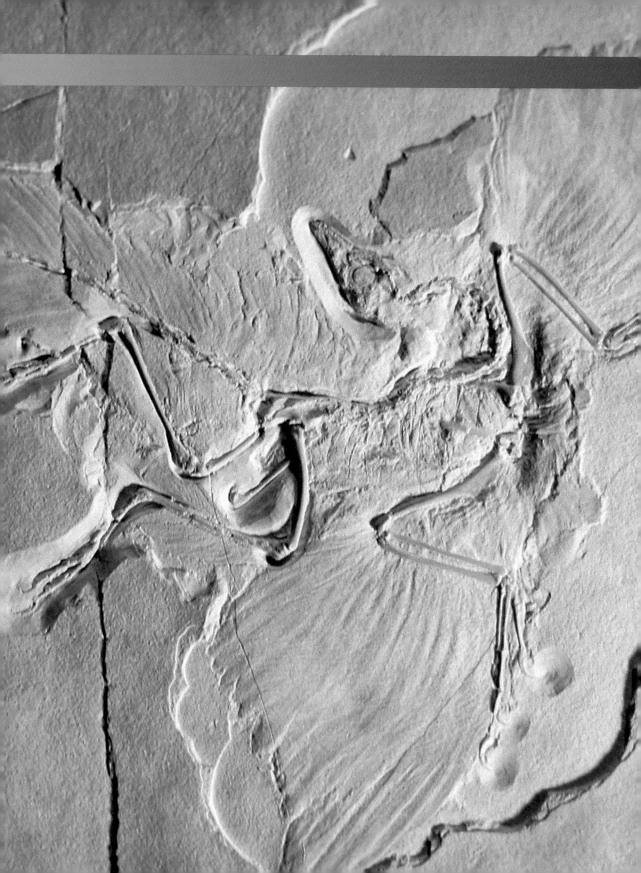

14

A Record of the Earth's History

magine a quiet forest. All is still. Suddenly, a blurry shape flies by close to the ground. Landing on a low branch, the shape shows itself to be a bird about the size of a crow. At least it *looks* like a bird. It has wings and feathers. But it also has a head like a lizard. Sharp teeth line its mouth, and its wings end in claws. Is this a creature from a movie? No, it is a real part of our past, preserved in the rock shown in the photo. Evidence, such as these remains, provides clues to what life on the earth was like long ago. In Chapter 14, you will learn about geologic time. You also will find out about the kinds of evidence scientists use to reconstruct the earth's history.

Organize Your Thoughts

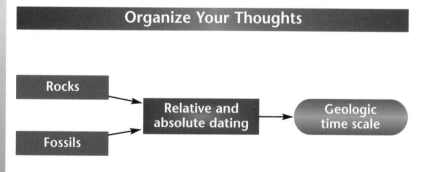

Goals for Learning

◆ To define geologic time

◆ To explain how fossils form

◆ To explain relative and absolute dating of rocks

◆ To outline major events in the earth's history

Geologic time

All the time that has passed since the earth formed

Does a year seem like a long time to you? Your idea of time depends on what you compare it to. Compared to events in your life, a year probably is a long time. Compared to the history of most nations, a year is not very long at all. Scientists who study the earth describe a long time in terms of millions or billions of years. For example, the carving of the Grand Canyon took about 6 million years. Compared to that amount of time, a year is not even noticeable.

Geologic Time

Most events in earth science are compared to **geologic time**— all the time that has passed since the earth formed. Scientists estimate that the earth is about 4.6 billion years old. Compared to this amount of time, even the Grand Canyon is fairly young.

When an event, such as a hurricane, happens today, it is recorded. Newspaper reports, videotapes, and photographs record the event. No such records exist for most of the earth's events. Yet much has happened in the earth's long history. Mountains have built up, continents have moved, living things have come and gone. These events left records in the rock of the earth's crust. As you will see, scientists study rock layers to learn what happened in the past and the order in which events took place.

The Colorado River has carved the Grand Canyon over millions of years.

Fossils are evidence that living things on the earth have changed over time. Fossils also show that the earth's climates haven't always been the same.

Fossils

Among the most important records of the earth's history are **fossils**. Fossils, like the one shown on page 332, are the traces or remains of organisms preserved in the earth's crust. Organisms are living things and include plants and animals. Fossils are evidence that certain kinds of life existed. Other living things may have been present on the earth in the past. However, unless these living things left fossils, scientists have no evidence of their existence.

It's not easy to become a fossil. When an organism dies, its soft parts usually decay. They might also be eaten by other creatures. The parts most likely to become fossils are the hard parts, such as wood, teeth, bones, and shells. Usually, these parts must be buried quickly in some way in order to become fossils. Most organisms that become fossils are buried by sediment on the ocean floor. Burial might also occur during sandstorms, volcanic eruptions, floods, or avalanches.

Types of Fossils

Most fossils preserve the shape of the organism but not the actual body matter. For example, some fossils form when minerals replace the original parts of a buried organism. This process is called **petrification**. The photo shows petrified wood. Over thousands of years, the wood was dissolved by groundwater and replaced by the minerals in the water.

What details can you see preserved in this petrified wood?

Another type of fossil forms when an organism leaves an imprint behind. For example, a plant or an animal may become buried in sediment that later forms rock. Eventually, the organism decays or dissolves. The space left in the rock, called a **mold**, has the shape of the plant or animal. If minerals fill the mold, a **cast** forms. The cast becomes a model of the original plant or animal. In the photo below, find both a mold and a cast of a trilobite. This sea animal lived 500 million years ago.

Many buried trilobites created the molds and casts in this rock.

*Fossils, such as this amber, offer a glimpse of
life from the past.*

Sometimes, the actual body matter of an organism is preserved as a fossil. For example, remains of woolly mammoths, ancient ancestors of elephants, have been found preserved in ice and frozen soil. The remains of saber-toothed tigers have been discovered trapped in petroleum deposits called tar pits. The insects in the photo on the left were trapped in tree sap. The sap hardened into a material called amber, preserving the actual body of each insect.

Lesson 1   R E V I E W

Write the answers to these questions on a sheet of paper.

1. What is geologic time?

2. What is a fossil?

3. What are three ways that fossils form?

4. Describe the process of petrification.

5. Explain how a cast forms from a buried organism.

Achievements in Science

Uncovering the History of Life

Fossils are keys to understanding the past. Paleontologists are scientists who uncover and study fossils. These scientists have learned much about the history of plant and animal life on the earth.

Fossils show what past climates were like. For example, fossils of palm and magnolia leaves have been found in Greenland. This shows that Greenland, an icy region today, had a warm, wet climate about 80 million years ago.

Fossils tell about an area's history. For example, paleontologists have found fossil shellfish in the Rocky Mountains. Since fossil shellfish are found in rocks formed under an ocean, this indicates that the Rocky Mountains were once underwater.

Fossils reveal past forms of life that are now extinct. Richard Owen was a British paleontologist who examined fossil teeth discovered in the 1820s. Other scientists thought the teeth belonged to a large lizard. Owen had a different idea. He thought the teeth belonged to a huge reptile that was unlike any known reptiles. In 1841, he proposed a name for this new group of animals—Dinosauria. The term *dinosaur* soon became part of scientific language.

How do paleontologists uncover fossils? When these scientists find part of a fossil in a rock, they dig the rock away from it. They start with large tools or even explosives. As they get closer to the fossil, they use smaller tools to carefully free the fossil. Then they use delicate tools and tiny brushes to clean the fossil.

Making a Model of a Fossil

Materials

- newspaper
- modeling clay
- seashell
- petroleum jelly
- plaster of paris powder
- plastic container
- water
- spoon

Purpose

How does a clay impression model a fossil formation? In this investigation, you will make a model of a mold and a cast.

Procedure

1. Cover your work space with newspaper. Flatten the modeling clay into a slab that is about 2 centimeters thick.

2. Gently press a seashell into the clay to form an impression.

3. Remove the seashell and inspect the impression. If the details of the shell cannot be seen clearly, repeat step 2.

4. Use your finger to gently coat the impression with a thin layer of petroleum jelly. Wash your hands.

5. In the container, mix the plaster of paris powder and water according to directions. Make enough plaster of paris to fill the impression. **Safety Alert: Wipe up any spills immediately. Avoid getting the plaster of paris on your hands or face.**

6. Pour the plaster of paris into the clay impression and allow it to harden overnight.

7. Remove the hard plaster of paris from the clay.

8. Clean your work space and wash the equipment.

Questions and Conclusions

1. What part of your model represents a mold?

2. What part of your model represents a cast?

3. How do the mold and cast compare?

Explore Further

Use a clean chicken or turkey bone and repeat the procedure. Then find out how a museum model is made from dinosaur fossils.

Objectives

After reading this lesson, you should be able to

◆ explain how a rock's relative age is determined.

◆ explain how a rock's absolute age is determined.

Relative dating

Method that compares two rock layers to find out which is older

Principle of superposition

In layers of sedimentary rocks, the oldest layer is on the bottom and the youngest layer is on the top if the layers have not been overturned.

To find the age of a fossil, scientists find the age of the rock in which the fossil was found. How is this done? It's not as difficult as you might think.

Principles of Relative Dating

One way to find the age of a rock is to compare it to other rocks. In this method, called **relative dating**, you place rock layers in order from oldest to youngest without using actual dates. Some basic principles can guide you when using relative dating.

If you are unpacking a box of books, you can be fairly certain that the book on the bottom was put in before the books on top. You can apply this simple idea to relative dating. Look at the layers of sedimentary rock shown in the diagram below. The oldest layer is at the bottom. The **principle of superposition** states that if sedimentary rock layers have not been overturned, the oldest rock layer is on the bottom and the youngest rock layer is on the top. Based on this principle, a fossil found in one layer of rock is older than a fossil found in a layer above it.

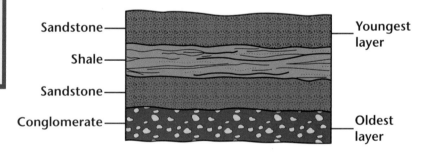

Sandstone — Youngest layer

Shale

Sandstone

Conglomerate — Oldest layer

Principle of superposition

Principle of crosscutting relationships

A feature, such as a rock structure or a fault, that cuts across rock layers is younger than the rock layers.

Index fossil

Fossil that can be used to establish the relative age of the rock in which the fossil occurs

? Did You Know?

Scientists estimate that only about 1 percent of all past organisms became fossils.

Suppose you saw a nail stuck in a tree trunk. You would realize that the tree grew first and the nail was later pounded into it. A similar principle is used to determine the relative ages of some rocks. According to the **principle of crosscutting relationships**, a rock that cuts through another rock must be younger than the rock it cuts. The diagram below illustrates this principle. The rock features in the diagram are numbered from oldest (1) to youngest (6).

The igneous rock pocket (5) formed when magma forced its way up through cracks in the existing rock layers. According to the principle of crosscutting relationships, this section of igneous rock is younger than the sedimentary rock layers (1 to 4).

The diagram also shows a fault cutting through layers of rock. Using the principle of crosscutting relationships, you can see that the fault (6) occurred after the pocket of igneous rock formed. So the fault is the youngest rock feature.

How do the rock layers in the diagram also show the principle of superposition?

Some fossils, called **index fossils**, can be used to establish the relative ages of rocks that contain these fossils. Index fossils, such as the trilobites shown on page 336, are useful because they are widespread and lived for a relatively short period of time. Therefore, when scientists find an index fossil anywhere in the world, they know the relative age of the rock in which the fossil was found.

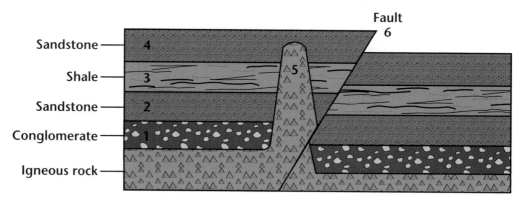

Principle of crosscutting relationships

Fault 6 — Sandstone 4 — Shale 3 — Sandstone 2 — Conglomerate 1 — Igneous rock

Absolute Dating Using Half-Life

Relative dating is useful, but **absolute dating** is more specific. Scientists use absolute dating to find the absolute age, or actual age, of a rock or fossil. Absolute dates are measured in years, just as your age is.

Scientists find the absolute age of a rock by studying certain **radioactive elements** the rock contains. Radioactive elements break apart, or decay, to form other elements. This decay happens at a constant rate. The length of time it takes for half of the atoms of a radioactive element to decay is the element's **half-life**. By comparing the amounts of different elements in a rock, scientists can determine the absolute age of the rock.

For example, the radioactive element carbon-14, a form of carbon, is used in absolute dating of some fossils. All living things contain carbon-14. When an organism dies, the carbon-14 starts to decay, forming nitrogen-14. The diagram below shows the rate of decay. The half-life of carbon-14 is 5,730 years. After 5,730 years, half of the carbon-14 is decayed. Every 5,730 years after that, half of the remaining carbon-14 decays. By measuring the amount of carbon-14 and nitrogen-14 in a sample, scientists can determine how many years ago the organism died.

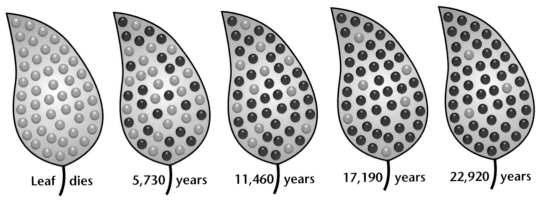

Leaf dies   5,730 years   11,460 years   17,190 years   22,920 years

Key:
○ Carbon-14
● Nitrogen-14

After about 50,000 years, almost all carbon-14 in an organism has decayed to nitrogen-14. Therefore, carbon-14 cannot be used to date fossils older than 50,000 years. Other radioactive elements with longer half-lives are used to determine the absolute age of older fossils and rocks.

For example, uranium-238 occurs in some igneous rocks and decays to form lead-206. The half-life of uranium-238 is about 4.5 billion years. Scientists can compare the uranium-238 content of a rock to its lead-206 content. From such a comparison, they can determine the absolute age of the rock. Using this method on meteorites, scientists have determined the age of the earth to be 4.6 billion years old.

This well-preserved fossil was discovered in Wyoming. According to absolute dating methods, this ancient fish lived about 40 million years ago.

Write the answers to these questions on a sheet of paper.

1. How does relative dating differ from absolute dating?

2. Define the principles of superposition and crosscutting relationships. Give an example of each.

3. How can a rock's absolute age be determined?

4. What is a radioactive element's half-life?

5. For what kind of fossils would uranium-238 be used to determine absolute age?

▼◄▲▼◄▲▼◄▲▼◄▲▼◄▲▼◄▲▼◄▲▼◄▲▼◄▲▼◄▲▼◄▲▼◄▲▼◄▲▼◄▲▼◄▲▼

Science at Work

Petroleum Engineer

Petroleum engineers travel the world searching for underground deposits of oil or natural gas. Once these deposits are located, petroleum engineers decide on the best way to recover, or get at, the oil or gas. To do this, they often use computer models and other technology. Then petroleum engineers work with geologists to set up drilling equipment and manage drilling operations. An important part of this job is making sure that people and the environment are not in danger.

Petroleum engineers work for petroleum companies, exploration companies, or governments. Petroleum engineers often work where oil or gas is being recovered or processed. These places include Alaska, Texas, Louisiana, Oklahoma, California, western and northern Canada, and countries overseas. Petroleum engineers also work on oil rigs, which are large ships that drill for oil that is located under oceans.

Petroleum engineers must have at least a bachelor's degree in petroleum engineering. Strong computer and technology skills are also required for their work. These engineers need to be good problem-solvers and careful planners. Because of the likelihood of travel, a petroleum engineer should be willing to learn about other cultures and languages.

14-2

INVESTIGATION

Making a Half-Life Model

Purpose

How does a radioactive element show age? In this investigation, you will model and graph the decay of a radioactive element.

Procedure

1. Copy the data table on a sheet of paper.

Materials

◆ 2 sheets of paper

◆ marking pen

◆ 16 beans

◆ clock or watch

◆ graph paper

| Time | Mass (grams) | |
	Radioactive Element	New Element
0		
1 half-life		
2 half-lives		
3 half-lives		

2. Label one sheet of paper *radioactive element* and another sheet of paper *new element*.

3. Place all of the beans on the sheet marked *radioactive element*. Each bean represents 1 gram of a radioactive element in a rock sample. At time 0, before any decay has occurred, record the mass in grams of the radioactive element.

4. Assume that the half-life of the beans is 1 minute. Note your starting time on the clock as time 0.

5. Wait 1 minute. Then remove half of the beans from the *radioactive element* paper and place them on the *new element* paper. Record the mass of each element at 1 half-life.

6. Repeat step 5 two times: at 2 half-lives and at 3 half-lives.

7. Draw a graph like the one shown here. Place the time in half-lives along the bottom axis and the mass of the radioactive element in grams along the side axis. Plot your data and connect the points.

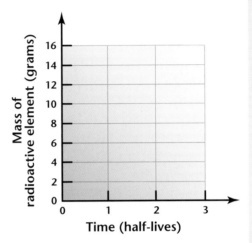

Questions and Conclusions

1. What do the beans that did not get moved represent?

2. What do the beans that did get moved represent?

3. How much of the radioactive element was left after 2 half-lives? After 3 half-lives?

4. How much of the radioactive element would be left after 4 half-lives?

Explore Further

This investigation shows only one of many different ways to make a half-life model. Design a half-life model yourself. You might shake pennies in a box and remove the "heads" or "tails" after each shake, or half-life. You might also use beans of different colors. Graph your data as you proceed. After a couple of half-lives are graphed, extend the graph to predict how many "radioactive atoms" will remain after additional half-lives. Check your predictions.

Geologic time scale

Outline of the events of the earth's history

Precambrian Era

Oldest and longest era of the earth's history; began about 4.6 billion years ago and ended about 540 million years ago

We know the earth has changed over time. But how the earth actually began is still a big question. Scientists use the evidence they have to suggest theories about the earth's origin.

Using evidence from the rock record and fossil record, scientists have developed the **geologic time scale**, shown on page 348. The geologic time scale is an outline of major events in the earth's history. Find the four major units, or eras, of geologic time. Notice how eras are divided into smaller units called periods. Some periods are divided into even smaller units called epochs. Refer to this table as you read about each era.

The Precambrian Era

The **Precambrian Era** is the oldest and longest era. It accounts for about 85 percent of all geologic time. The Precambrian Era began with the formation of the earth and ended about 540 million years ago.

Most Precambrian rocks are igneous or metamorphic. They form the foundation of the continents. These ancient rocks are exposed in some areas where the earth's crust has lifted and eroded. Precambrian rocks can be seen in the Black Hills of South Dakota, the Appalachian Mountains in the eastern United States, and the Ozark Mountains of Missouri.

Simple organisms probably first appeared at least 3.5 billion years ago, early in the Precambrian Era. These organisms may have included relatives of algae, fungi, and bacteria. The fossil record contains limited evidence of Precambrian organisms.

The Geologic Time Scale

Era	Period	Epoch	Years Before the Present (approximate)		Forms of Life	Physical Events
			Began	Ended		
Cenozoic	Quaternary	Recent	11,000		Humans dominate	West Coast uplift continues in U.S.; Great Lakes form
		Pleistocene	2,000,000	11,000	Primitive humans appear; mammoths	Ice age
	Tertiary	Pliocene	7,000,000	2,000,000	Modern horse, camel, elephant develop	North America joined to South America
		Miocene	23,000,000	7,000,000	Grasses; grazing animals thrive	North America joined to Asia; Columbia Plateau
		Oligocene	38,000,000	23,000,000	Mammals progress; elephants in Africa	Himalayas start forming; Alps continue rising
		Eocene	53,000,000	38,000,000	Ancestors of modern horse, other mammals	Coal forming in western U.S.
		Paleocene	65,000,000	53,000,000	Many new mammals appear	Uplift in western U.S. continues; Alps rising
Mesozoic	Cretaceous		145,000,000	65,000,000	Dinosaurs die out; flowering plants	Uplift of Rockies and Colorado Plateau begins
	Jurassic		208,000,000	145,000,000	First birds appear; giant dinosaurs	Rise of Sierra Nevadas and Coast Ranges
	Triassic		245,000,000	208,000,000	First dinosaurs and mammals appear	Palisades of Hudson River form
Paleozoic	Permian		280,000,000	245,000,000	Trilobites die out	Ice age in South America; deserts in western U.S.
	Pennsylvanian		310,000,000	280,000,000	First reptiles, giant insects; ferns, conifers	Coal-forming swamps in North America and Europe
	Mississippian		345,000,000	310,000,000	Early insects	Limestone formation
	Devonian		395,000,000	345,000,000	First amphibians appear	Mountain building in New England
	Silurian		435,000,000	395,000,000	First land animals (spiders, scorpions)	Deserts in eastern U.S.
	Ordovician		500,000,000	435,000,000	First vertebrates (fish)	Half of North America submerged
	Cambrian		540,000,000	500,000,000	Trilobites, snails; seaweed	Extensive deposition of sediment in inland seas
Precambrian			4,600,000,000	540,000,000	First jellyfish, bacteria, algae	Great volcanic activity, lava flows, metamorphism of rocks; evolution of crust, mantle, core

The Paleozoic Era

The **Paleozoic Era** began about 540 million years ago and ended about 245 million years ago. It was a time of great development of life in the oceans. At times, oceans covered large portions of the continents. Paleozoic rocks contain fossils of trilobites, sponges, and shellfish. The first land plants and animals also developed during this era. In the geologic time scale on page 348, note the progression of life from amphibians to insects to reptiles. Many ancient insects were huge. Some dragonflies had the wingspan of eagles!

During the Paleozoic Era, the earth's crust underwent many changes. For example, the Appalachian Mountains formed during this time as the crust buckled over millions of years. Much of the coal, oil, and natural gas we use today for energy formed from the organisms that lived in large swamps and shallow seas during this era. Many rock layers built up over the dead organic matter. Heat and pressure slowly turned the organic matter into coal, oil, and natural gas.

Compare the trilobite model above with the fossils shown on page 336.

The Mesozoic Era

The **Mesozoic Era** began about 245 million years ago and ended 65 million years ago. Life on land flourished during this time. Trees similar to our palm and pine trees were common. Small mammals and birds first appeared. But this era is often called the Age of Reptiles because they were the major form of life on land. The most dominant of the reptiles were the dinosaurs.

In many ways, the kinds of dinosaurs were like the kinds of animals today. Some ate meat and some ate plants. Some were larger than an elephant, while others were as small as a chicken. Some were fierce and others were gentle. Some traveled in herds and some were loners. Even their color probably varied, though we cannot tell this from the fossil record.

The end of the Mesozoic Era is marked by the end of the dinosaurs. Why the dinosaurs died out, or became extinct, during this time is still a mystery.

This is a fossil model of the largest Tyrannosaurus rex *skeleton ever discovered. It is displayed at The Field Museum in Chicago.*

Cenozoic Era

Era described as the Age of Mammals; began about 65 million years ago and continues today

Did You Know?

If you compared the earth's entire history to a one-year calendar, the Precambrian Era would be the first $10\frac{1}{2}$ months. Dinosaurs would appear around December 12 and become extinct by December 27. The first humans would show up during the last few hours of New Year's Eve.

The Cenozoic Era

We are living in the **Cenozoic Era**. It began about 65 million years ago. During this era, the Alps and the Himalayas formed as the earth's plates continued to collide. Late in the era, several ice ages occurred. An ice age is a period of time when glaciers cover large portions of the land. About 2 million years ago, glaciers carved out huge basins and formed the Great Lakes.

Although dinosaurs became extinct at the close of the Mesozoic Era, mammals survived and flourished. The Cenozoic Era is known as the Age of Mammals. In this era, mammals, including humans, became the dominant form of life. The variety of mammals grew. The population, or total number, of each kind of mammal grew as well. At the same time, the kinds and numbers of birds, reptiles, fish, insects, and plants also increased.

Scientists estimate that about 30 million kinds of animals and plants live on the earth today. This is a small percent of all the kinds of organisms that have ever existed. Scientists also believe that about 100 kinds of organisms become extinct each day. Two factors that threaten the survival of plants and animals are pollution and the destruction of the natural environment. Many people are working to save animals and plants from extinction.

As time continues, living things and the earth that supports them will continue to change.

Technology Note

Scientists use fossils to find the ages of rocks. Scientists also use fossils to find deposits of oil. Some fossils, called conodonts, were formed in a variety of colors. The colors are related to how hot the rock was when the fossil formed. This is important because oil forms underground only at certain temperatures. The colors of the conodonts, then, help scientists locate rock layers that might contain oil.

Write the answers to these questions on a sheet of paper.

1. What is the geologic time scale?

2. Describe the Precambrian Era.

3. Name two forms of life that first appeared during each of the Paleozoic, Mesozoic, and Cenozoic Eras.

4. What time periods were spanned by the Paleozoic, Mesozoic, and Cenozoic Eras?

5. For each era of geologic time, name a major change that occurred in the earth's crust during that era.

Science in Your Life

Cutting Down on Fossil Fuels

Petroleum, coal, and natural gas are fossil fuels. Deposits of fossil fuels are found in layers of underground rock. They formed there long ago from decayed plants and animals. Today fossil fuels are burned to create energy. They currently supply at least 60 percent of the world's electrical needs. They also are used to make cosmetics, paints, dry-cleaning chemicals, asphalt, and many other products.

Fossil fuels are nonrenewable. This means there is a limited supply of fossil fuels. They won't last forever, and we are using them up quickly. Because of this, scientists are improving ways to use renewable sources of energy. Renewable energy includes wind, hydroelectric, solar, geothermal, and nuclear energy. You can read about these forms of energy in Appendix B.

Make a list of ways you use gasoline, electricity, motor oil, coal, and natural gas. Then list other products you use that are made from fossil fuels. What can you do to reduce your use of fossil fuels?

- Geologic time is all the time that has passed since the earth formed—about 4. 6 billion years.

- Rocks contain clues about events that happened in the earth's past.

- Fossils are evidence that certain organisms existed.

- Fossils form when plant or animal remains become replaced with minerals, leave an imprint, or become preserved.

- Relative dating is a method used to find the relative age of a rock layer by comparing it to other layers.

- The principle of superposition states that the youngest layer in sedimentary rock is the top layer.

- The principle of crosscutting relationships states that a rock feature that cuts through other rock layers is younger than those layers.

- Absolute dating is a method used to determine the actual age of a rock layer.

- Absolute dating relies on the decay of radioactive elements in a rock or fossil. How fast a radioactive element decays depends on its half-life.

- The events in the earth's history occurred over geologic time and are outlined on the geologic time scale.

- Earth's history is divided into four eras: Precambrian, Paleozoic, Mesozoic, and Cenozoic. Each era is unique in terms of the living things that developed and the changes that took place in the earth's crust.

Science Words

absolute dating, 342	geologic time scale, 347	Paleozoic Era, 349	principle of superposition, 340
cast, 336	half-life, 342	petrification, 335	radioactive
Cenozoic Era, 351	index fossil, 341	Precambrian Era, 347	element, 342
fossil, 335	Mesozoic Era, 350	principle of	relative dating, 340
geologic time, 334	mold, 336	crosscutting relationships, 341	

Chapter 14 REVIEW

Word Bank
___

absolute dating

cast

fossil

geologic time

half-life

index fossil

mold

petrification

superposition

relative dating

Vocabulary Review

Choose the word or phrase from the Word Bank that best matches each definition. Write the answer on your paper.

1. principle stating that a rock layer is younger than the layer below it and older than the layer above it

2. method used to determine how old a rock layer is by comparing it to another rock layer

3. trace or remains of an organism preserved in the earth's crust

4. impression left in a rock by an organism

5. method that determines the actual age of a rock or fossil

6. fossil that provides clues to the age of the rock in which the fossil occurs

7. process by which original plant or animal parts are replaced with minerals

8. model of an organism

9. total amount of time since the earth was formed

10. length of time it takes for half of the atoms of a radioactive element to decay

Concept Review

Choose the word or phrase that best completes each sentence. Write the letter of the answer on your paper.

11. The geologic time scale divides the history of the earth into four _____.
   A epochs   **B** eras   **C** periods   **D** events

12. Scientists study _____ to learn about the history of life on the earth.
   A mammals   **C** radioactive elements
   B reptiles   **D** fossils

354 *Chapter 14 A Record of the Earth's History*

13. To find the absolute age of a rock, scientists use _____.
A radioactive uranium   **C** the principle of superposition
B relative dating   **D** crosscutting relationships

14. To find the relative age of a rock, scientists use _____.
A carbon-14   **C** absolute dating
B index fossils   **D** half-lives

15. During the _____ Era, dinosaurs and other reptiles were the major forms of life on the earth.
A Mesozoic   **C** Precambrian
B Paleozoic   **D** Cenozoic

16. A radioactive element decays to form _____.
A an index fossil   **C** carbon-14
B petrified wood   **D** another element

17. According to the principle of crosscutting relationships, a rock feature that cuts across other rock layers is _____ than the rock layers.
A older   **B** younger   **C** harder   **D** sharper

18. During the Cenozoic Era, the Great Lakes basins were carved out by _____.
A glaciers   **B** rivers   **C** wind   **D** mudslides

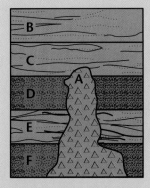

Critical Thinking

Write the answer to each of the following questions.

19. In the diagram, which lettered rocks are younger than rock D? Explain your answer in terms of two scientific principles.

20. An organism dies and becomes a fossil. Later scientists discover the fossil and find it contains 100 units of carbon-14 and 300 units of nitrogen-14. How many half-lives have occurred? How many years ago did the organism die?

Test-Taking Tip   Before you begin a test, look it over quickly. Try to set aside enough time to complete each section.

Appendix A: Metric and Customary Measurement

Metric Measures

Length
1,000 meters (m) = 1 kilometer (km)
100 centimeters (cm) = 1 m
10 decimeters (dm) = 1 m
1,000 millimeters (mm) = 1 m
10 cm = 1 decimeter (dm)
10 mm = 1 cm

Area
100 square millimeters (mm^2) = 1 square centimeter (cm^2)
10,000 cm^2 = 1 square meter (m^2)
10,000 m^2 = 1 hectare (ha)

Volume
1,000 cubic meters (m^3) = 1 cubic centimeter (cm^3)
1,000 cubic centimeters (cm^3) = 1 liter (L)
1 cubic centimeter (cm^3) = 1 milliliter (mL)
100 cm^3 = 1 cubic decimeter (dm^3)
1,000,000 cm^3 = 1 cubic meter (m^3)

Capacity
1,000 milliliters (mL) = 1 liter (L)
1,000 L = 1 kiloliter (kL)

Mass
100 grams (g) = 1 centigram (cg)
1,000 kilograms (kg) = 1 metric ton (t)
1,000 grams (g) = 1 kg
1,000 milligrams (mg) = 1 g

Temperature Degrees Celsius (°C)
0°C = freezing point of water
37°C = normal body temperature
100°C = boiling point of water

Time
60 seconds (sec) = 1 minute (min)
60 min = 1 hour (hr)
24 hr = 1 day

Customary Measures

Length
12 inches (in.) = 1 foot (ft)
3 ft = 1 yard (yd)
36 in. = 1 yd
5,280 ft = 1 mile (mi)
1,760 yd = 1 mi
6,076 feet = 1 nautical mile

Area
144 square inches (sq in.) = 1 square foot (sq ft)
9 sq ft = 1 square yard (sq yd)
43,560 sq ft = 1 acre (A)

Volume
1,728 cubic inches (cu in.) = 1 cubic foot (cu ft)
27 cu ft = 1 cubic yard (cu yard)

Capacity
8 fluid ounces (fl oz) = 1 cup (c)
2 c = 1 pint (pt)
2 pt = 1 quart (qt)
4 qt = 1 gallon (gal)

Weight
16 ounces (oz) = 1 pound (lb)
2,000 lb = 1 ton (T)

Temperature Degrees Fahrenheit (°F)
32°F = freezing point of water
98.6°F = normal body temperature
212°F = boiling point of water

To change	To	Multiply by	To change	To	Multiply by
centimeters	inches	0.3937	meters	feet	3.2808
centimeters	feet	0.03281	meters	miles	0.0006214
cubic feet	cubic meters	0.0283	meters	yards	1.0936
cubic meters	cubic feet	35.3145	metric tons	tons (long)	0.9842
cubic meters	cubic yards	1.3079	metric tons	tons (short)	1.1023
cubic yards	cubic meters	0.7646	miles	kilometers	1.6093
feet	meters	0.3048	miles	feet	5,280
feet	miles (nautical)	0.0001645	miles (statute)	miles (nautical)	0.8684
feet	miles (statute)	0.0001894	miles/hour	feet/minute	88
feet/second	miles/hour	0.6818	millimeters	inches	0.0394
gallons (U.S.)	liters	3.7853	ounces avdp	grams	28.3495
grams	ounces avdp	0.0353	ounces	pounds	0.0625
grams	pounds	0.002205	pecks	liters	8.8096
hours	days	0.04167	pints (dry)	liters	0.5506
inches	millimeters	25.4000	pints (liquid)	liters	0.4732
inches	centimeters	2.5400	pounds advp	kilograms	0.4536
kilograms	pounds avdp	2.2046	pounds	ounces	16
kilometers	miles	0.6214	quarts (dry)	liters	1.1012
liters	gallons (U.S.)	0.2642	quarts (liquid)	liters	0.9463
liters	pecks	0.1135	square feet	square meters	0.0929
liters	pints (dry)	1.8162	square meters	square feet	10.7639
liters	pints (liquid)	2.1134	square meters	square yards	1.1960
liters	quarts (dry)	0.9081	square yards	square meters	0.8361
liters	quarts (liquid)	1.0567	yards	meters	0.9144

Fossil Fuels

We fly through the air in planes. We roll down highways in cars. On the coldest days, our homes are warm. Our stores are full of products to satisfy our needs and wants.

The power that runs our lives comes from fossil fuels. A fossil is the remains of ancient life. Fossil fuels formed from the remains of dead matter—animals and plants. Over millions of years, forests of plants died, fell, and became buried in the earth. Over time, the layers of ancient, dead matter changed. The carbon in the animals and plants turned into a material we now use as fuel. Fossil fuels include coal, oil, natural gas, and gasoline.

Fossil fuels power our lives and our society. In the United States, electricity comes mainly from power plants that burn coal. Industries use electricity to run machines. In our homes, we use electricity to power lightbulbs, TVs, and everything else electric. Heat and hot water for many homes come from natural gas or oil, or from fuels that come from oil. Of course, cars and trucks run on gasoline, which is also made from oil.

Powering our society with fossil fuels has made our lives more comfortable. Yet our need for fossil fuels has caused problems. Fossil fuels are a nonrenewable source of energy. That means that there is a limited supply of these fuels. At some point, fossil fuels will become scarce. Their cost will increase. And one day the supply of fossil fuels will run out. We need to find ways now to depend less and less on fossil fuels.

Fossil fuels cause pollution. The pollution comes from burning them. It is like the exhaust from a car. The pollution enters the air and causes disease. It harms the environment. One serious effect of burning fossil fuels is global warming. Carbon dioxide comes from the burning of fossil fuels. When a large amount of this gas enters the air, it warms the earth's climate. Scientists believe that warming of the climate will cause serious problems.

Renewable Energy

Many people believe that we should use renewable fuels as sources of energy. Renewable fuels never run out. They last forever.

What kinds of fuels last forever? The energy from the sun. The energy in the wind. The energy in oceans and rivers. We can use these forms of energy to power our lives. Then we will never run out of fuel. We will cut down on pollution and climate warming. Using renewable energy is not a dream for the future. It is happening right now—right here—today.

Energy from the Sun

As long as the sun keeps shining, the earth will get energy from sunlight. Energy from the sun is called solar energy. It is the energy in light. When you lie in the sun, your skin becomes hot. The heat comes from the energy in sunlight. Sunlight is a form of renewable energy we can use forever.

We use solar energy to make electricity. The electricity can power homes and businesses. Turning solar energy into electricity is called photovoltaics, or PV for short. Here's how PV works.

Flat solar panels are put near a building or on its roof. The panels face the direction that gets the most sunlight. The panels contain many PV cells. The cells are made from silicon—a material that absorbs light. When sunlight strikes the cells, some of the light energy is absorbed. The energy knocks some electrons loose in the silicon. The electrons begin to flow. The electron flow is controlled. An electric current is produced. Pieces of metal at the top and bottom of each cell make a path for electrons. The path leads the electric current away from the solar panel. The electric current flows through wires to a battery. The battery stores the electrical energy. The electrical wiring in a building is connected to the battery. All the electricity used in the building comes from the battery.

Today, PV use is 500 times greater than it was 20 years ago. And PV use is growing about 20 percent per year. Yet solar energy systems are still not perfect. PV cells do not absorb all the sunlight that strikes them, so some energy is lost. Solar energy systems also are not cheap. Still, every year, PV systems are improved. The cost of PV electricity has decreased. The amount of sunlight PV cells absorb has increased.

On a sunny day, every square meter of the earth receives 1,000 watts of energy from sunlight. Someday, when PV systems are able to use all this energy, our energy problems may be solved.

Energy from the Wind

Sunlight warms different parts of the earth differently. The North Pole gets little sunlight, so it is cold. Areas near the equator get lots of sunlight, so they are warm. The uneven warming of the earth by the sun creates the wind. As the earth turns, the wind moves, or blows. The blowing wind can be used to make electricity. This is wind energy. Because the earth's winds will blow forever, the wind is a renewable source of energy.

Wind energy is not new. Hundreds of years ago, windmills created energy. The wind turned the large fins on a windmill. As the fins spun around, they turned huge stones inside the mill. The stones ground grain into flour.

Modern windmills are tall, metal towers with spinning blades, called wind turbines. Each wind turbine has three main parts. It has blades that are turned by blowing wind. The turning blades are attached to a shaft that runs the length of the tower. The turning blades spin the shaft. The spinning shaft is connected to a generator. A generator changes the energy from movement into electrical energy. It feeds the electricity into wires, which carry it to homes and factories.

Wind turbines are placed in areas where strong winds blow. A single house may have one small wind turbine near it to produce its electricity. The electricity produced by the wind turbine is stored in batteries. Many wind turbines may be linked together to produce electricity for an entire town. In these systems, the electricity moves from the generator to the electric company's wires. The wires carry the electricity to homes and businesses.

Studies show that in the United States, 34 of the 50 states have good wind conditions. These states could use wind to meet up to 20 percent of their electric power needs. Canada's wind conditions could produce up to 20 percent of its energy from wind too. Alberta already produces a lot of energy from wind, and the amount is expected to increase.

Energy from Inside the Earth

Deep inside the earth, the rocks are burning hot. Beneath them it is even hotter. There, rocks melt into liquid. The earth's inner heat rises to the surface in some places. Today, people have developed ways to use this heat to create energy. Because the inside of the earth will always be very hot, this energy is renewable. It is called geothermal energy (*geo* means earth; *thermal* means heat).

Geothermal energy is used where hot water or steam from deep inside the earth moves near the surface. These areas are called "hot spots." At hot spots, we can use geothermal energy directly. Pumps raise the  hot water, and pipes carry it to buildings. The water is used to heat the space in the buildings or to heat water.

Geothermal energy may also be used indirectly to make electricity. A power plant is built near a hot spot. Wells are drilled deep into the hot spot. The wells carry hot water or steam into the power plant. There, it is used to boil more water. The boiling water makes steam. The steam turns the blades of a turbine. This energy is carried to a generator, which turns it into electricity. The electricity moves through the electric company's wires to homes and factories.

Everywhere on the earth, several miles beneath the surface, there is hot material. Scientists are improving ways of tapping the earth's inner heat. Someday, this renewable, pollution-free source of energy may be available everywhere.

Energy from Trash

We can use the leftover products that come from plants to make electricity. For example, we can use the stalks from corn or wheat to make fuel. Many leftover products from crops and lumber can fuel power plants. Because this fuel comes from living plants, it is called bioenergy (*bio* means life or living). The plant waste itself is called biomass.

People have used bioenergy for thousands of years. Burning wood in a fireplace is a form of bioenergy. That's because wood comes from trees. Bioenergy is renewable, because people will always grow crops. There will always be crop waste we can burn as fuel.

Some power plants burn biomass to heat water. The steam from the boiling water turns turbines. The turbines create electricity. In other power plants, biomass is changed into a gas. The gas is used as fuel to boil water, which turns the turbine.

Biomass can also be made into a fuel for cars and trucks. Scientists use a special process to turn biomass into fuels, such as ethanol. Car makers are designing cars that can run on these fuels. Cars that use these fuels produce far less pollution than cars that run on gas.

Bioenergy can help solve our garbage problem. Many cities are having trouble finding places to dump all their trash. There would be fewer garbage dumps if we burned more trash to make electricity.

Bioenergy is a renewable energy. But it is not a perfect solution to our energy problems. Burning biomass creates air pollution.

Energy from the Ocean

Have you ever been knocked over by a small wave while wading in the ocean? If so, you know how much power ocean water has. The motion of ocean waves can be a source of energy. So can the rise and fall of ocean tides. There are several systems that use the energy in ocean waves and tides. All of them are very new and still being developed.

In one system, ocean waves enter a funnel. The water flows into a reservoir, an area behind a dam where water is stored. When the dam opens, water flows out of the reservoir. This powers a turbine, which creates electricity. Another system uses the waves' motion to operate water pumps, which run an electric generator. There is also a system that uses the rise and fall of ocean waves. The waves compress air in a container. During high tide, large amounts of ocean water enter the container. The air in the container is under great pressure. When the high-pressure air in the container is released, it drives a turbine. This creates electricity.

Energy can also come from the rise and fall of ocean tides. A dam is built across a tidal basin. This is an area where land surrounds the sea on three sides. At high tide, ocean water is allowed to flow through the dam. The water flow turns turbines, which generate electricity. There is one serious problem with tidal energy. It damages the environment of the tidal basin and can harm animals that live there.

The oceans also contain a great deal of thermal (heat) energy. The sun heats the surface of the oceans more than it heats deep ocean water. In one day, ocean surfaces absorb solar energy equal to 250 billion barrels of oil! Deep ocean water, which gets no sunlight, is much colder than the surface.

Scientists are developing ways to use this temperature difference to create energy. The systems they are currently designing are complicated and expensive.

Energy from Rivers and Dams

Dams built across rivers also produce electricity. When the dam is open, the flowing water turns turbines, which make electricity. This is called hydroelectric power (*hydro* means water). The United States gets 7 percent of its electricity from hydroelectric power. Canada gets up to 60 percent of its electricity from hydroelectric plants built across its many rivers.

Hydroelectric power is a nonpolluting and renewable form of energy—in a way. There will always be fresh water. However, more and more people are taking water from rivers for different uses. These uses include drinking, watering crops, and supplying industry. Some rivers are becoming smaller and weaker because of the water taken from them. Also, in many places dams built across rivers hurt the environment. The land behind the dam is "drowned." Once the dam is built, fish may not be able swim up or down the river. In northwestern states, salmon have completely disappeared from many rivers that have dams.

Energy from Hydrogen Fuel

Hydrogen is a gas that is abundant everywhere on the earth. It's in the air. It is a part of water. Because there is so much hydrogen, it is a renewable energy source. And hydrogen can produce energy without any pollution.

The most likely source of hydrogen fuel is water. Water is made up of hydrogen and oxygen. A special process separates these elements in water. The process produces oxygen gas and hydrogen gas. The hydrogen gas is changed into a liquid or solid. This hydrogen fuel is used to produce energy in a fuel cell.

Look at the diagram on page 363. Hydrogen fuel (H_2) is fed into one part of the fuel cell. It is then stripped of its electrons. The free electrons create an electric current (e). The electric current powers a lightbulb or whatever is connected to the fuel cell.

Meanwhile, oxygen (O_2) from the air enters another part of the fuel cell. The stripped hydrogen (H+) bonds with the oxygen, forming water (H_2O). So a car powered by a fuel cell has pure water leaving its tailpipe. There is no exhaust to pollute the air.

When a regular battery's power is used up,

the battery dies. A fuel cell never runs down as long as it gets hydrogen fuel.

A single fuel cell produces little electricity. To make more electricity, fuel cells come in "stacks" of many fuel cells packaged together. Stacked fuel cells are used to power cars and buses. Soon, they may provide electric power to homes and factories.

Hydrogen Fuel Cell

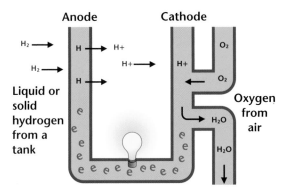

Hydrogen fuel shows great promise, but it still has problems. First, hydrogen fuel is difficult to store and distribute. Today's gas stations would have to be changed into hydrogen-fuel stations. Homes and factories would need safe ways to store solid hydrogen.

Second, producing hydrogen fuel by separating water is expensive. It is cheaper to make hydrogen fuel from oil. But that would create pollution and use nonrenewable resources. Scientists continue to look for solutions to these problems.

Energy from Atoms

Our sun gets its energy—its heat and light—from fusion. Fusion is the joining together of parts of atoms. Fusion produces enormous amounts of energy. But conditions like those on the sun are needed for fusion to occur. Fusion requires incredibly high temperatures.

In the next few decades, scientists may find ways to fuse atoms at lower temperatures. When this happens, we may be able to use fusion for energy. Fusion is a renewable form of energy because it uses hydrogen atoms. It also produces no pollution. And it produces no dangerous radiation. Using fusion to produce power is a long way off. But if the technology can be developed, fusion could provide us with renewable, clean energy.

Today's nuclear power plants produce energy by splitting atoms. This creates no air pollution. But nuclear energy has other problems. Nuclear energy is fueled by a substance we get from mines called uranium. There is only a limited amount of uranium in the earth. So it is not renewable. And uranium produces dangerous radiation, which can harm or kill living things if it escapes the power plant. Used uranium must be thrown out, even though it is radioactive and dangerous. In 1999, the United States produced nearly 41 tons of radioactive waste from nuclear power plants. However, less uranium is being mined. No new nuclear power plants have been built. The amount of energy produced from nuclear power is expected to fall. People are turning toward less harmful, renewable energy sources: the sun, wind, underground heat, biomass, water, and hydrogen fuel.

Fuel That U.S. Electric Utilities Used to Generate Electricity in 2000

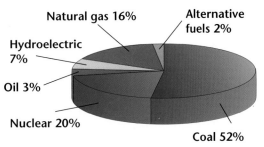

Source: U.S. Dept. of Energy Hydropower Program

Appendix C: The Solar System

The planets in our solar system are very different from each other. Some are huge balls of gas, and others are small, rocky worlds. Some are frozen, and others are burning hot. Some have violent storms raging in their atmosphere, and others hav[e] almost no atmosphere. The table below lists many facts about each planet. As you study these facts, look for similarities, differences, and patterns.

Features	Mercury	Venus	Earth	Mars	Jupiter	Saturn	Uranus	Neptune	Pluto
Unique Characteristics	fastest moving planet; closest planet to sun	hottest planet; brightest planet in Earth's night sky	only planet that has liquid water and supports life	reddish color; only planet explored by exploration robots	fastest rotation; largest planet; Great Red Spot	biggest ring system; great storms	rotates on its side; blue-green color	storms; blue-green color; Great Dark Spot	coldest and smallest planet; longest revolution time
Diameter (kilometers)	4,879	12,014	12,756	6,794	142,984	120,536	51,118	49,528	2,390
Relative Mass (Earth = 1)	0.055	0.82	1	0.11	318	95	15	17	0.002
Average Distance from Sun (millions of kilometers)	58	108	150	228	779	1,434	2,873	4,496	5,870
Rotation (Earth time)	59 days	243 days*	1 day	24 hours and 38 minutes	10 hours	11 hours	17 hours*	16 hours	6 days*
Revolution (Earth time)	88 days	224 days	365 days	687 days	12 years	29 years	84 years	164 years	248 years
Surface Temperature (°C)	−183 to 427	460	−89 to 58	−82 to 0	−150	−170	−200	−210	−220
Atmospheric Composition	very thin: sodium and helium gas	thick: carbon dioxide gas	thick: nitrogen and oxygen gas	thin: carbon dioxide gas	thick: hydrogen and helium gas	thick: hydrogen and helium gas	thick: hydrogen, helium, and methane gas	thick: hydrogen, helium, and methane gas	thin: methane ga[s]
Surface Composition	rocky	rocky	rocky	rocky	gaseous	gaseous	gaseous	gaseous	rocky
Number of Moons	0	0	1	2	60	31	22	11	1
Ring System	no	no	no	no	yes	yes	yes	yes	no

*planet rotates from east to west, the opposite direction of Earth's rotation

Source: NAS[A]

Mercury Venus Earth Mars

Pluto

Neptune

Uranus

Saturn

Jupiter

Appendix D: Space Exploration

Our knowledge of outer space has grown tremendously since the space age began in the 1950s. Orbiters, landers, probes, satellites, and space stations—as well as crews and scientists—continue to uncover new information about the solar system and beyond. The following timeline displays some of the important missions of space exploration. Each entry lists the name of the spacecraft, the country sponsoring it, and the mission's significance.

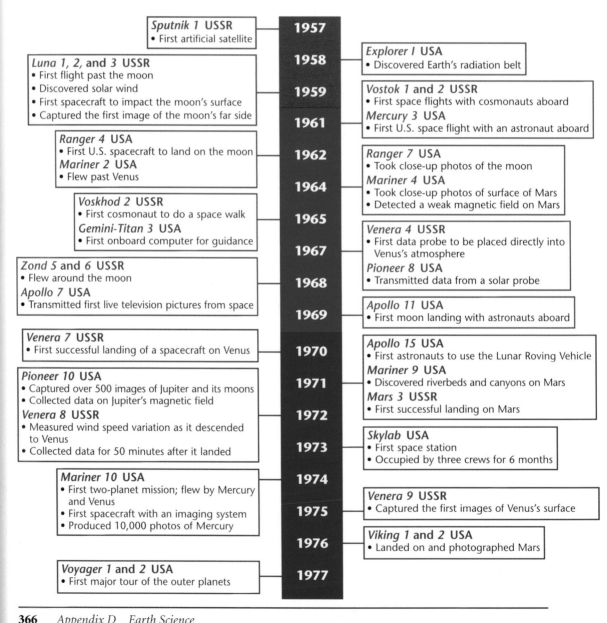

Sputnik 1 USSR
- First artificial satellite

1957

Explorer I USA
- Discovered Earth's radiation belt

1958

Luna 1, 2, and **3** USSR
- First flight past the moon
- Discovered solar wind
- First spacecraft to impact the moon's surface
- Captured the first image of the moon's far side

1959

Vostok 1 and **2** USSR
- First space flights with cosmonauts aboard

Mercury 3 USA
- First U.S. space flight with an astronaut aboard

1961

Ranger 4 USA
- First U.S. spacecraft to land on the moon

Mariner 2 USA
- Flew past Venus

1962

Ranger 7 USA
- Took close-up photos of the moon

Mariner 4 USA
- Took close-up photos of surface of Mars
- Detected a weak magnetic field on Mars

1964

Voskhod 2 USSR
- First cosmonaut to do a space walk

Gemini-Titan 3 USA
- First onboard computer for guidance

1965

Venera 4 USSR
- First data probe to be placed directly into Venus's atmosphere

Pioneer 8 USA
- Transmitted data from a solar probe

1967

Zond 5 and **6** USSR
- Flew around the moon

Apollo 7 USA
- Transmitted first live television pictures from space

1968

Apollo 11 USA
- First moon landing with astronauts aboard

1969

Venera 7 USSR
- First successful landing of a spacecraft on Venus

1970

Apollo 15 USA
- First astronauts to use the Lunar Roving Vehicle

Mariner 9 USA
- Discovered riverbeds and canyons on Mars

Mars 3 USSR
- First successful landing on Mars

1971

Pioneer 10 USA
- Captured over 500 images of Jupiter and its moons
- Collected data on Jupiter's magnetic field

Venera 8 USSR
- Measured wind speed variation as it descended to Venus
- Collected data for 50 minutes after it landed

1972

Skylab USA
- First space station
- Occupied by three crews for 6 months

1973

Mariner 10 USA
- First two-planet mission; flew by Mercury and Venus
- First spacecraft with an imaging system
- Produced 10,000 photos of Mercury

1974

Venera 9 USSR
- Captured the first images of Venus's surface

1975

Viking 1 and **2** USA
- Landed on and photographed Mars

1976

Voyager 1 and **2** USA
- First major tour of the outer planets

1977

1980

STS-1 Columbia **USA**
- First winged, reusable space shuttle to be launched

Venera 13 **USSR**
- First color views of Venus's surface

Voyager 1 **USA**
- Flew past Titan, one of Saturn's moons

Solar Maximum Mission **USA**
- Monitored the sun, especially solar flares

1981

1982

Venera 15 **and** *16* **USSR**
- Produced maps of Venus

1983

1984

Suisei **Japan**
- Flew past and studied comet Halley

Soyuz T-14 **USSR**
- First relief mission to replace cosmonauts on *Soyuz-T13*

1985

Mir **USSR**
- First space station to conduct research and deploy other spacecraft

1986

Ginga **Japan**
- Studied sources of gamma rays and X-rays in the Milky Way galaxy

Voyager 2 **USA**
- Flew past Uranus

1987

1988

Voyager 2 **USA**
- Flew past Neptune

Magellan **USA**
- Began mapping the surface of Venus

1989

STS-31 Discovery **USA, Europe**
- Deployed the Hubble Space Telescope

Soyuz TM-1 **USSR**
- First commercial passenger to make a space shuttle flight

Galileo **USA**
- Flew past Venus

1990

1991

1992

Ulysses **Europe and USA**
- Orbited Jupiter on its way to the sun

STS-61 Endeavor **USA**
- Repaired the Hubble Space Telescope

1993

1994

Clementine **USA**
- Generated the first lunar topographic map

Galileo **USA**
- Began orbiting Jupiter

1995

1996

NEAR **USA**
- Orbited and studied asteroids near Earth

Mars Pathfinder **USA**
- Returned data about Mars, including thousands of images
- Landed on Mars and released an exploration robot to explore its surface

Cassini **Europe**
- Began a 7-year flight to Saturn

1997

1998

International Space Station
- First orbiting research facility

1999

Stardust **USA**
- Collected sample from a comet

IMAGE **USA**
- First weather satellite to monitor space storms

2000

2001

Mars 2001 Odyssey **USA**
- Mapping surface minerals, looking for water, and studying potential radiation hazards to future missions

Muses-C **Japan**
- Collected sample from an asteroid

2002

2003

Mars Express **Europe**
- Will attempt to study Mars's surface and atmosphere in great detail

Deep Impact **USA**
- Will attempt to excavate the interior of a comet

2004

2005

Venus Express **Europe**
- Will attempt to study Venus's atmosphere in great detail

Europa **USA**
- Will attempt to orbit Jupiter's moon Europa

BepiColumbo **Europe**
- Will attempt to orbit Mercury

2006 and beyond

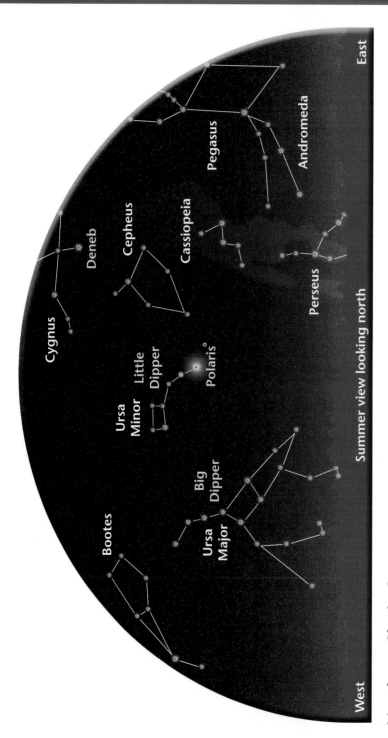

Summer view looking north

Northern Sky in Summer

If you look in the northern sky in August, you may see the stars in these constellations. The Big Dipper is low and toward the west. Cygnus, also called the Northern Cross, is almost directly overhead. The Little Dipper is upside-down. Polaris is the last star in the Little Dipper's handle.

Compare the Little Dipper here to its winter position shown on page 370. Can you see how the Little Dipper appears to rotate around Polaris during the year? The other stars in the Northern Hemisphere appear to rotate around Polaris, too.

Southern Sky in Summer

If you look in the southern sky in August, you may see the stars in the constellations shown here. Find the constellation Aquila, the Eagle. Altair is the brightest star in this constellation. High in the sky, almost straight up, is the constellation Lyra, the Lyre. Lyra contains a bright star named Vega. Three stars—Altair, Vega, and Deneb (in the high northern sky)—form the Summer Triangle. The faint band of starlight stretching across the sky from south to north is the Milky Way.

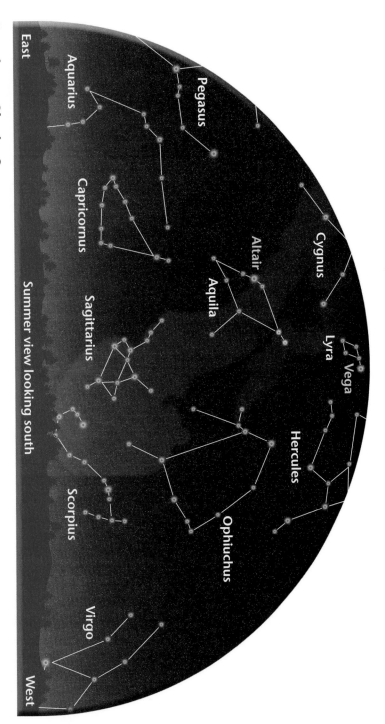

East

Aquarius

Pegasus

Capricornus

Cygnus

Altair

Aquila

Lyra

Vega

Sagittarius

Hercules

Scorpius

Ophiuchus

Virgo

West

Summer view looking south

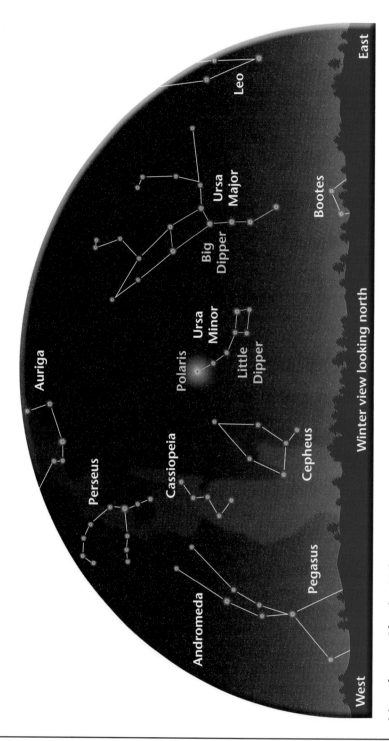

Winter view looking north

West

East

Leo

Bootes

Ursa Major

Big Dipper

Ursa Minor

Polaris

Little Dipper

Cepheus

Cassiopeia

Perseus

Auriga

Andromeda

Pegasus

Northern Sky in Winter

If you look in the northern sky in February, you may see the stars in the constellations shown here. Toward the east, the Big Dipper appears to stand on its handle. Which two stars in the Big Dipper always line up to point to Polaris? The Little Dipper appears to hang from Polaris, also called the North Star. Compare this view to the summer sky on page 368. Polaris remains in the same position in the northern sky all year long. Because of this, it is a good reference star, telling which way is north.

Southern Sky in Winter

If you look in the southern sky in February, you may see the stars in the constellations shown here. Find Orion in the center. Can you see why the ancient stargazers named this constellation the Hunter? Orion contains two supergiants: Betelgeuse and Rigel.

Three other bright stars make up Orion's belt. Canis Major, also called the Great Dog, contains the star Sirius, which is the brightest star in the sky. Leo, toward the east, looks like a backward question mark.

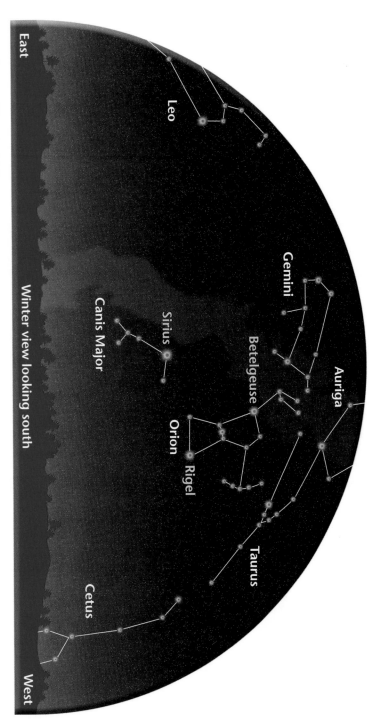

East

Winter view looking south

West

Leo

Gemini

Betelgeuse

Auriga

Canis Major

Sirius

Orion

Rigel

Taurus

Cetus

Appendix F: The Periodic Table of Elements

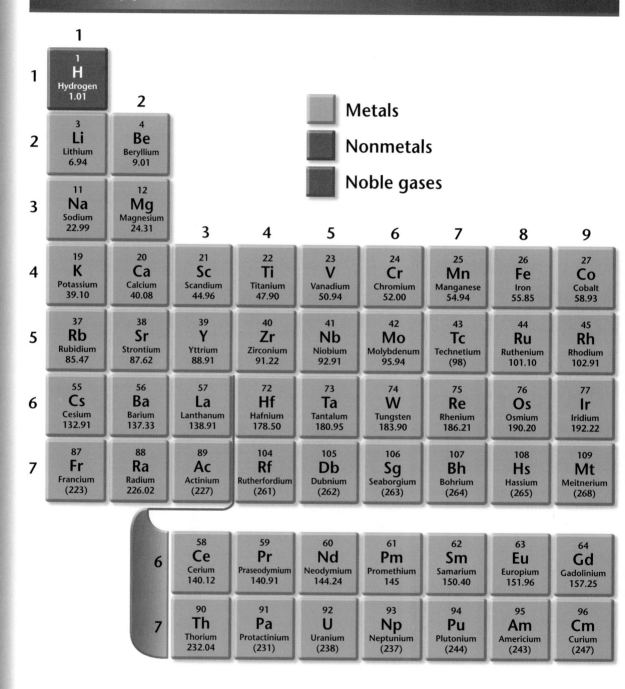

			13	**14**	**15**	**16**	**17**	**18**

Atomic number
Element symbol
Element name
Average atomic mass

| 2 He Helium 4.00 |

| 5 B Boron 10.81 | 6 C Carbon 12.01 | 7 N Nitrogen 14.01 | 8 O Oxygen 16.00 | 9 F Fluorine 19.00 | 10 Ne Neon 20.18 |

| 13 Al Aluminum 26.98 | 14 Si Silicon 28.09 | 15 P Phosphorus 30.97 | 16 S Sulfur 32.07 | 17 Cl Chlorine 35.45 | 18 Ar Argon 39.95 |

| **10** | **11** | **12** |

| 28 Ni Nickel 58.70 | 29 Cu Copper 63.55 | 30 Zn Zinc 65.39 | 31 Ga Gallium 69.72 | 32 Ge Germanium 72.59 | 33 As Arsenic 74.92 | 34 Se Selenium 78.96 | 35 Br Bromine 79.90 | 36 Kr Krypton 83.80 |

| 46 Pd Palladium 106.42 | 47 Ag Silver 107.90 | 48 Cd Cadmium 112.41 | 49 In Indium 114.82 | 50 Sn Tin 118.69 | 51 Sb Antimony 121.75 | 52 Te Tellurium 127.60 | 53 I Iodine 126.90 | 54 Xe Xenon 131.30 |

| 78 Pt Platinum 195.09 | 79 Au Gold 196.97 | 80 Hg Mercury 200.59 | 81 Tl Thallium 204.40 | 82 Pb Lead 207.20 | 83 Bi Bismuth 208.98 | 84 Po Polonium 209 | 85 At Astatine (210) | 86 Rn Radon (222) |

| 110 Uun Ununnilium (269) | 111 Uuu Unununium (272) | 112 Uub Ununbium (277) | | 114 Uuq Ununquadium (289) | | 116 Uuh Ununhexium (289) |

| 65 Tb Terbium 158.93 | 66 Dy Dysprosium 162.50 | 67 Ho Holmium 164.93 | 68 Er Erbium 167.26 | 69 Tm Thulium 168.93 | 70 Yb Ytterbium 173.04 | 71 Lu Lutetium 174.97 |

| 97 Bk Berkelium (247) | 98 Cf Californium (249) | 99 Es Einsteinium (254) | 100 Fm Fermium (257) | 101 Md Mendelevium (258) | 102 No Nobelium (259) | 103 Lr Lawrencium (260) |

Note: *The atomic masses listed in the table reflect current measurements.*
The atomic masses listed in parentheses are those of the element's most stable or most common isotope.

1 ALBANIA
2 ANDORRA
3 BELGIUM
4 BOSNIA & HERZEGOVINA
5 CROATIA
6 CZECH REPUBLIC
7 DENMARK
8 HUNGARY
9 LIECHTENSTEIN
10 LUXEMBOURG
11 MALTA
12 MOLDOVA
13 MONACO
14 NETHERLANDS
15 SERBIA & MONTENEGRO
16 SLOVAKIA
17 SLOVENIA
18 SWITZERLAND
19 THE FORMER
    YUGOSLAV REP.
    OF MACEDONIA

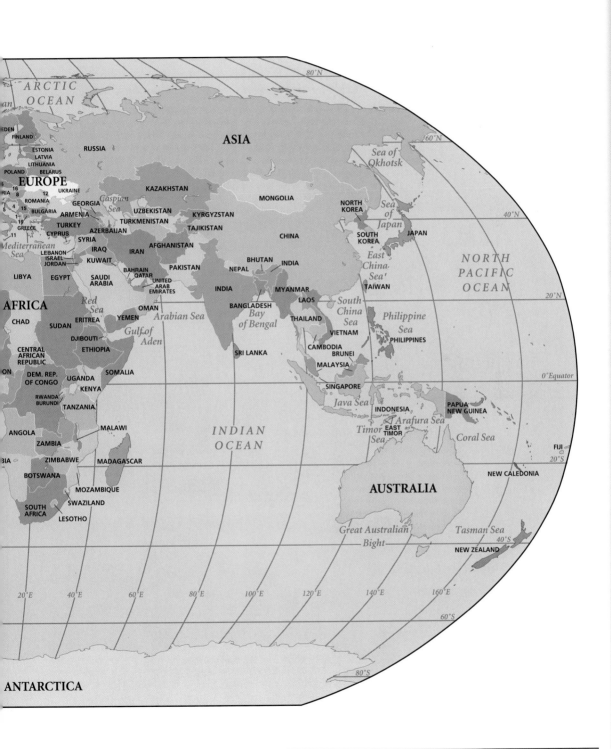

ARCTIC
OCEAN

FINLAND
ESTONIA
LATVIA
LITHUANIA
POLAND   BELARUS
EUROPE
ROMANIA
BULGARIA
GREECE
TURKEY
CYPRUS
SYRIA
LEBANON
ISRAEL
JORDAN
Mediterranean
Sea
LIBYA   EGYPT

RUSSIA

ASIA

KAZAKHSTAN

UKRAINE
GEORGIA   Caspian
ARMENIA   Sea   UZBEKISTAN   KYRGYZSTAN
AZERBAIJAN   TURKMENISTAN   TAJIKISTAN

IRAQ   IRAN   AFGHANISTAN
KUWAIT
BAHRAIN
QATAR   PAKISTAN
UNITED
ARAB   NEPAL
EMIRATES

MONGOLIA

CHINA

NORTH
KOREA
SOUTH
KOREA

BHUTAN
INDIA

Sea of
Okhotsk

Sea
of
Japan   JAPAN

60°N

80°N

40°N

AFRICA
Red
Sea
CHAD   SUDAN   ERITREA   YEMEN
DJIBOUTI
CENTRAL   ETHIOPIA
AFRICAN
REPUBLIC
DEM. REP.   UGANDA
OF CONGO
KENYA
RWANDA
BURUNDI   TANZANIA

SAUDI
ARABIA

OMAN

Gulf of
Aden

Arabian Sea

INDIA

BANGLADESH
SRI LANKA

MYANMAR

LAOS

THAILAND

CAMBODIA

MALAYSIA

SINGAPORE

East
China
Sea'

TAIWAN

South
China
Sea

VIETNAM

BRUNEI

Bay
of Bengal

Philippine
Sea

PHILIPPINES

NORTH
PACIFIC
OCEAN

20°N

0°Equator

ANGOLA
ZAMBIA
ZIMBABWE
BOTSWANA

SOMALIA

MALAWI

MADAGASCAR

INDIAN
OCEAN

Java Sea   INDONESIA

Timor   EAST
Sea   TIMOR

Arafura Sea

PAPUA
NEW GUINEA

Coral Sea

FIJI

NEW CALEDONIA

20°S

MOZAMBIQUE
SOUTH   SWAZILAND
AFRICA   LESOTHO

Great Australian
Bight

AUSTRALIA

Tasman Sea

NEW ZEALAND

40°S

20°E   40°E   60°E   80°E   100°E   120°E   140°E   160°E

60°S

ANTARCTICA

80°S

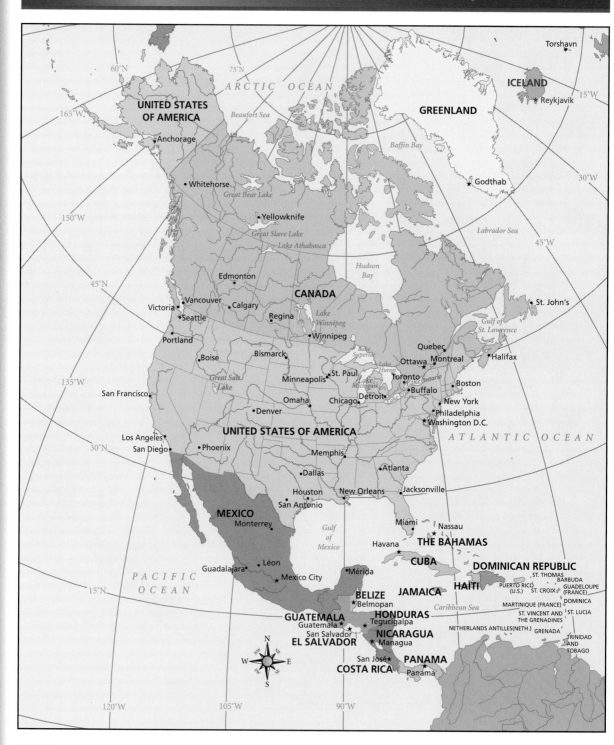

Glossary

A

Absolute dating (ab´sə lüt dā´ting) Method that determines the actual age of a rock or fossil (p. 342)

Absolute magnitude (ab´sə lüt mag´nə tüd) How bright a star actually is (p. 109)

Air mass (âr´ mas´) Large section of the atmosphere with the same temperature and humidity throughout (p. 239)

Air pressure (âr´ presh´ər) Force of air against a unit of area (p. 231)

Alluvial fan (ə lü´vē əl fan´) Fan-shaped area of land deposited where a mountain stream moves onto flat land (p. 289)

Altitude (al´tə tüd´) Height above the earth's surface (p. 212)

Anemometer (an´ə mom´ə tər) Instrument used to measure wind speed (p. 233)

Apparent magnitude (ə par´ənt mag´nə tüd) How bright a star looks (p. 109)

Asteroid (as´tə roid) Rocky object, smaller than a planet, that orbits a star (p. 100)

Asteroid belt (as´tə roid belt´) Region between Mars and Jupiter where most asteroids orbit the sun (p. 100)

Astronomer (ə stron´ə mər) Scientist who studies outer space and objects in it (p. 4)

Astronomy (ə stron´ə mē) Study of outer space and objects in it (p. 2)

Atmosphere (at´mə sfir) Envelope of gas surrounding an object in space (p. 82)

Atom (at´əm) Smallest particle of an element that has the characteristics of that element (p. 138)

Axis (ak´sis) Imaginary line through the earth that connects the North and South Poles (p. 29)

B

Barometer (bə rom´ə tər) Instrument used to measure air pressure (p. 231)

Benthos (ben´thos) Organisms that live on the ocean floor (p. 271)

Black hole (blak´ hōl´) Region in space with tremendous gravity, caused by the collapse of a huge star (p. 119)

C

Cast (kast) Type of fossil that forms when minerals fill a mold; a model of an organism (p. 336)

Cenozoic Era (sen´ə zō´ik ir´ə) Era described as the Age of Mammals; began about 65 million years ago and continues today (p. 351)

Chemical property (kem´ə kəl prop´ər tē) Characteristic that describes how a substance changes into a different substance (p. 133)

Chemical rock (kem´ə kəl rok´) Sedimentary rock that forms from chemicals dissolved in water (p. 187)

Chemical weathering (kem´ə kəl weŦH´ər ing) Breaking apart of rocks caused by a change in their chemical makeup (p. 281)

Cinder cone (sin´dər kōn´) Small volcano with steep sides and explosive eruptions; made of ash and rock (p. 314)

Cirque (sərk) Bowl-like basin in a mountain that is carved out by an alpine glacier (p. 295)

Cirrus cloud (sir´əs kloud´) High, wispy cloud made of ice crystals (p. 213)

a	hat	e	let	ī	ice	ô	order	ü	put	sh	she		a	in about
ā	age	ē	equal	o	hot	oi	oil	ü	rule	th	thin	ə	e	in taken
ä	far	èr	term	ō	open	ou	out	ch	child	ŦH	then		i	in pencil
â	care	i	it	ó	saw	u	cup	ng	long	zh	measure		o	in lemon
													u	in circus

Clastic rock (klas´tik rok´) Sedimentary rock made mainly from fragments of other rocks (p. 186)

Cleavage (klē´vij) Ability to split along flat surfaces (p. 165)

Climate (klī´mit) Average weather of a region over a long period of time (p. 247)

Cold front (kōld´ frunt´) Boundary ahead of a cold air mass that is pushing out and wedging under a warm air mass (p. 239)

Comet (kom´it) Ball of ice, rock, frozen gases, and dust that orbits the sun (p. 101)

Compass rose (kum´pəs rōz´) Part of a map that shows the major compass directions (p. 9)

Composite volcano (kəm poz´it vol kā´nō) Tall volcano; formed from quiet lava flows that alternate with eruptions of rock and ash (p. 315)

Compound (kom´pound) Substance formed when the atoms of two or more elements join chemically (p. 141)

Condense (kən dens´) Change from a gas to a liquid (p. 211)

Conglomerate (kən glom´ ər it) Clastic rock made of rounded pebbles cemented together (p. 186)

Constellation (kon´stə lā´shən) Pattern of stars seen from Earth (p. 121)

Continent (kon´tə nənt) One of the seven major land areas of the earth (p. 27)

Continental drift (kon´tə nən´təl drift´) Theory that the major landmasses of the earth move (p. 309)

Continental shelf (kon´tə nən´təl shelf´) Part of a continent that extends from a shoreline out into an ocean (p. 270)

Continental slope (kon´tə nən´təl slōp´) Steep slope between the continental shelf and the deep ocean floor (p. 270)

Contour interval (kon´tùr in´tər vəl) Vertical distance between contour lines on a topographic map (p. 16)

Contour line (kon´tùr līn´) Line on a map that connects points of equal elevation (p. 15)

Convection current (kən vek´shən kėr´ənt) Circular motion of a gas or liquid as it heats (p. 311)

Core (kôr) Dense center of the earth made of solid and melted metals (p. 308)

Crater (krā´tər) Circular low area surrounded by a rim, usually caused by an object hitting the ground (p. 70)

Crust (krust) Outer layer of the earth (p. 308)

Crystal (kris´tl) Basic shape that a mineral tends to take (p. 164)

Cumulus cloud (kyü´myə ləs kloud´) Puffy, white cloud occurring at medium altitudes (p. 213)

Current (kėr´ənt) Large stream of water flowing in oceans, in rivers, and in some large lakes (p. 269)

D

Degree (di grē´) Unit for measuring angles in a circle or sphere (p. 42)

Delta (del´tə) Fan-shaped area of land formed when sediment is deposited where a river empties into a lake or an ocean (p. 289)

Deposition (dep´ə zish´ən) Dropping of eroded sediment (p. 289)

Divide (də vīd´) Ridge that separates drainage basins (p. 261)

Drainage basin (drā´nij bā´sn) Land area that is drained by a river and its tributaries (p. 261)

E

Earthquake (ėrth´kwāk´) Shaking of the earth's crust (p. 322)

Earth science (ėrth´ sī´əns) Study of the earth's land, water, air, and outer space (p. 2)

Element (el´ə mənt) Substance that cannot be changed or separated into other kinds of substances (p. 137)

Epicenter (ep´ə sen´tər) Point on the earth's surface directly over the focus of an earthquake (p. 324)

Equator (i kwā´tər) Line of 0° latitude halfway between the poles (p. 42)

Erosion (i rō´zhən) Wearing away and moving of weathered rock and soil (p. 286)

Evaporate (i vap´ə rāt´) Change from a liquid to a gas (p. 211)

Extrusive rock (ek strü´siv rok´) Igneous rock that forms from cooled lava on the earth's surface (p. 183)

F

Fault (fòlt) Break in the earth's crust along which movement occurs (p. 318)

Floodplain (flud´plān´) Low, flat area that a river covers when it overflows its banks (p. 288)

Focus (fō´kəs) Point inside the earth where rock first moves, starting an earthquake (p. 324)

Fog (fog) Stratus cloud that forms near the ground (p. 212)

Folding (fōld´ing) Bending of rock layers that are squeezed together (p. 317)

Foliated rock (fō´lē ā´təd rok´) Metamorphic rock in which minerals have been rearranged into visible bands (p. 192)

Fossil (fos´əl) Trace or remains of an organism preserved in the earth's crust (p. 335)

Fracture (frak´chər) Tendency to break with jagged edges (p. 165)

Front (frunt) Moving boundary line between two air masses (p. 239)

Full moon (fùl´ mün´) Phase of the moon when the earth is between the sun and the moon (p. 66)

Fusion (fyü´zhən) Process by which particles combine to form a new particle (p. 108)

G

Galaxy (gal´ək sē) Group of billions of stars (p. 122)

Geologic time (jē´ə loj´ik tīm´) All the time that has passed since the earth formed (p. 334)

Geologic time scale (jē´ə loj´ik tīm skāl´) Outline of the events of the earth's history (p. 347)

Geologist (jē ol´ə jist) Scientist who studies the solid parts of the earth and how they change (p. 3)

Geology (jē ol´ə jē) Study of the solid parts of the earth (p. 2)

Geyser (gī´zər) Place where hot groundwater and steam blast into the air (p. 260)

Glacier (glā´shər) Thick mass of ice that covers a large area (p. 294)

Gravity (grav´ə tē) Force of attraction between any two objects (p. 56)

Greenhouse effect (grēn´hous´ ə fekt´) Warming of the atmosphere because of trapped heat energy from the sun (p. 88)

Grid (grid) Set of horizontal and vertical lines on a map (p. 38)

Groundwater (ground´ wô´tər) Water that sinks into the ground (p. 257)

H

Hachure (ha shùr´) Short line that points toward the center of a depression on a topographic map (p. 16)

Half-life (haf´ līf´) Length of time it takes for half of the atoms of a radioactive element to decay (p. 342)

Hardness (härd´nəs) Ability of a mineral to resist being scratched (p. 159)

Hemisphere (hem´ə sfir) Half of the earth (p. 49)

a	hat	e	let	ī	ice	ô	order	ù	put	sh	she		a	in about
ā	age	ē	equal	o	hot	oi	oil	ü	rule	th	thin	ə	e	in taken
ä	far	ėr	term	ō	open	ou	out	ch	child	ᵮH	then		i	in pencil
â	care	i	it	ò	saw	u	cup	ng	long	zh	measure		o	in lemon
													u	in circus

High (hī) Cold area of high air pressure (p. 240)

Horn (hôrn) Jagged, pyramid-shaped peak formed by the intersection of three or more cirques (p. 295)

Humidity (hyü mid´ə tē) Amount of water vapor in the air (p. 232)

Hurricane (hėr´ə kān´) Severe tropical storm with high winds that revolve around an eye (p. 245)

I

Igneous rock (ig´nē əs rok´) Rock formed from melted minerals that have cooled and hardened (p. 178)

Index fossil (in´deks fos´əl) Fossil that can be used to establish the relative age of the rock in which the fossil occurs (p. 341)

International date line (in´tər nash´ə nəl dāt´ līn´) Imaginary line that defines the start of a day (p. 33)

Intrusive rock (in trü´siv rok´) Igneous rock that forms underground from cooled magma (p. 181)

Ionosphere (ī on´ə sfir) Layer of the atmosphere containing ions, or electrically charged particles (p. 209)

Isobar (ī´sə bär) Line on a weather map connecting areas of equal air pressure (p. 240)

L

Latitude (lat´ə tüd) Angle that describes the distance north or south of the equator (p. 42)

Lava (lä´və) Magma that comes out onto the earth's surface (p. 183)

Legend (lej´ənd) List of map symbols and their meanings (p. 8)

Light-year (līt´ yir´) Distance that light travels in one year (p. 114)

Longitude (lon´jə tüd) Angle that describes the distance east or west of the prime meridian (p. 46)

Low (lō) Warm area of low air pressure (p. 240)

Lunar eclipse (lü´nər i klips´) Passing of the moon through the earth's shadow (p. 67)

Luster (lus´tər) How a mineral reflects light (p. 158)

M

Magma (mag´mə) Hot, liquid rock inside the earth (p. 181)

Magnitude (mag´nə tüd) Brightness of a star (p. 109)

Mantle (man´tl) Layer of the earth that surrounds the core (p. 308)

Map (map) Drawing that shows part of the earth's surface as seen from above (p. 7)

Maria (mär´ē ə) Low, flat plains on the moon's surface that appear as dark areas (p. 70)

Mass (mas) Amount of material that an object contains (p. 56)

Matter (mat´ər) Anything that has mass and takes up space (p. 132)

Meander (mē an´dər) Looping curve in a river (p. 288)

Mechanical weathering (mə kan´ə kəl weᴛʜ´ər ing) Breaking apart of rocks without changing their mineral composition (p. 280)

Meridian (mə rid´ē ən) Line of longitude (p. 46)

Mesosphere (mes´ə sfir) Third layer of the atmosphere; the coldest layer (p. 209)

Mesozoic Era (mes´ə zō´ik ir´ə) Era characterized by dinosaurs; began about 245 million years ago and ended about 65 million years ago (p. 350)

Metamorphic rock (met´ə môr´fik rok´) Rock that has been changed by intense heat, pressure, and chemical reactions (p. 179)

Meteor (mē´tē ər) Brief streak of light seen when an asteroid enters the earth's atmosphere and burns up (p. 100)

Meteorite (mē′tē ə rīt′) Piece of rock that hits the surface of a planet or moon after traveling through space (p. 70, 101)

Meteorologist (mē′tē ə rol′ə jist) Scientist who studies the air and weather (p. 4)

Meteorology (mē′tē ə rol′ə jē) Study of the earth's air and weather (p. 2)

Metric system (met′rik sis′təm) System of measurement used by scientists (p. 3)

Mid-ocean ridge (mid′ ō′shən rij′) Mountain chain on the ocean floor (p. 270)

Milky Way galaxy (mil′kē wā′ gal′ək sē) Group of stars to which our solar system belongs (p. 123)

Mineral (min′ər əl) Element or compound found in the earth (p. 154)

Mixture (miks′chər) Two or more elements or compounds mixed together, but not joined chemically (p. 144)

Mold (mōld) Type of fossil that forms when the shape of a plant or an animal is left in a rock (p. 336)

Moon (mün) Natural satellite that orbits a planet (p. 78)

Moraine (mə rān′) Ridge of sediment deposited by a glacier (p. 296)

Mouth (mouth) Place where a river flows into a larger body of water (p. 289)

N

Nebula (neb′yə lə) Cloud of gas and dust in space (p. 117)

Nekton (nek′ton) Free-swimming ocean animals (p. 271)

Neutron star (nü′tron stär′) Very small, very dense star that remains after a supernova (p. 119)

New moon (nü′ mün′) Phase of the moon when the moon is between the sun and the earth (p. 66)

Nonfoliated rock (non fō′lē ā′təd rok′) Metamorphic rock that does not show bands (p. 192)

Normal fault (nôr′məl fôlt′) Break in the crust in which the overhanging block of rock has slid down (p. 318)

North Pole (nôrth′ pōl′) Point farthest north on the earth (p. 29)

Nova (nō′və) Brilliant explosion of a collapsed red giant (p. 118)

Nucleus (nü′klē əs) Atom's center, which is made of protons and neutrons (p. 138)

O

Oceanographer (ō′shə nog′rə fər) Scientist who studies the oceans (p. 4)

Oceanography (ō′shə nog′rə fē) Study of the earth's oceans (p. 2)

Orbit (ôr′bit) Curved path that an object follows as it revolves around another object (p. 56)

Organic rock (ôr gan′ik rok′) Sedimentary rock that forms from the remains of living things (p. 188)

Oxbow lake (oks′bō′ lāk′) C-shaped body of water formed when a meander is cut off from the rest of the river (p. 288)

Oxidation (oks′sə dā′shən) Process in which minerals combine with oxygen to form new substances (p. 281)

P

Paleozoic Era (pā′lē ə zō′ik ir′ə) Era marked by great development in sea life; began about 540 million years ago and ended about 245 million years ago (p. 349)

Pangaea (pan jē′ə) Single landmass from which Alfred Wegener thought the continents separated millions of years ago (p. 309)

a	hat	e	let	ī	ice	ô	order	ú	put	sh	she		a	in about
ā	age	ē	equal	o	hot	oi	oil	ü	rule	th	thin	ə	e	in taken
ä	far	ėr	term	ō	open	ou	out	ch	child	ᴛʜ	then		i	in pencil
â	care	i	it	ȯ	saw	u	cup	ng	long	zh	measure		o	in lemon
													u	in circus

Parallel (par´ə lel) Line of latitude (p. 42)

Petrification (pet´rə fə kā´shən) Replacement of the original parts of a buried organism with minerals (p. 335)

Phases of the moon (fāz´əz ov ᴛнə mün´) Changes in the moon's appearance as it orbits the earth (p. 66)

Physical property (fiz´ə kəl prop´ər tē) Characteristic of a substance or an object that can be observed without changing the substance into a different substance (p. 133)

Planet (plan´it) Large object in space that orbits a star such as the sun (p. 78)

Plankton (plangk´tən) Tiny organisms that live at or near the ocean surface (p. 271)

Plate (plāt) Large section of the earth's crust that moves (p. 310)

Plate tectonics (plāt´ tek ton´iks) Theory that the earth's surface is made of large sections of crust that move (p. 335)

Polar easterly (pō´lər ē´stər lē) Wind near a pole; blows from the east (p. 223)

Porous (pôr´əs) Containing many spaces through which air and water can move (p. 259)

Precambrian Era (prē´kam´brē ən ir´ə) Oldest and longest era of the earth's history; began about 4.6 billion years ago and ended about 540 million years ago (p. 347)

Precipitation (pri sip´ə tā´shən) Moisture that falls to the earth from the atmosphere (p. 216)

Prevailing westerly (pri vā´ling wes´tər lē) Wind generally between 30°N and 60°N latitudes (or 30°S and 60°S); blows from the west (p. 223)

Prime meridian (prīm´ mə rid´ē ən) Line of 0° longitude (p. 46)

Principle of crosscutting relationships (prin´sə pəl ov krós´kut´ing ri lā´shən ships) A feature, such as a rock structure or a fault, that cuts across rock layers is younger than the rock layers (p. 341)

Principle of superposition (prin´sə pəl ov sü´pər pə zish´ən) In layers of sedimentary rocks, the oldest layer is on the bottom and the youngest layer is on the top if the layers have not been overturned (p. 340)

Property (prop´ər tē) Characteristic that describes matter (p. 133)

Psychrometer (sī krom´ə tər) Instrument used to measure relative humidity (p. 232)

R

Radioactive element (rā´dē ō ak´tiv el´ə mənt) Element that breaks apart, or decays, to form another element (p. 342)

Rain gauge (rān´gāj´) Instrument used to measure the amount of rainfall (p. 234)

Red giant (red´ jī´ənt) Star that has expanded after using up its hydrogen (p. 118)

Relative dating (rel´ə tiv dāt´ing) Method that compares two rock layers to find out which is older (p. 340)

Relative humidity (rel´ə tiv hyü mid´ə tē) Amount of water vapor in the air compared to the maximum amount of water vapor the air can hold (p. 232)

Reservoir (rez´ər vwär) Artificial lake created by placing a dam across a river (p. 263)

Reverse fault (ri vėrs´ fôlt´) Break in the crust in which the overhanging block of rock has been raised (p. 318)

Revolution (rev´ ə lü´shən) Movement of one object in its orbit around another object in space (p. 60)

Richter scale (rik´tər skāl´) Scale used to measure the strength of an earthquake (p. 324)

Rock (rok) Natural, solid material made of one or more minerals (p. 178)

Rock cycle (rok´ sī´kəl) Series of natural changes that cause one type of rock to become another type of rock (p. 194)

Rotation (rō tā´shən) Spinning of the earth or other object in space (p. 29)

Runoff (run´óf´) Water that runs over the earth's surface and flows into streams (p. 257)

S

Salinity (sə lin´ə tē) Saltiness of water (p. 267)

Scale (skāl) Part of a map that shows the relationship between map distance and actual distance (p. 10)

Sea-floor spreading (sē´flôr´ spred´ing) Theory that the ocean floor spreads apart as new crust is formed at mid-ocean ridges (p. 310)

Seamount (sē´mount) Underwater mountain that is usually a volcano (p. 270)

Sediment (sed´ə mənt) Solid material, such as sand, soil, pebbles, and organic matter, that is carried in air, water, or ice and settles out (p. 185)

Sedimentary rock (sed´ə mən´tər ē rok´) Rock formed from pieces of other rock and organic matter that have been pressed and cemented together (p. 179)

Seismograph (sīz´mə graf) Instrument that detects and records earthquake waves (p. 323)

Shield volcano (shēld´ vol kā´nō) Low, broad volcano with a wide crater; formed from thin layers of lava (p. 315)

Sinkhole (singk´hōl´) Funnel-shaped depression that results when the roof of a cave collapses (p. 260)

Soil (soil) Mixture of tiny pieces of weathered rock and the remains of plants and animals (p. 282)

Solar eclipse (sō´lər i´klips) Passing of the moon between the earth and the sun (p. 67)

Solar system (sō´lər sis´təm) A star, such as the sun, and all of the objects that revolve around it in space (p. 79)

South Pole (south´ pōl´) Point farthest south on the earth (p. 29)

Specific gravity (spi sif´ik grav´ə tē) Mineral's weight compared to the weight of water (p. 165)

Spring (spring) Place where groundwater flows naturally out of the ground (p. 260)

Standard time zone (stan´dərd tīm´ zōn´) Area that has the same clock time (p. 32)

Star (stär) Glowing ball of hot gas that makes its own energy and light (p. 78)

States of matter (stāts´ ov mat´ər) Basic forms in which matter exists, including solid, liquid, and gas (p. 132)

Stratosphere (strat´ə sfir) Second layer of the atmosphere; includes the ozone layer (p. 209)

Stratus cloud (strā´təs kloud´) Low, flat cloud that forms in layers (p. 212)

Streak (strēk) Color of the mark a mineral makes on a white tile (p. 158)

Strike-slip fault (strīk´slip´ fólt´) Break in the crust in which the blocks of rock move horizontally past each other (p. 318)

Submersible (səb mėr´sə bəl) Small underwater research vessel (p. 4)

Subsoil (sub´soil´) Layer of soil directly below the topsoil (p. 282)

Sunspot (sun´spot´) Dark area on the sun's surface that gives off less energy than the rest of the sun (p. 82)

a	hat	e	let	ī	ice	ô	order	ù	put	sh	she		a	in about
ā	age	ē	equal	o	hot	oi	oil	ü	rule	th	thin		e	in taken
ä	far	ėr	term	ō	open	ou	out	ch	child	ᴛʜ	then	ə	i	in pencil
â	care	i	it	ó	saw	u	cup	ng	long	zh	measure		o	in lemon
													u	in circus

Supergiant (sü´pər jī´ənt) One of the largest stars, formed when a star expands after using up its hydrogen; larger than a red giant (p. 118)

Supernova (sü´pər nō´və) Brilliant explosion of a collapsed supergiant (p. 119)

T

Telescope (tel´ə skōp) Instrument that collects light, making faint objects easier to see and enlarging distant objects (p. 70)

Texture (teks´chər) Size of crystals in an igneous rock (p. 182)

Thermocline (thėr´mō klīn) Ocean layer between about 300 and 1,000 meters below the surface, where the temperature drops sharply (p. 268)

Thermosphere (thėr´mə sfir) Outermost layer of the atmosphere; includes most of the ionosphere (p. 209)

Tides (tīdz) Regular rising and falling of the earth's major bodies of water (p. 68)

Topographic map (top´ə graf´ik map´) Map that shows the shape and elevation of the land surface (p. 15)

Topsoil (top´soil´) Top layer of soil, rich with oxygen and decayed organic matter (p. 282)

Tornado (tôr nā´dō) Powerful wind storm with a whirling, funnel-shaped cloud and extremely low pressure (p. 245)

Trade wind (trād´ wind´) Strong, reliable wind just north or south of the equator; blows from the east (p. 223)

Trench (trench) Deep valley on the ocean floor (p. 270)

Tributary (trib´yə ter´ē) River that joins another river of equal or greater size (p. 261)

Troposphere (trop´ə sfir) Bottom layer of the atmosphere, extending from ground level up to about 16 kilometers above the earth (p. 208)

Tsunami (sü nä´mē) Large sea wave caused by vibrations of the earth (p. 325)

U

Unit (yü´nit) Known amount used for measuring (p. 3)

Universe (yü´nə vėrs´) Everything that exists (p. 123)

V

Vent (vent) Round opening through which magma reaches the surface of the earth (p. 313)

Volcano (vol kā´nō) Mountain that develops where magma pushes up through the earth's surface (p. 313)

W

Warm front (wôrm´ frunt´) Boundary ahead of a warm air mass that is pushing out and riding over a cold air mass (p. 239)

Water cycle (wò´tər sī´kəl) Movement of water between the atmosphere and the earth's surface (p. 256)

Water table (wò´tər tā´bəl) Top of the groundwater layer (p. 259)

Water vapor (wò´tər vā´pər) Water in the form of a gas (p. 211)

Wave (wāv) Up-and-down motion of water caused by energy moving through the water (p. 268)

Weather (weŦH´ər) State of the atmosphere at a given time and place (p. 230)

Weathering (weŦH´ər ing) Breaking down of rocks on the earth's surface (p. 280)

White dwarf (wīt´ dwôrf´) Small, white, hot, dense star that remains after a nova (p. 118)

Wind belt (wind´ belt´) Pattern of wind movement around the earth (p. 222)

Wind cell (wind´ sel´) Continuous cycle of rising warm air and falling cold air (p. 221)

Wind vane (wind´ vān´) Instrument used to find wind direction (p. 233)

Index

A

Absolute dating, 342–343
Absolute magnitude, 109
Achievements in Science
  Almanacs, 57
  Artificial Glaciers, 299
  Balloon Pilots, 210
  Black Holes, 120
  Celebrating Earth Day, 6
  Cloud Seeding, 218
  Creating New Elements, 140
  Doppler Radar, 241
  Field Guides for Rocks and
    Minerals, 184
  Global Positioning
    Systems, 39
  Protecting the
    Environment, 272
  The Rock Cycle Theory, 196
  The Struggle to Accept the
    Solar System, 91
  The Theory of Sea-Floor
    Spreading, 312
  A Trip Around the World,
    30
  Uncovering the History of
    Life, 337
  Working with Metals, 156
Africa, 27
Agricola, Georgius, 184
Air, 145
Air masses, 239
Air pressure, 231–232
  measuring, 236–237
Air temperature, 230
Air-traffic controller, 45
Aldrin, Buzz, 71
Aleutian Islands, 313

Alluvial fan, 289
Almanacs, 57
Alpine glaciers, 294, 295–296
Alternative energy sources,
  358–363
Altitude, 212
Aluminum, 154, 171
  recycling, 172
Alvin (submersible),
  4, 312
Amber, 336
Americium, 140
Andes, 317
Anemometer, 233
Aneroid barometer, 231
Angle of light, 63–64
Antarctica, 27, 294
Antarctic Ocean, 28
Apatite, 160
Apollo missions, 65, 71
Appalachian Mountains, 347,
  349
Apparent magnitude, 109
Arctic Ocean, 28
Armstrong, Neil, 71
Army Signal Service, 238
Artificial glaciers, 299
Artificial satellites, 69
Asia, 27
Asteroid belt, 100
Asteroids, 100–101
Astronauts, 71, 80
Astronomers, 4, 97, 111, 115,
  119
Astronomical distance
  see Stars, distances of
Astronomy, 2
Atlantic Ocean, 28, 268
Atlantic time zone, 34

Atmosphere, 82
  defined, 204
  gases in, 204–206
  layers of, 208–209
Atmospheric scientist, 235
Atoms, 138
Australia, 27
Axis, 29, 31

B

Bacteria, 206
Balloon pilots, 210
Banneker, Benjamin, 57
Barometer, 231–232, 239
Bar scale, 10
Basalt, 183, 198
Bauxite, 171, 172
Bays, 268
Beaches, 290
Benthos, 271
Berkelium, 140
Big Dipper, 115, 121
Biodegradable materials, 134
Biosphere, 3, 188, 205–206,
  249, 271, 335–337,
  347–351, 361
Black Hills, 347
Black holes, 119, 120
Bopp, Thomas, 101
Break pattern of minerals,
  165
Bronze, 156
Building products, minerals
  used in, 171

C

Calcite, 154, 160, 188
  making, 190–191
Calcium, 160

Calcium carbonate, 187
California Current, 269
Californium, 140
Carbon-14, 342–343
Carbon dioxide, 88, 89, 145, 205
Carbon dioxide cycle
   see Oxygen-carbon dioxide cycle
Carbonic acid, 281
Careers
   see Science at Work
Carson, Rachel, 272
Cartographer, 12, 47
Cascade Range, 317
Cassini (spacecraft), 94
Cast, 336
Castle Geyser, 260
Caves, 260, 281, 283
Celsius scale, 230
Cenozoic Era, 351
Centimeter, 11
Central Standard Time (CST), 35
Central time zone, 34
Cernan, Eugene, 71
Chalk, 188
Channeling machines, 193
Charon, 96
Chemical change
   see Chemical properties
Chemical engineer, 146
Chemical properties, 133
Chemical rocks, 187
Chemical weathering, 281, 284–285
Chlorine, 141
Chromosphere, 82
Cinder cones, 314
Cinders, 314
Cirques, 295
Cirrus clouds, 213
Clastic rocks, 186–187
Cleavage, 165

Climates, 247
   factors that affect, 248
Climate zones, 247–248, 250
Clouds, 211–213, 229, 255
   formation of, 211
   observing, 215
   seeding, 218
   types of, 212–213
Coal, 188, 189, 198
Cold front, 239
Colorado River, 263
Color of minerals, 157, 164
   observing, 162–163
Color of stars, 110
Comets, 101
Compass directions, 9
Compass roses, 9, 11
Composite volcanoes, 315
Compounds, 141–142, 145, 154, 204
   formulas for, 143–144
Computers, 4
Concave mirror, 72
Condensation, 211
Conglomerate, 186, 198
Conodonts, 351
Constellations, 121, 368–371
Continental climate, 248
Continental drift, 309
Continental glaciers, 294, 297–298
Continental shelf, 270
Continental slope, 270
Continents, 27
Contour interval, 16
Contour lines, 15–17
Convection currents, 311
Convex lens, 72
Copernicus, Nicolaus, 91
Copper, 153, 155, 156, 170
Core, 308
Corundum, 160
Crater, 70
Crust, 308

Crystals, 164
Cumulus clouds, 213, 217
Curium, 140
Currents
   convection, 311
   ocean, 269
Cuyahoga River, 272
Cycles
   see Nitrogen cycle
   see Oxygen-carbon dioxide cycle
   see Rock cycle
   see Water cycle

D

Day, 29, 31
Dead Sea, 257
Degrees, 42, 43, 230
Delta, 289
Density
   see Specific gravity of minerals
Deposition, 289
Depression, 16
Deserts, 300
   steppes and, 249
Diamond, 138, 154, 159, 160, 171
Did You Know?
   Alvin (submersible), 4
   ancient maps, 9
   Army Signal Service, 238
   atmosphere composition, 204
   atmosphere layers, 209
   comets, 101
   crystals, 164
   Dead Sea, 257
   diamond and graphite, 138
   dinosaur extinction, 350
   fossils, 186, 341
   geologic time scale, 351
   greenhouse effect, 89
   hydrogen, 143

Did You Know? (continued)
  items left on the moon, 71
  Large and Small
    Magellanic Clouds, 122
  lead, 139
  malachite, 171
  Mimas, 94
  minerals in food, 160
  Minnesota lakes, 262
  mirrors, 158
  moonquakes, 323
  moon's far side, 65
  Mount Waialeale, 234
  Niagara Falls, 287
  ocean water, 267
  plasma, 132
  plate movement, 311
  Pluto, 96
  pumice, 183
  Sahara desert, 300
  space technology, 5
  standard time zones, 32
  starlight, 114
  sunlight traveling to Earth,
    81
  volcano types, 314
  water on Mars, 90
Dinosaurs, 337, 350
Divides, 261
Dolomite, 154
Doppler radar, 241
Drainage basin, 261

E

Earth, 88–89
  atmosphere of, 203–217
  earth-moon system, 55–68
  surface temperature of, 88
  gravitational pull of, 56
  layers of, 308
  revolution of, 60
  rotation of, 29, 31,
    36–37, 60
  shape of, 26

Earth (continued)
  surface features of, 27–28
  unique features of, 88–89
  water in, 255–274
Earth chemistry, 131–149
Earth Day, 6
Earthquakes, 310, 319,
    322–325
  causes of, 322
  locating, 327–328
  predicting, 325
  strength and effect of,
    324–325
Earthquake waves, 323
Earth science, 2
  importance of, 5
  tools used in, 3–4
Eastern Hemisphere, 49
Eastern time zone, 34
Eclipses, 67
Einsteinium, 140
Electrons, 138
Elements, 137–139, 204
  creating new, 140
Elevations, 16
Elliptical galaxy, 122
El Niños, 5
Energy
  alternative sources, 358–363
  nuclear, 143
  renewable and
    nonrenewable sources, 352,
    358–363
  solar, 83
Environment, degradation of,
    134, 189, 207, 214, 272,
    291–293, 301, 352, 358
Environment, protecting, 6,
    214, 235, 272, 302
Environmental Protection
    Agency (EPA), 272
Environmental science
    technician, 214
Epicenter, 324

Equator, 42
Equivalence scale, 11
Erosion, 195
  comparing, 292–293
  glaciers as cause of, 294–298
  people as cause of, 291
  river, 286
  role of gravity in, 301
  water as cause of, 286–290
Europa, 93
Europe, 27
Evaporation, 211
  exploring, 265–266
Extrusive rocks, 183

F

Fahrenheit scale, 230
Faults, 318
  models of, 320–321
Federal Emergency
    Management Agency,
    250
Feldspar, 154, 160, 182, 281
Fermium, 140
Field guides for rocks and
    minerals, 184
Finger Lakes, 298
Fission, 143
Floating, measuring the effect
    of salt water on, 273–274
Floodplain, 288
Floodplain manager, 302
Fluorite, 160
Fog, 212
Folding, 317
  models of, 320–321
Folding plates, 317
Foliated rocks, 192
Forces, 56, 68, 80, 100,
    118–119, 120, 194–195,
    231, 240, 279–301,
    307–325
Formulas for compounds, 143
Fossett, Steve, 30

Fossil fuels, cutting down on, 352
Fossils, 186, 335, 337
    ages of, 340–343
    index, 341
    model of, 338–339
    types of, 335–336
Fracture, 165
Franklin, Benjamin, 57
Front, 239
Full moon, 66
Fusion, 108, 118

G

Galaxies, 122–123
Galilei, Galileo, 91
Galileo (spacecraft), 92
Ganymede, 93
Garnet, 171
Gases, 81–82, 88–89, 92, 94, 95, 100, 101, 108, 117, 131, 132, 145, 183, 192, 204–211, 257, 362–363
    in atmosphere, 204–206
Geographic information system, 12
Geologic time, 334
    eras in, 347–351
Geologic time scale, 347–348
Geologists, 3, 155, 178
Geology, 2
Geosynchronous operational environmental satellites (GOES), 246
Geysers, 260
Glaciers, 294
    alpine, 294
    artificial, 299
    continental, 294, 297–298
    erosion caused by, 294–298
Global ocean, 28
Global positioning system (GPS), 17, 30, 39, 69

Global winds, 222–223
Gneiss, 192, 198
Gold, 137, 154, 155, 157, 159, 170, 171
    properties of, 161
Grand Canyon, 334
Grand Tetons, 318
Granite, 182
Graphite, 138, 154, 170
Gravity, 56, 80, 118
    effect of, 56
    glaciers and, 295
    role of, in erosion, 301
    tides and, 68
Great Bear, 121
Great Lakes, 262, 298, 351
Great Red Spot, 92
Greenhouse effect, 88, 89
Greenland, 294
Greenwich, England, 46
Greenwich meridian, 46
Grid, 38
Groundwater, 257, 259
Gulf of Alaska, 268
Gulf of Mexico, 261
Gulfs, 268
Gulf Stream, 269
Gypsum, 154, 160, 187

H

Hachures, 16
Hailstones, 217, 234
Hale, Alan, 101
Hale-Bopp, 101
Half-life, 342–343
    model of, 345–346
Halite, 154
Hardness of minerals, 159–160
    observing, 162–163
Hawking, Stephen, 120
Heat, 82, 88, 108, 117, 143, 161, 179, 192, 194–195, 211, 221, 256, 269, 309, 311, 359–363

Heat lightning, 244
Helium, 81
Hemispheres, 49
High, 240
Himalayas, 317
Horn, 295
Hubble Space Telescope, 116, 119
Humid continental climate, 249
Humidity, 232
Humid subtropical climate, 249
Hurricanes, 229, 245, 334
Hutton, James, 196
Hydroelectric dam, 263
Hydroelectric power plant operator, 264
Hydroelectric power plants, 263
Hydrogen, 81, 143
Hydrologic cycle
    see Water cycle
Hydrosphere
    see Atmosphere
    see Water cycle
    see Water on the earth

I

Ice cap climate, 249
Ice crystals, 216
Igneous rocks, 178, 181–183, 194, 347
Impurities, 157
Index fossils, 341
Indian Ocean, 28
Inner planets, 86–90
International date line, 33
International Space Station (ISS), 62
Intrusive rocks, 181–182
Investigations
    Comparing Erosion, 292–293

Investigations (continued)
 Describing Location on
  a Round Surface, 40–41
 Exploring Evaporation,
  265–266
 Exploring Light Angle,
  63–64
 Finding Specific Gravity,
  168–169
 Identifying Rocks, 197–198
 Locating an Earthquake,
  327–328
 Making Calcite, 190–191
 Making a Constellation
  Model, 125–126
 Making a Half-Life Model,
  345–346
 Making a Map, 13–14
 Making a Model of a Fossil,
  338–339
 Making a Model of an
  Orbit, 58–59
 Making a Model of Rain,
  219–220
 Making Models of Folding
  and Faults, 320–321
 Measuring Air Pressure,
  236–237
 Measuring the Effect of
  Salt Water on Floating,
  273–274
 Measuring Physical
  Properties of Objects,
  135–136
 Modeling Distances in the
  Solar System, 98–99
 Modeling the Earth's
  Rotation, 36–37
 Observing Brightness,
  112–113
 Observing Chemical
  Weathering, 284–285
 Observing Clouds, 215
 Observing Color, Streak,
  and Hardness, 162–163
 Observing Sunspots, 84–85
 Reading a Topographic
  Map, 19–20
 Separating a Mixture,
  147–148
 Using a Weather Map,
  242–243
Io, 93
Ionosphere, 209
Iron, 139, 155, 156, 160
Irregular galaxy, 122
Isobars, 240

J

Jeweler, 167
Juan de Fuca plate, 313
Jupiter, 92–93

K

Kilauea Volcano, 315

L

Lake Erie, 272
Lake Havasu, 263
Lakes, 262
Lake Superior, 262
Lake Winnipeg, 298
Landforms
 see Alluvial fan
 see Beaches
 see Caves
 see Deltas
 see Faults
 see Floodplains
 see Lakes
 see Meanders
 see Mountains
 see Oxbow lakes
 see Rivers
 see River valley
 see Sand dunes
 see Sea stack
 see Volcanoes
Landslides, 301

Large and Small Magellanic
  Clouds, 122
Latitude, 42–44
 locating points by, 48
Lava, 183, 194
Lead, 139, 170
Light, angle of, 63–64
Lightning, 132
 heat, 244
Light pollution, 124
Light-years, 114–115
Lignite, 189
Limestone, 188, 192, 198
Liquids, 131, 132, 192
Lithosphere
 see Crust
 see Earth, layers of
 see Mantle
Little Ghost Nebula, 117
Longitude, 46
 locating points by, 48
Low, 240
Lunar eclipse, 67
Luster of minerals, 158, 159,
  164
L-waves, 323

M

Magellan (spacecraft), 88
Magma, 181, 183, 192, 194,
  309, 310, 311
Magnetorheological (MR)
  fluid, 316
Magnitude, 109–110
Mantle, 308
Map legends, 8
Mapmaker, 47
Map projection, 47
Maps, 7
 grid system on, 38
 making, 13–14
 topographic, 15–17
Map scales, 10–11

Marble, 192, 193, 198
Maria, 70
Marine climate, 248
Mariner 10 (spacecraft), 86
Marine west coast climate, 249
Mars, 89–90
Mass, 56
Matter, 131, 132
    properties of, 133
    states of, 132
Matterhorn, 295
Meanders, 288
Measurement, 3
    see also Investigations
Mechanical weathering, 280
Mediterranean climate, 249
Mediterranean Sea, 268
Melroy, Pamela Ann, 62
Mendelevium, 140
Mercator projection, 47
Mercury, 80, 86
Mercury barometer, 231
Meridians, 46
Mesosphere, 209
Mesozoic Era, 350, 351
Metallic luster, 158
Metals, working with, 156
Metamorphic rocks, 179, 192, 195, 347
Meteor, 100
Meteor Crater, 101
Meteorite, 70, 101
Meteorologists, 4, 5, 69, 241, 246
Meteorology, 2
Metric system, 3
Metric units, 3
Metric and customary measurement, 356–357
Mica, 154, 182
Mid-ocean ridges, 270, 309
Milky Way galaxy, 107, 123
Mimas, 94

Minerals, 153–172, 170, 179
    common uses of, 170–171
    defined, 154
    features of, 154
    field guides for, 184
    locating and mining, 155
    properties of, 157–160, 164–166
Mining, 155
Mississippi River, 288
Missouri River, 288
Mixtures, 144–145
    separating, 147–148
Model, 7
Mohs' scale of hardness, 159–160
Mold, 336
Mono Lake, 187
Moon, 78–79
    Apollo missions to, 71
    movement of, 65–68
    phases of, 66
    revolution of, 65
    rotation of, 65
    surface of, 70
Moraines, 296, 297
Mountains, 317–318
Mountain time zone, 34
Mount St. Helens, 313
Mount Waialeale, 234
Mouth, 289

N

National Aeronautics and
    Space Administration
    (NASA), 116
National Radio Astronomy
    Observatory, 111
National Weather Service
    (NWS), 238, 246
Natural resouces, 83,
    154–155, 172, 178, 214,
    258–259, 262–263,
    358–363

Natural satellite, 69
Nazca plate, 310
Nebula, 117
Nekton, 271
Nelson, Gaylord, 6
Neptune, 95–96
Neutron star, 119
Neutrons, 138
New moon, 66
Newton, Isaac, 91
Niagara Falls, 287
Night, 29, 31
Nitrogen, 139, 145, 204, 206
Nitrogen cycle, 206
Nobelium, 140
Nonfoliated rocks, 192
Normal fault, 318
Norphel, Chewang, 299
North America, 27
    map of, 376
North American plate, 322
North Atlantic Drift, 269
Northern Hemisphere, 49, 60, 61
North Pole, 29, 43
North Star, 121
North wind, 233
Notes
    alpine glaciers, 296
    atoms, 139
    climate types, 248
    degrees, 43
    diamonds, 170
    Earth's origin, 347
    Earth's surface temperature, 88
    fossils, 335
    glacier formation, 294
    granite, 182
    Hale-Bopp comet, 101
    ice shelves, 297
    iron, 308
    Kilauea Volcano, 315
    landslides, 301

Notes (continued)
map symbols, 11
matter, 142
meanders, 288
mine shafts, 155
photosynthesis, 205
saltwater bodies, 268
solar system motion, 79
star color, 110
system definition, 3
theory definition, 309
tide factors, 68
topographic maps, 16
water cycle, 216, 257
world ocean, 28
Nova, 118
Nuclear energy, 143
Nuclear reactions, 82, 108,
117, 143, 363
Nucleus, 138

O

Obsidian, 183, 198
Ocean currents, 269
Ocean floor, 270
age of, 309
Ocean life, 271
Oceanographers, 4
Oceanography, 2
Ocean waves, 268
Odyssey (orbiter), 90
Ohio River, 288
Orbit, 56
model of, 58–59
Organic rocks, 188
Orthographic projection, 47
Outer planets, 92–96
Owen, Richard, 337
Oxbow lake, 288
Oxidation, 281
Oxygen-carbon dioxide cycle,
205
Oxygen, 139, 145, 154, 204
Ozark Mountains, 347

Ozone, 207
Ozone holes, 207

P

Pacific Ocean, 28, 261, 268
Pacific time zone, 34
Paleontologists, 337
Paleozoic Era, 349
Pangaea, 309
Parallels, 42
Paricutín, 314
Park, mapping, 18
Parker Dam, 263
Periodic Table of Elements,
139, 140, 372–373
Petrification, 335
Petroleum engineer, 344
Phases of moon, 66
Phosphorus, 160
Photogrammetry, 48
Photosynthesis, 205
Photovoltaic (PV) cell, 102
Physical change
see Physical properties
Physical properties, 133
measuring, 135–136
Piton de la Fournaise, 307
Plains, 270
Planets, 78–79
inner, 86–90
outer, 92–96
Plankton, 271
Plasma, 132
Plastic, 134
Plates, 310
Plate tectonics, 310–311
Pluto, 96
Plutonium, 140
Polar climates, 248, 249
Polar easterlies, 223
Pollution
laws on, 214
light, 124
Poor Richard's Almanack, 57

Porous, 259
Precambrian Era, 347, 351
Precious metals, 171
Precipitation, 216–217,
234, 256–257, 259
Prevailing westerlies, 223
Prime meridian, 46
Principle of crosscutting
relationships, 341
Principle of superposition, 340
Properties, 133
of gold, 161
Protons, 138
Proxima Centauri, 114
Psychrometer, 232
Pulitzer, Joseph, 57
Pumice, 183, 198
P-waves, 323, 325
Pyrite, 157, 158, 159

Q

Quartz, 137, 154, 157, 160,
170, 171, 182, 187
Quick test, 160

R

Radioactive elements, 342
Rain, 216
model of, 219–220
Rainbows, 203
Raindrops, 217
Rain gauge, 234
Ratio, 11
Recycling, 134, 172
Red giant, 118
Reflecting telescopes, 72
Refracting telescopes, 72
Relative dating, 340–341
Relative humidity, 232
Reservoirs, 263
Reverse fault, 318
Revolution, 60
Rhyolite, 198
Richter scale, 324

River deposits, 289
River erosion, 286
Rivers, 261–262
River valley, life of, 287–288
Robinson projection, 47
Rock cycle, 194–195
    theory of, 196
Rock record, 334–336
Rocks, 177–198
    ages of, 340
    chemical, 187
    clastic, 186–187
    defined, 178
    elements in, 139
    extrusive, 183
    field guides for, 184
    foliated, 192
    identifying, 197–198
    igneous, 178, 181–183, 347
    intrusive, 181–182
    metamorphic, 179, 192,
        195, 347
    nonfoliated, 192
    organic, 188
    sedimentary, 177, 179,
        185–188, 189, 195
    types of, 178–179
Rock salt, 187
Rotation, 29, 60
Runoff, 257, 259
Rust, 133

S

Salinity, 267
Salt, physical properties of, 133
Salt water, 257, 267
    measuring its effect on
        floating, 273–274
San Andreas fault, 318, 322
Sand dunes, 300
Sandstone, 187, 192, 198

Satellites, 78–79
    artificial, 69
    natural, 69
Saturn, 94
Savannah, 249
Schist, 192, 198
Schmitt, Harrison, 71
Science at Work
    Air-Traffic Controller, 45
    Astronomer, 97
    Atmospheric Scientist, 235
    Cartographer, 12
    Chemical Engineer, 146
    Environmental Science
        Technician, 214
    Floodplain Manager, 302
    Hydroelectric Power Plant
        Operator, 264
    Jeweler, 167
    Petroleum Engineer, 344
    Seismologist, 326
    Space Shuttle and
        International Space
        Station Crews, 62
    Stonemason, 180
    Telescope Technician, 111
Science in Your Life
    Cutting Down on Fossil
        Fuels, 352
    Erosion Caused by People,
        291
    The Good and Bad of Coal,
        189
    Lasting Plastic, 134
    Light Pollution, 124
    Living on a Tectonic Plate,
        316
    Mapping a Park, 18
    Natural and Artificial
        Satellites, 69

Ozone: Protector and
    Pollutant, 207
Recycling Aluminum, 172
A Solar House, 83
Time Zones, 35
Your Climate Zone, 250
Your Water Budget, 258
Science Myths
    air vs. oxygen, 145
    deserts, 300
    dinosaurs and people, 349
    distance between the earth
        and the sun, 61
    facing north, 9
    heat lightning, 244
    light-year, 114
    mineral characteristics, 160
    ocean floor, 271
    raindrops, 217
    rocks vs. minerals, 179
    gravity in space, 80
Science, nature of, xviii–xix
Scientific method, xviii–xix
    see also Investigations
Seaborg, Glenn, 140
Seaborgium, 140
Sea-floor spreading, 309–310,
    312
Seamount, 270
Seas, 268
Seasons, 60–61
Sea stack, 290
Sediment, 185
Sedimentary rocks, 177, 179,
    185–188, 189, 195
Seismic tomography, 319
Seismograph, 323
Seismologist, 326
Shale, 186, 198
Shield volcanoes, 315
Shooting stars, 100
Silent Spring, 272

Silicon, 154
Silver, 155, 171
Sinkhole, 260
Sirius, 110, 114
Slate, 192, 198
Sleet, 216
Snow, 216
Society
    see Technology and society
Sodium, 141
Sodium chloride, 141, 267
Soil, 282
Solar and Heliospheric
    Observatory (SOHO),
    82
Solar cell, 102
Solar eclipse, 67
Solar flares, 77
Solar house, 83
Solar system, 77–101, 364–365
    asteroids in, 100–101
    comets in, 101
    distances in, 98–99
    inner planets in, 86–90
    objects in, 79–80
    outer planets in, 92–96
    sun in, 81–82
Solar wind, 101
Solids, 131, 132, 154
South America, 27
Southern Hemisphere, 49, 61
Southern Ocean, 28
South Pole, 29, 43
Space, growing minerals in,
    164
Space exploration, 366–367
Space shuttle, 62
Specific gravity of minerals,
    165–166, 168–169
Spiral galaxies, 123
Spirit of Freedom (hot air
    balloon), 30
Spring, 260

Standard time zones, 32–34, 35
Stars, 78–79, 108–110, 132
    birth of, 117
    brightness of, 108–110
    color of, 110
    death of, 118–119
    distances of, 114–115
    observing brightness of,
        112–113
Steel, 156
Stellar equilibrium
    see Stars, birth of
    see Stars, death of
Steppes, deserts and, 249
Stonemason, 180
Storms, 244–245
Stratosphere, 209
Stratus clouds, 212
Streak of minerals, 158–159
    observing, 162–163
Streak plate, 158
Strike-slip fault, 318
Subarctic climate, 249
Submersible, 4
Subsoil, 282
Sugar, physical properties of,
    133
Sulfur, 154, 157
Sun, 81–82
Sunspots, 82
    observing, 84–85
Supergiant, 118
Supernova, 119
S-waves, 323, 325

T

Table salt, 141
Talc, 160
Tar pits, 336
Technology and society, 3–5,
    17, 30, 39, 48, 65, 69, 71,
    72, 83, 102, 116, 134,
    140, 143, 155, 156, 161,

Technology and society
(continued)
    170–171, 172, 188–189,
    193, 207, 218, 224, 238,
    241, 246, 263, 272, 283,
    291, 299, 312, 316, 319,
    324–325, 342–343, 352,
    358–363, 366–367
Technology Notes
    cave mapping, 283
    coal, 188
    conodonts, 351
    global positioning system
        (GPS), 17
    gold, 161
    Hubble Space Telescope,
        116
    hydroelectric power plants,
        263
    map projections, 47
    marble, 193
    nuclear fission, 143
    photogrammetry, 48
    photovoltaic (PV) cell, 102
    telescopes, 72
    weather balloons, 5
    weather satellites, 246
    wind power 224
Tectonic plate, living on, 316
Telescopes, 70, 72, 108
Telescope technician, 111
Temperature, 230
Temperate climates, 248, 249
Texture of rocks, 182
Theories, xix, 91, 196,
        309–312, 347, 350
Thermocline, 268
Thermometers, 230
Thermosphere, 209
Thunderheads, 244
Thunderstorms, 244
Tides, 68
Titan, 94

Topaz, 160, 171
Topographic maps, 15–17
    reading, 19–20
    using, 16–17
Topsoil, 282
Tornadoes, 245
Tourmaline, 171
Trade winds, 223
Trench, 270
Tributaries, 261
Trilobites, 336, 349
Tropical climates, 248, 249
Tropical desert, 249
Tropical rain forest, 249
Tropic of Cancer, 42
Tropic of Capricorn, 42
Troposphere, 208, 209, 244
Tsunamis, 325
Tundra climate, 249

U

Universe, 123
Uranus, 95
Ursa Major, 121

V

Vent, 313
Venus, 87–88
Volcanoes, 155, 194, 307
    formation of, 313
    types of, 314–315

Voyager (spacecraft), 92, 95
Warm front, 239
Wasatch Range, 318
Water, 131
    as cause of erosion,
        286–290
    on the earth, 255–274
    properties of ocean,
        267–268
    salt, 257, 267
    sources of fresh, 259–263
Water budget, 258
Water cycle, 216, 256–257
Water table, 259, 260
Water vapor, 211, 232
Wave deposits, 290
Wave erosion, 290
Waves
    earthquake, 323
    ocean, 268
Weather, 230
    collecting data on, 238
    conditions and
        measurements, 230–234
    patterns and predictions,
        238–240
Weather balloons, 5, 238
Weathering, 195, 280
    chemical, 281, 284–285
    mechanical, 280

Weather maps, 240, 242–243
Weather satellites, 238, 246
Weather stations, 238
Wegener, Alfred, 309
Western Hemisphere, 49
White Cliffs of Dover, 188
White dwarf, 118
Wind belts, 222
Wind cells, 221
Wind erosion and deposits,
    300
Wind farms, 224
Windmills, 224
Wind patterns, 221–223
Wind speed and direction, 233
Wind turbine, 224
Wind vane, 233
*The World Almanac and Book
    of Facts*, 57
World map, 374–375
World ocean, 28

Y

Yellowstone River, 287

Z

Zinc, 160

Photo Credits

Cover background—Courtesy of U.S. Geological Survey; cover inset—© Antony Edwards/Image Bank/Getty Images; pp. iii, xx—© James Randklev/Corbis; p. x—© Francois Gohier/Photo Researchers, Inc.; p. 4 (left)—© Norbert Wu Photography; p. 4 (right)—Courtesy of NASA Jet Propulsion Laboratory; p. 5—© Brecelj Bojan/Corbis/Sygma; p. 7—© Air Photographics, Inc.; p. 12—© Gibson Stock Photography; p. 18—© Bruce Iverson Photomicrography; p. 24—Courtesy of KidSat, NASA Jet Propulsion Laboratory; p. 35—© Bonnie Kamin/Index Stock Imagery; p. 45—© David Lawrence/Corbis; p. 54—Courtesy of NASA Goddard Space Flight Center; pp. 56, 61, 67, 78, 79, 81, 88, 96, 100, 104, 118, 256 (image of sun)—Courtesy of Solar and Heliospheric Observatory (European Space Agency, NASA); pp. 56, 66, 67, 68, 74 (image of moon)—Courtesy of NASA; p. 62—Courtesy of NASA; p. 68 (left)—© Peter Gregg/Color-Pic Inc.; p. 68 (right)—© Peter Gregg/Color-Pic Inc.; p. 71—Courtesy of NASA, Apollo 17; p. 76—© The Stocktrek Corp/Brand X Pictures/Alamy.com; p. 79, 86, 100, 104, 364—Courtesy of NASA, Mariner 10, U.S. Geological Survey Astrogeology Team; p. 78, 79, 87, 88, 100, 104, 364—Courtesy of Magellan Project, NASA Jet Propulsion Laboratory; p. 79, 89, 100, 104, 364—Courtesy of NASA, Hubble Heritage Team (STScI/AURA); p. 90—Courtesy of NASA Jet Propulsion Laboratory; p. 79, 92, 100, 104, 364—Courtesy of NASA, Hubble Heritage Team (STScI/AURA); p. 93—Courtesy of NASA Jet Propulsion Laboratory; p. 79, 94, 100, 365—Courtesy of NASA, Hubble Heritage Team (STScI/AURA); p. 79, 95 (top), 104, 365—Courtesy of NASA, U.S. Naval Observatory; p. 79, 95 (bottom), 96, 104, 365—Courtesy of NASA Jet Propulsion Laboratory; p. 97—© Addison A. Geary/Stock Boston; p. 101 (top)—© Francois Gohier/Photo Researchers, Inc.; p. 101 (bottom)—© Dennis di Cicco/Corbis; p. 106—Courtesy of NASA, European Southern Observatory; p. 111—Courtesy of National Radio Astronomy Observatory, Associated Universities, Inc., National Science Foundation; p.115—Courtesy of Sébastien Giguère (www.astrosurf.com/sg); p. 117—Courtesy of NASA, Hubble Heritage Team (STScI/AURA); p. 119 (left)—Courtesy of NASA, Chandra X-ray Observatory Center, MPE; p. 119 (right)—Courtesy of NASA, STScI; pp. 122, 123—Courtesy of National Optical Astronomy Observatory, Association of Universities for Research in Astronomy, National Science Foundation; p. 124—Courtesy of NASA, National Oceanic and Atmospheric Administration, DMP; p. 130—© Michael T. Sedam/Corbis; p. 134—© Bill Banaszewski/Visuals Unlimited; p. 137—© Tom McHugh/Photo Researchers, Inc.; p. 141 (left)—© Photo Reseachers, Inc.; p. 141 (center)—© Yoav Levy/Phototake; pp. 141 (right), 164 (left)—© A.J. Copley/Visuals Unlimited; p. 144—© John Sohlden/Visuals Unlimited; p. 146—© Bob Daemmrich/The Image Works, Inc.; p. 154—© Stan Osolinski/Dembinsky Photo Associates; p. 155 (left)—© Mark A. Schneider/Photo Reseachers, Inc.; p. 155 (right)—© Lester V. Bergman/Corbis; p. 157—© Ken Lucas/Visuals Unlimited; p. 158 (left)—© Alan Curtis/Leslie Garland Picture Library/Alamy.com; p. 158 (right)—© Mark A. Schneider/Dembinsky Photo Associates; p. 164 (right)—© Doug Sokell/Visuals

Unlimited; p. 167—© Reporters Press Agency/eStock Photo; p. 172—© David Young-Wolff/Stone/Getty Images; p. 175 (top)—© Ken Lucas/Visuals Unlimited; p. 175 (bottom)—© José Manuel Sanchis Calvete/Corbis; p. 176—© Manfred Gottschalk/Animals Animals; p. 178—© Hubert Stadler/Corbis; p. 179 (top)—© W. Cody/Corbis; p. 179 (bottom)—© David Muench/Corbis; p. 180—© Annie Griffiths Belt/Corbis; p. 182—© Doug Sookell/Visuals Unlimited; p. 183—© Mark A. Schneider/Photo Researchers, Inc.; p. 186 (left)—© John D. Cunningham/Visuals Unlimited; p. 186 (right)—© Jonathan Blair/Corbis; p. 187—© John Gerlach/Visuals Unlimited; p. 192 (top)—© Ann Swengel/Visuals Unlimited; p. 192 (bottom)—© Greg Pease/Stone/Getty Images; p. 202—© Royalty Free/Corbis; p. 207—Courtesy of NASA; p. 212—© Visuals Unlimited; p. 213 (top)—© David Matherly/Visuals Unlimited; p. 213 (bottom)—© Royalty Free/Corbis; p. 214—© Jerry Mason/Science Photo Library/Photo Researchers, Inc.; p. 216—© A.J. Copley/Visuals Unlimited; p. 228—© NASA/Science Photo Library/Photo Researchers, Inc.; p. 231—© Leonard Lessin/Photo Researchers, Inc.; p. 233—© E.R. Degginger/Color-Pic Inc.; p. 234—© Runk/Schoenberger/Grant Heilman Photography; p. 235—© Shepard Sherbell/Corbis/SABA; p. 238—Courtesy of the National Oceanic and Atmospheric Administration; p. 245—© Royalty Free/Corbis; p. 249 (top)—© Kurt Scholz/SuperStock; p. 249 (center)—© Dominique Braud/Dembinsky Photo Associates; p. 249 (bottom)—© Kjell B. Sandved/Visuals Unlimited; p. 254—© Doug Wilson/Corbis; p. 260 (left)—Courtesy of U.S. Geological Survey; p. 260 (right)—© AP/Wide World Photos; p. 263—© Lester Sloan/Woodfin Camp & Associates; p. 264—© Lester Lefkowitz/Corbis; p. 278—© Visuals Unlimited; p. 280—© Royalty Free/Corbis; p. 281 (left)—© John Prior Images/Alamy.com; p. 281 (right)—© John Lemker/Earth Scenes/Animals Animals; p. 282—© Adam Woolfitt/Corbis; p. 286—© Royalty Free/Corbis; p. 288—Courtesy of NASA Jet Propulsion Laboratory; p. 290—© Randy Wells/Stone/Getty Images; p. 291—© John Sohlden/Visuals Unlimited; p. 294—© Gerald & Buff Corsi/Visuals Unlimited; p. 295 (top)—© Visuals Unlimited; p. 295 (bottom)—© Donald Johnston/Stone/Getty Images; p. 296—© Lawrence Dodge; p. 301—Courtesy of Terry Taylor, Colorado State Patrol; p. 302—© Patti McConville/Image Bank/Getty Images; p. 306—© Sylvain Grandadam/Image Bank/Getty Images; p. 314—© Tom Bean/Corbis; p. 315 (top)—Courtesy of U.S. Geological Survey; p. 315 (bottom)—© Stone/Getty Images; p. 316—© Dana White/PhotoEdit; p. 322—Courtesy of U.S. Geological Survey; p. 325—© Robert Yager/Stone/Getty Images; p. 326—© PhotoEdit; p. 332—© Francois Gohier/Photo Researchers, Inc.; p. 334—© Danny Lehman/Corbis; p. 335—© Phil Degginger/Stone/Getty Images; p. 336 (top)—© A.J. Copley/PhotoDisc; p. 336 (bottom)—© Howard Grey/Stone/Getty Images; p. 343—© Kaj R. Svensson/ Photo Researchers, Inc.; p. 344—© Keith Wood/Stone/Getty Images; p. 349—© A.J. Copley/Visuals Unlimited; p. 350—© Phil Martin/PhotoEdit; p. 352—© Michael Newman/PhotoEdit; pp. 358, 360, 361—© Royalty Free/Corbis